ZIMBOLICIOUS ANTHOLOGY 8:

An Anthology of Zimbabwean Literature and Arts

Edited by **Tendai Rinos Mwanaka**
Matthew Kunashe Chikono

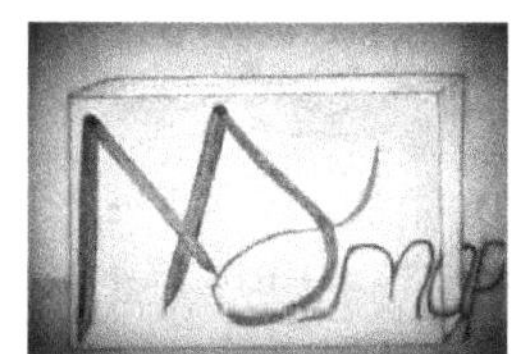

Mwanaka Media and Publishing Pvt Ltd,
Chitungwiza Zimbabwe
*
Creativity, Wisdom and Beauty

Publisher: *Mmap*
Mwanaka Media and Publishing Pvt Ltd
24 Svosve Road, Zengeza 1
Chitungwiza Zimbabwe
mwanaka@yahoo.com
mwanaka13@gmail.com
https://www.mmapublishing.org
www.africanbookscollective.com/publishers/mwanaka-media-and-publishing
https://facebook.com/MwanakaMediaAndPublishing/

Distributed in and outside N. America by African Books Collective
orders@africanbookscollective.com
www.africanbookscollective.com

ISBN: 978-1-77933-166-3
EAN: 9781779331663

TABLE OF CONTENTS

Nyarawo Iwe!: *Chengetai Nyagumbo*
Zvazopera!: *Chengetai Nyagumbo*
Vazukuru!!: *Chengetai Nyagumbo*
Hazvisi zvangu..: *Chengetai Nyagumbo*
Sarapavana: *Chengetai Nyagumbo*
The New Voices in Zimbabwe's Publishing Arena: *Matthew K Chikono*
Mmap Multi-disciplinary Series

About editors

Tendai Rinos Mwanaka is a multidisciplinary artist, editor, publisher and producer with 26 individual books and over 27 curated anthologies published in US, Northern Ireland, UK, Cameroon and Zimbabwe. As publisher of Mwanaka Media and Publishing, he has edited and published at least 118 titles from authors from all continents of the world here: https://www.africanbookscollective.com/publishers/mwanaka-media-and-publishing. He has 3 music albums playing in at least 18 radio stations in US, Canada, UK, France, Israel, Brazil and Australia and hundreds of paintings and drawings, thousands of photographs, some exhibited, published and sold. His art pieces have appeared in over 400 journals in over 35 countries and his books and writing is translated into at least 11 languages. His music can be licensed here https://www.songtradr.com/tendai.mwanaka Find him here: https://m.facebook.com/tendai.mwanaka

Matthew Kunashe Chikono is a short story writer and editor from Chitungwiza, Zimbabwe. He has published two solo short story collections; *Dreams of Paradise* and *Blue Threads and other stories.* He edited two anthologies *The Rules of the City* and *Prima Volume 1.* www.facebook.com/passionatewriterspen

CONTRIBUTORS' BIO NOTES

Hasan Simani, born on 15 August 1992 at Matibi hospital in Mwenezi South of Zimbabwe. He is a talented poet, Applied Psychology Lecturer at University of Zimbabwe and counsellor known for his ability to touch hearts with his evocative poems and his dedication to promoting mental health awareness. With a Master's degree in Counseling Psychology with Great Zimbabwe University and B.Sc. Honours Psychology with University of Zimbabwe, Hasan combines his passion for writing and his expertise in psychology to create powerful pieces that resonate deeply with his readers. Hasan Simani is also a devoted Muslim in Zimbabwe.

Moira Marangwanda-Chipanda is an avid reader, passionate writer and literary enthusiast who dabbles in scripts and poetry. Her poems *The Heel* and *The Eye Of The Mind* were featured in Our Stories Redefined Poetry Anthology (2021). Her play *Naked Failure* was performed at Mitambo International Theatre Festival. More of her work can be found on www.momosramblings@wordpress.com

Nelia Nkazimulo Mutema: I am a poetess aged 20 , I strongly believe that poetry is the best means of communication as it can heal any wounds, I am talking about emotional wounds .

Fabian Choto is a writer who was born on 26 October 1979 in Harare. His rural home is in Choto village, Chief Svosve in Wedza under Mashonaland East Province. Fabian popularly known as poet of the people is a published author who published his Shona anthology *Wajaira* in 2017, followed by his English poetry anthology *Wisdom and Foolishness.* He then contributed his poems to the recently published poetry anthologies namely *Chingoma Chokwedu, Essential Verses, Dzinobva Muropa and Zimbolicious Anthology Volume 8.* In his early writings the poet presented his Shona poems at Muninga Dzepfungwa at Radio Zimbabwe with Aaron Chiundura Moyo and Musavengana Nyasha.Then by that time he presented his poems at Mabhuku neVanyori and AM Zimbabwe with Rebecca Chisamba. He has had his works in the country's well known newspapers such as *The Sunday Mail, Herald, Manica Post, Kwayedza* and magazines such as *Parade, Outpost* and others.

Tafadzwa Chiwanza is an accountant and a poet by calling. He grew up in Harare. Chiwanzas works has appeared in local publications such as *The standard Mail, The Queensdale Report* and *Jikinya.* He has published two poetry collections *No bird singing now?* and *The rest is silence.*

Kudakwashe P. Simbi saw the light of the earth on the 12th of May 1996 in Rusape. Simbi is an alumni from the University of Zimbabwe who studied B.A Honours Degree in English. He is a published author and poet. He contributed in quite a number of anthologies such as Speak, The bleeding tree, Essential voices, Pariah in Paradise, Bullfrog Vibrations: The Drumbeat, Zimbolicious volume 7, Voices of Africa: A Call For Freedom Anthology, Prima Anthology; Prose and Poetry from Africa Volume 1 just to mention a few.

Ayanda Valeria Sithole's artistic journey began in 2019 where she recited her first poetry titled Women With Towels under her director and videographer Vusimuzi Vector SA. Since then,her poetic majesty evolved and articulated stage performances and anthology series. Winner of Gambinga Poetry Competition [2020], securing 2nd place. Authorship in an anthology titled Poetic Minds Combined [2020], a South African taste and she was the only Zimbabwean. The book was published by Charles Hoby the founder of Ava's Publishers. World poetry anthology book titled Mercy And Poetic Healing [3 September 2021], published at Author Press, India. Voiced in Voices Season 1 [2021] an inaugural season of 100 poems,10 themes,10 poets in 100 days. First book titled Maverick Thoughts [2022] laced in deep and hidden emotions embodied in creative writing and uncommon. Honoured at the AfriCan Honoree Awards [31 July 2023]by the Founder Anthea Thyssen as one of the best poetry authors in Africa.

Chenjerai Mhondera is a rabbi, the dissident reporter, a book reviewer, previewer, proofreader, editor and a Lord of Controversies. He comes from the spirit world, and lives in the World. He is the author of A Case of Love and Hate (Zimbabwe), Masasi aChinoz (Zimbabwe). His works also appear in over seventy publications; online journals and blogs, magazines and anthologies. Among the lot - including Best New African Poets (BNAP) 2015 Anthology (Cameroon), BNAP 2016 Anthology, BNAP 2017 Anthology, BNAP 2018 Anthology, BNAP 2019 Anthology, BNAP 2020 Anthology, BNAP 2021 Anthology, BNAP 2022 Anthology, Zimbolicious Poetry Vol. 1 (USA, 2016), Zimbolicious Poetry Vol. 2 (Cameroon, 2017), Zimbolicious Poetry Vol. 3 (Zimbabwe, 2018), Zimbolicious Poetry Vol. 5 (Zimbabwe, 2020)

Handson Chirefu was born in Nyajena, Masvingo Province in 1969. He went to Bondolfi and Gokomere Schools in Masvingo. He is married and has two children. Chirefu is a teacher and has published two novels in English. Currently is an English lecturer at Masvingo Teachers' College.

My name is **Qinisela Possenti Ndlovu**, born on 28 January 1970 in Tsholotsho, Zimbabwe. I stay in Trenance and currently Lecturer at Bulawayo Poly in Business Communication and Public Relations.

Gamuchirai Susan Muchirahondo is a female Zimbabwean writer aged 25. She has been published in the Best New African Poets Anthology for 2018, 2019 and 2021 and 2022. She has also been published in the Zimbolicious Anthology Vol.7. She mainly writes about tragic romances, mental health issues and is a novelist and children's book author.

David Chasumba is an award-winning Zimbabwean Author and Poet. His debut short story collection, *The Mad Man on First Street and Other Short Stories*, won the NAMA (National Arts Merit Award) in 2023 for Outstanding First Creative Published Work in Zimbabwe. His short stories were published in four anthologies; A Bundle of Joy and Other Short Stories from Africa, Momaya Short Story Review: (Treasure) (2015), Small Worlds anthology- University of Brighton Literature Society (2014) and Reflections anthology by University of Brighton Literature Society (2015). His short story, Crossing the Rubicon, was longlisted for the Fish Publishing Short Story Competition (2013-14). He published four short stories with Kalahari Review. He has recently published three poems in Ipikai Poetry Journal and a poem, *There are still poets* in Mosi oa Tunya Review Issue 2. David has two MA degrees from University of Sussex and Canterbury Christ Church University. David lives in Bexhill on sea. X: @davidchasumba22

Oscar Gwiriri was born on 15 June 1975 at Gwiriri Village, Chief Mutasa, Zimbabwe. He learnt at Manunure Primary School and Dangamvura High School, Mutare. He is published in more than sixty books, both fiction and text books. His two books *Hatiponi* and *Chitima nditakure* were nominated for NAMA awards in 2019. Oscar is a Certified Forensic Investigations Professional (CFIP), as well as a Certified Information Systems Security Professional (CISSP) who also holds a *Master of Science in Strategic Management Degree, Bachelor of Business Administration, Associates of Arts in Business Administration, Diploma in Logistics and Transport (CILT, UK), Diploma in Workplace Safety and Health, Commanding United Nations Peacekeeping Operations Certificate*, and many other professional qualifications. Gwiriri is a guru in writing in his vernacular language, Shona.

Jabulani Mzinyathi is a published poet and novelist. His published works are the following: Under The Steel Yoke, Righteous Indignation, In The Steel Talons, Along The Way(poetry collections) and a chiShona novel, Mumambure. Jabulani Mzinyathi is currently a lawyer in Zimbabwe. He also holds qualifications in alternative dispute resolution methods, human capital management, journalism, public relations , international relations and education. He strives towards high levels of self actualisation and will never stop.

I'm **Onward Mutapurwa**, a Zimbabwean boy born in a local city of Chipinge. Right now I am a political scientist and about my poetic career have been published with creative minds, a journal of the creative arts, Zimbolicious and the recent Best New African Poets 2020 and 2022 as well as The Mental Health Anthology.

Jeremiah Maengedze is a passionate Zimbabwean author from Chiredzi, Masvingo Province.A finalist in the "Writing Ukraine Prize" of 2023,he co-authored the anthology "Advice" by Blue Star Publications.

Chengetai Nyagumbo was born in 1991. She was bred and born in Chitungwiza. She is a poet, and short story writer. She likes to write in her vernacular language. Her moniker is Dr. Amai.

My name is **Aisha Chikodzi**. I am 13 years old. I am a student at the Heritage school.I like hockey and tennis. In my free time I read books and poems, and occasionally stay on social media. I love listening to music because it is calming and relaxing.

Lin Barrie: 0772922148. Art by Lin Barrie': https://wineandwilddogs.art/art/ Contemporary African Art: http://www.contemporary-african-art.com/lin-barrie-art.html Wallpapers by Lin Barrie: https://robinsprong.com/product-category/designers/lin-barrie/ African Wild dogs on Facebook: A-Celebration-of-Painted-Wolves https://www.facebook.com/hlolwa/ Chilo Gorge Safari Lodge website: http://www.chilogorge.com/

Blessing Barnet Chiniko is an avid and passionate poet dedicated to fighting stigma and bringing attention to social issues. He has a degree in law and a masters in water policy

Introduction

Zimbolicious Anthology volume 8: an anthology of Zimbabwean literature and arts is finally here. Despite the current economic and political situation in our country; poets, writers, artists, and other creatives have defied the odds and continued to churn their works and submit to produce this marvelous anthology. Thumbs up to everyone who submitted. This eighth installment continues the tradition of giving new writers the platform to shine and to the seasoned writers, a shebeen to meet again and prolong the tradition.

Stories in the fiction section tackle numerous themes that have become a norm in our today society. Matthew K Chikono, Tendai R Mwanaka and David Chasumba give us stories that reflect on family disputes, role of religion in disrupting families, sexual assault, first love, taboo relationships, regret, lost loved ones in the liberation war, and a name to the tombstone of the unknown soldier.

Poems of heart breaks, loneliness, grief and self-reflection in the poetry section shows how the local poets are not shunning to expose to the world their lyrical mastery. Hope, love and dreams of better Zimbabwe continues to fill in the pages of our local wordsmiths. Young poets like Aisha Chikodza dazzle us with their words whilst debutant Nelia Mutema joins in seasoned poets like Edward Dzonze, Jabulani Mzinyathi and Chenjerai Mhondera to bestow to us the best the local poetic scenery has to offer. This installment also feature poems in chiShona from poets Kudakwashe Simbi and Chengetai Nyagumbo and isiNdebele from Qinisela Possenti Ndlovu.

Artwork by father-son sculpturing duo Rangarirai and Fair Makunde whose display serves to remind the readers that Zimbolicious isn't about fiction and poetry only, but every form of art is still being bred in every part of Zimbabwe and the world at large by Zimbabweans.

The anthology is also lit with Tendai Mwanaka's magnificent photography ranging from the beautiful Domboshava scenery to paintings by Lin Barrie and wire installations by Johnson Zuze at Pikicha Gallery in Harare.

The non-fiction piece by Matthew Kunashe Chikono focuses on the expanding publishing field in Zimbabwe despite the shrinking economic benefits. New and old writers have a lot to say on the subject matter.

We hope you continue to read and follow the Zimbolicious anthology series. Enjoy.

Vestiges of Colonialism: Artworks by Moffat Takadiwa

Photography by Tendai Rinos Mwanaka

Is an arresting, beautiful and provocative installations by Mbare Artist Moffat Takadiwa, curated by Fadzai Muchemwa, which was shown at the National Art Gallery of Zimbabwe, Harare, in March 2023. We will be showing you this exhibition in this volume interspersed with fictions from Zimbabwean storytellers in the forthcoming sections. We start this exhibition with an installation he titled *Walk of Shame.* These are toothbrushes in several colours arranged as a carpet, also depicting the Star of David.

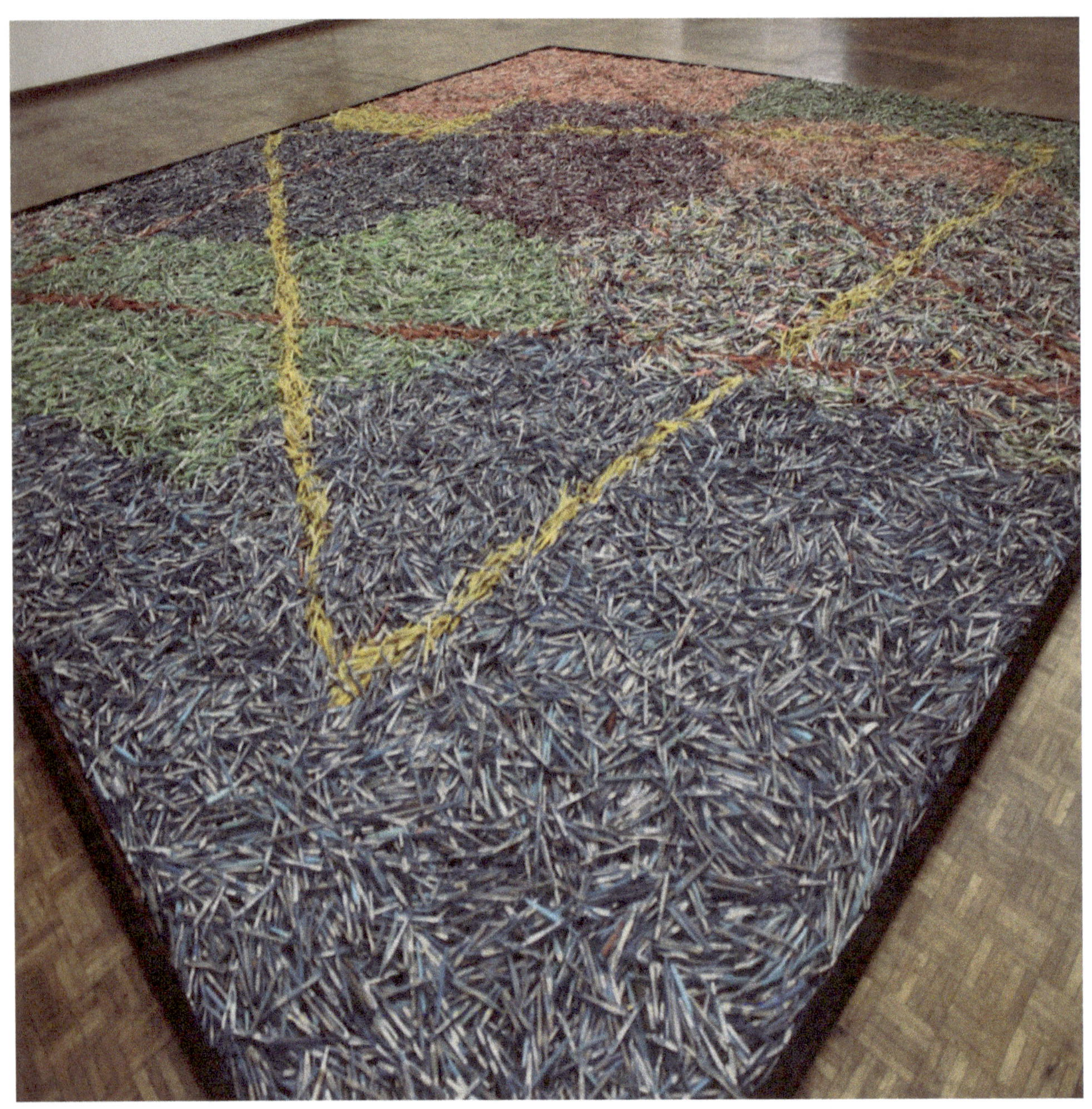

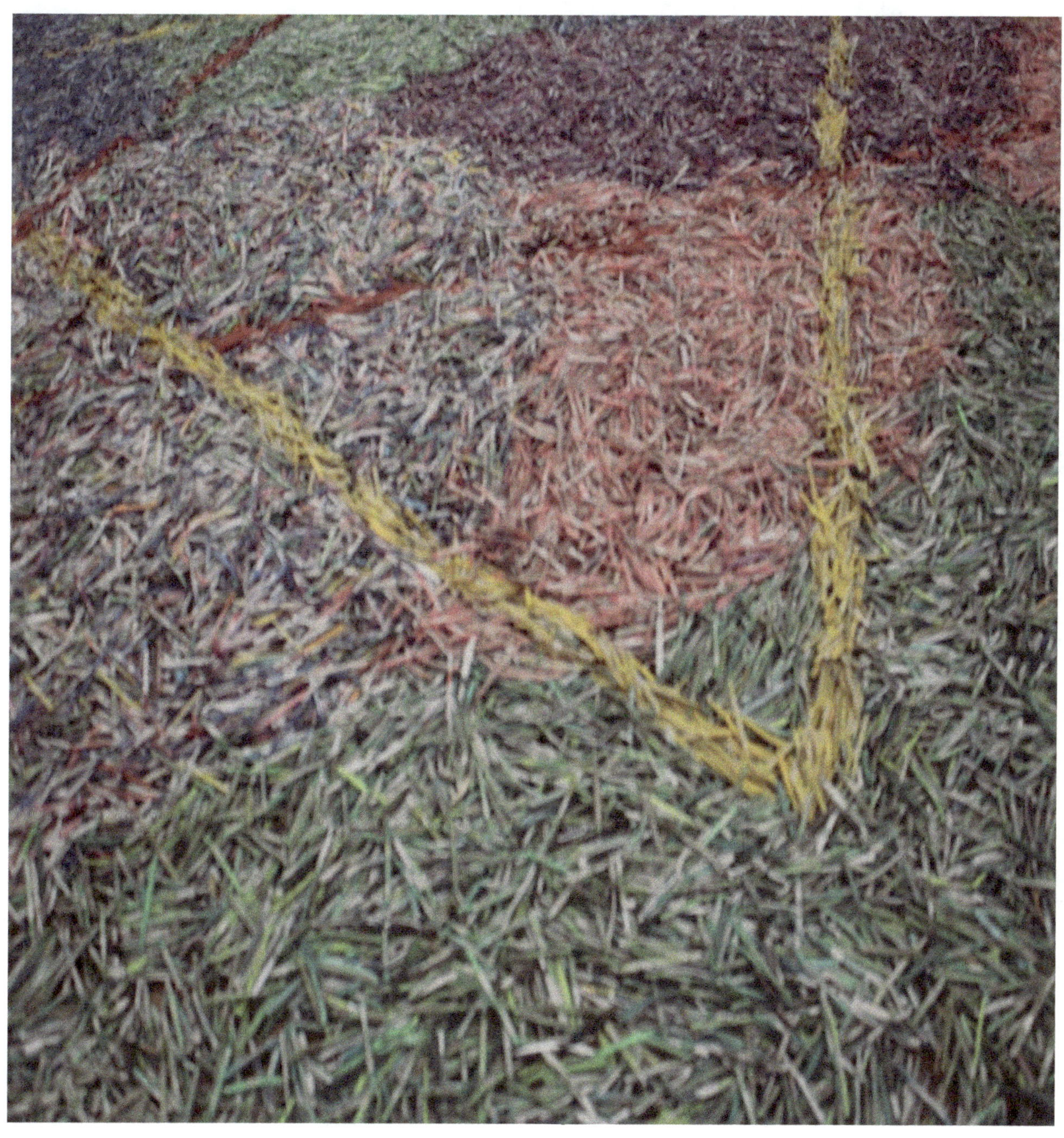

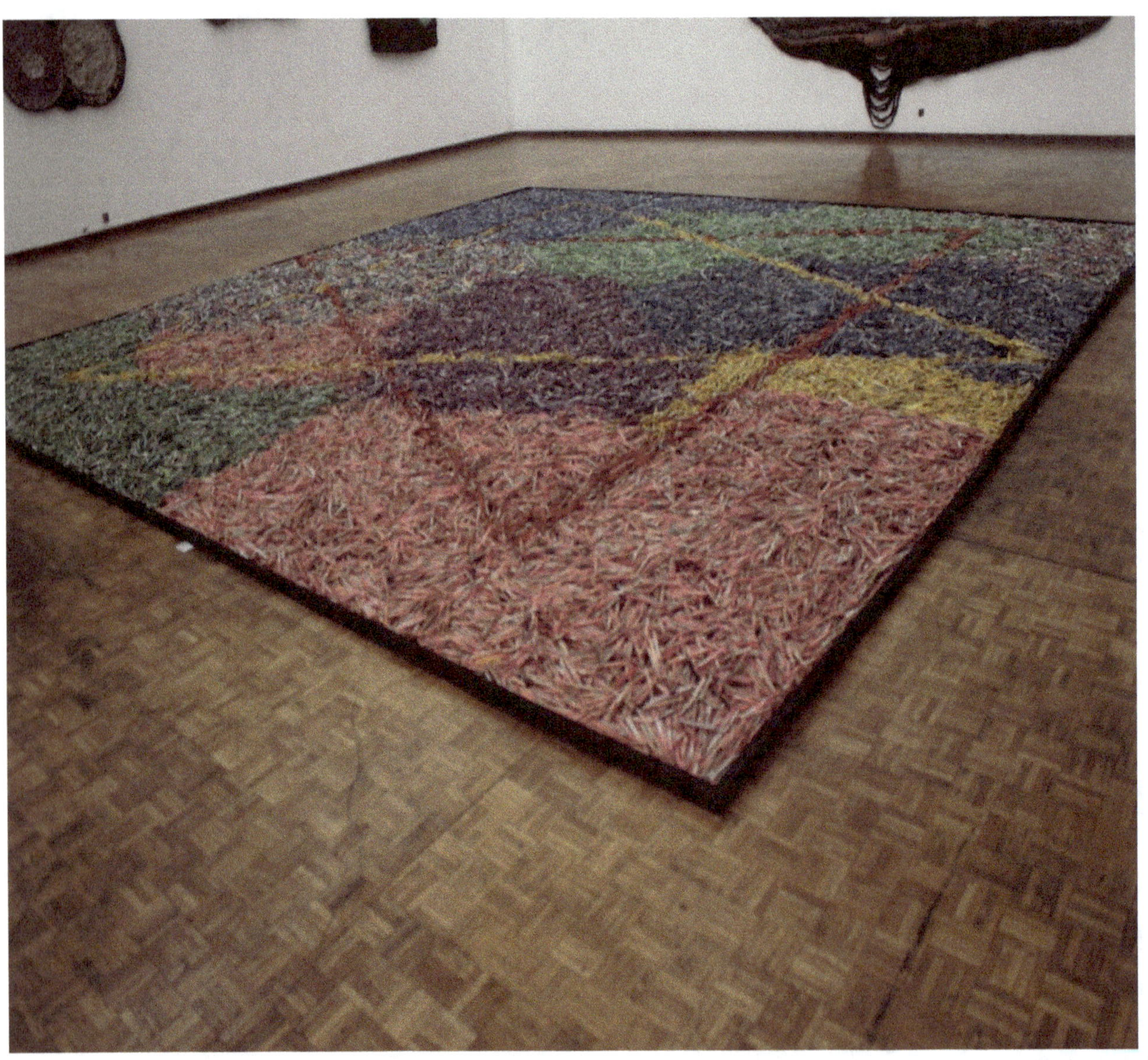

Where did all the birds go?

Matthew Kunashe Chikono

After the news-paper had packed their cameras and left, Lukia walked over to the river bank where her aunt had been left standing alone. She was gazing into the water as if someone was about to come out of it. Lukia relied her father's message to her. Lukia had known the message wouldn't be well received, she was just a messenger hoping not to get shot. Her aunt stood for a moment staring into Lukia's eyes, her face twitching as evil thoughts ran wild in her mind.

"Your mother, she is the one who send you, isn't she?" Aunty Firidha said heaving in anger, "My brother would never say such things to me, that wife of his is always imposing her will. Go and tell her that if she doesn't like the way I am handling the situation she should come and tell me herself."

Lukia lowered her head, utterly disgusted by her aunt, and started walking back home. It was a kilometer or so from the river to the homestead where she lived with her family. It wasn't the distance that made her heart unsettle - she was accustomed to the distance - but the thought of vanishing whilst walking past the woodlot between the river and her family's homestead. Disappearing without leaving a trace, just like her sister.

Handling the situation, that was what her aunt had called it. The way she had been handling the situation was to dress like a teenage and talk about how her niece had been taken by the mermaid that lived in the River Save whenever the camera people arrived. Aunt Firidha had become the self-appointed family spokesperson, Lukia's father had sent her to tell her aunt to stop doing that after she had left with another group of camera people who had arrived that morning. Her aunt had went berserk on her, accusing Lukia's mother of being a horrible sister-in-law.

The woodlot Lukia had to pass on her way from the river consisted of pine and gum trees. If someone was to abduct her, they would have an excellent place to set an ambush for her. Lukia listened carefully as she walked through the whistling pine trees that Friday afternoon. If an attacker was to show themselves, Lukia wasn't going to scream for help. No, she couldn't, she had to fight for herself. At sixteen, Lukia was as healthy as any child of her age. Village life had toughened her since birth.

The woodlot was quiet, too quiet to make Lukia feel relaxed though. Not a sound of a chirping cricket could be heard. Lukia also realised there weren't any birds singing in the trees too. For a moment she wondered where all the birds had gone. She thought maybe they had day jobs in the fields where they caught worms and ate maize cobs and would return to their nests in the evening. Lukia missed the birds.

When she was younger she had been taught by someone that the absence of singing birds was a permutation of something bad going to happen-like getting kidnapped in the woodlot.

Often lately, Lukia had been getting thoughts of being abducted whenever she was alone. She had also started having nightmares about men putting a black bag on her head and taking her with them and she unable to scream for help. She couldn't scream if anything like that were to happen to her. Not a single word had passed from her mouth since birth. The invading thoughts of being kidnapped had started after her sister's disappearance, about a fortnight earlier. Lukia wanted to believe her sister had been kidnapped and would be returned to them as soon as her father paid a certain number of heifers. Her father had dozens of those and surely could afford to exchange some, if not all, for the safe return of her eldest daughter. The kidnapping story was more feasible in Lukia's mind than the story her family was dishing out to the public; their daughter had been taken by the mermaid of Save River and would be returned to them if they perform the necessary ceremony and ritual at the riverbank.

It was way past lunch when Lukia finally arrived home. The three mud huts and a bricked cottage was the only home she had ever known. A strange car was parked outside. Obviously, she didn't know whom it belonged to, none of their relatives or fellow villagers owned cars. Lukia prayed it wasn't the news people again trying to write a story about her missing sister. Over the past few days she had grown to hate everyone who asked about Eustancia.

Lukia crunched and silently moved closer to one of the hut the family used as a kitchen. That was where her mother would receive visitors. The smell of cooking chicken made her mouth to water. They only cooked chicken for important guest, not journalists or camera people. A sigh of relief left her mouth, she was certain that she had been saved a trip to the river.

She wasn't going to bulge in the house without knowing how important the visitor was, she didn't want to embarrass her family or herself. First, she listened through the wall and could hear a muffled voice. It was her mother's, recounting for the thousandth time the night of Eustancia's disappearance.

"Then I told her to go to the river to fetch a bucket of water for the chickens, you know the rains haven't fallen well this month. It was almost seven in the evening when I realised she wasn't back yet," Lukia's mother's voice broke a bit, "knowing my daughter well, my maternal instinct told me that something was wrong. I sent her father and her uncle to look for her."

At that moment the story was interrupted whilst her mother sobbed. Lukia could hear her uncle, Aunt Firidha's young brother, telling her not to cry for it was a bad omen to mourn for someone who was not yet dead. Despite her uncle being the youngest in her father's family, he sounded wise most of the time that Lukia was both surprised and impressed at the same time.

After few minutes or so, her mother regained her composure and continued the story," They followed her all by the way to the river. They couldn't find her, but what they did find on the riverside was her bucket, her sandals, and her wrapping cloth neatly folded on top of the bucket."

With the tale complete, Lukia made her way into the hut to see whom the story was being narrated to. She entered the room to find her uncle sitting on the only bench in the house with rich-looking man. He was dark and had a well-rounded belly. On the other side of the room, her mother sat on the mat with the fairest of the woman of the country. The woman looked familiar but Lukia couldn't figure out where she had seen her before.

Lukia shook hands with each of the strangers and went to hid herself behind her mother. Lukia's mother apologised for her behavior and told the strangers about her daughter's condition.

"Lukia doesn't speak but she could hear and knows sign language. She is Eustancia's younger sister, three years apart." her mother continued," You see pastor, our whole family is not doing well and we need your help."

Pastor. The man was the pastor at a church Eustancia attended. The woman was his wife, now Lukia remembered where she had seen the woman before. Few days before her disappearance, Eustancia had dragged Lukia to church. It was strange since Eustancia was the only one in the whole family who went to church. It made sense for Eustancia to go to church; she was nineteen and looking for a husband. After the service, Eustancia had pointed to the pastor's wife and whispered into Lukia's ear," She is your father's girlfriend. I saw them kissing last week behind the grocery store."

Lukia didn't know how to react when she had heard the gossip. Now with the woman sitting comfortable beside her mother she didn't know what it meant. She wondered again how the holiest of the woman in the village had managed to meet her father who didn't go to church and spent his time at beer halls with loud noises. No answer came here. Lukia kept her eyes on the door waiting for her father to bust in and do something.

Nothing happened. Her father come back home early evening, hours after the pastor and his wife had left. He didn't come alone, he was in company of two men. They didn't go inside the house, but straight to the cattle kraal where they stood and pointed at different heifers at irregular intervals. After an hour or so the two men left. Her father went to the kitchen where Lukia was preparing supper in the presence of her mother.

"The village headman and the witch doctor just left." He proclaimed. No one said anything, not even his two younger siblings.

"The doctor said we should pay him one beast and another cow shall be slaughtered for the ceremony," her father continued, "the headman had agreed that the ceremony be done two nights from now."

"You can't do the ceremony that night," Lukia's mother's finally spoke, "Eustancia's pastor will be doing an all-night church service at the river bank to bring back my daughter."

Her father stood up, upsetting the bench. He puffed with anger, "You think you are now the man of the house who does all the thinking? Did you think this through? What if you are upsetting the mermaid by doing the Jesus stuff at the river? Do you think my daughter will be safe?"

Aunt Firidha intervened and tried to sooth her brother's anger by kneeling on the floor and begging for the soft side of the Hog totem. Her older brother didn't have time for that, he even lashed at her, "Don't pretend you even care Firidha! You are enjoying the attention the news people are giving you. You think you are going to be a celebrity because you will be on TV and YouTube? You need to get another husband and leave my house. Or go and beg the first one to take you back."

Lukia continued cooking on the fire place, she didn't have the voice to give her opinion. She could see her uncle sitting quietly in the dim hut, listening and waiting for the perfect moment to chip in. In the end it didn't matter; her father was the first to storm out of the hut, probably to a beer hall, her aunt unable to look at her sister-in-law escaped to her sleeping quarters, and her mother with red eyes, from the loss of the battle of words, excused herself and went to cry in her bedroom.

Lukia continued cooking and she knew that night only her uncle and her would be having supper. The trio wouldn't be back until the following morning. The scene that had played in front of Lukia wasn't a new one. Fighting had been happening almost every day since Eustancia had vanished. They were the same and always solved nothing.

"Everyone is on edge these days," her uncle finally Said, "they should calm down and solve this like a real family."

Lukia dished the dried okra she had cooked as the relish for the night. She handed it along with a plate of sadza and a dish of water for him to wash his hands. Her uncle starting eating near the fireplace where the light was better. Lukia took that opportunity to closely look at the man her sister had called 'the devil of the family'.

He was around twenty eight, dark and short. He was the sweetest member of the family, after Eustancia of course. Lukia couldn't imagine what the horrible thing he had done to Eustancia many times that she would consider telling the police and calling him a devil.

"It's considered rude to stare at people like that while they are eating." Her uncle said eventually noticing her.

Lukia hand mentioned what she thought she would never tell anyone. "Maybe Eustancia left to find her real father because everyone in this family is horrible to her, especially you. You deserve to go to jail for taking advantage of her."

"That was a lot of words and I didn't understand any of it, well, except for father and Eustancia. What I think is she has eloped with that boyfriend of hers who works in Harare. She should have appreciated how much your mother and father loves you." Her uncle said.

Our father, the words echoed in Lukia's ears. My father, Lukia thought, he is not Eustancia's father. She wanted to scream until her father heard that the daughter he had raised for 19 years wasn't his. Lukia knew it, Eustancia knew it and her mother knew it but her father and his siblings didn't.

For two whole days none of the family members spoke to Lukia, except for her uncle. To be fair no one in the family spoke to anyone. With the day of ceremony to appease the mermaid of the river, the family hated each other more. Lukia's mother had decided not to heed to her husband, and was determined to let the pastor host his church service at the river the same night as the ceremony.

On the morning of that day, Lukia's uncle joked that it was better to ask both the spirit of the river and the Holy Spirit for the safe return of Eustancia. The joke was received with stony and awkward silence. He shrugged and went on with his life, which on that day included slaughtering a cow to be consumed at the riverbank during the ceremony.

Lukia helped cook and carry pots of food and beer. There was lots of it, traditional millet beer, pots and jars filled to the brim. It was an essential component of the ceremony. Lukia knew only a cup would be used for the ceremony, the rest was to lure villagers to grace the event. Who wouldn't want free beer?

Apparently the pastor, his promiscuous wife, and their congregation didn't want the free beer. The presence of the ancient liquid was so repulsive to the pastor's wife that she started crying. Lukia desperately wanted to ask her if fermented millet was worse than adultery among the Ten Commandments. Lukia searched the overcrowded River bank for her father. She wanted to see if he was also watching the drama his extra marital partner was acting. She found him standing a distance away, his back turned from the church people. He doesn't want people to notice the chemistry between him and the pastor's wife, Lukia thought, or Eustancia lied there is nothing at all between them.

She kept one eye on the pastor's wife and another on her father. The moment a tear dropped from the wife's eye, a dozen handkerchiefs were offered to her. Being a woman of God she only accepted her husband's only. Her fellow women from church spread cloth on the ground for her to sit whilst she recovered. Lukia smiled, it was funny. How can a woman like that do it with her father? She prayed that her father would come over to her and explain his side of the story.

Her prayer was answered. Suddenly his father turned and started walking towards her. People who had turned up for the ceremony eyed him sympathetically whilst they made way for him to pass. However a hint of anger was on his face. Lukia knew he was coming to vent off. Everyone vented off to her. They came to complain about others to her. They told her their secrets. She was a mute and wasn't supposed to say a single word about. Lukia listened without complaining.

"Look at your aunt over there." His father hissed when he was in earshot, "Dressed like a common whore for the cameras."

Aunty Firidha was dressed in a tiny dress that left her ugly legs bare. A thick layer of makeup was on her face. She looked pretty. Aunty Firidha was directing and giving instructions to the small newspaper interns who had came to cover the event. She was enjoying herself.

"I don't think she cares for my daughter at all." His father said with a resigned look on his face.

Lukia stared at his face and let her hands drop. She didn't have it in her to tell his father Eustancia wasn't his biological daughter. As if he had read her mind his father said, "Eustancia is my daughter, I raised her for 19 years."

Their father-daughter moment was interrupted by screams. A fight had started. From afar Lukia could see the pastor punching his wife. No, not his wife. He was punching the witch doctor who had slapped his wife. The church people were now trying to form a wall to protect their holy one. The horde of beer people stumbled and staggered to help the village headman who had been trapped in the middle trying to broker peace between the two camps.

Lukia could see no one caring about her sister.

Lukia's noticed her mother on the ground. Her father noticed his wife in need of comfort and protection and dashed over to console her, or scold her. Lukia wasn't sure what would happen. Her uncle stood a distance away, tearing with his mouth the meat from the cow he had slaughtered. Aunty Firidha stood alone with her hands on her waist, her army of newspaper interns scrambling away to take pictures of the great twist to the boring ceremony.

Lukia started walking away, upstream were she knew there were no hippos or crocodiles. She could hear the sound of the uproar turning in a whisper behind her. She looked at the slow moving water and begged it to bring her sister back. There was no answer. She asked the river if her sister had left all the madness, left her and her horrible family to a better life. She strained her ears not to miss a whisper from the river. There was silence, not even the birds chirped to console her on that September sunset. Lukia wondered again, where all the birds had gone.

Bhiro nePen

Photography by Tendai Rinos Mwanaka

Another Vestiges of Colonialism installation of Takadiwa is titled Bhiro nePen (ball point pen). It is made up of pen refills in yellow and green, and computer keyboard parts weaved together. We all know the importance of a pen, and the keyboard's function as a pen, but on the deeper level he is alluding to and mocking the political stand of ZANUPF that Nyika haitorwe ne bhiro ne paper (a country cannot be taken by pen and paper, i.e. election), but by a gun!

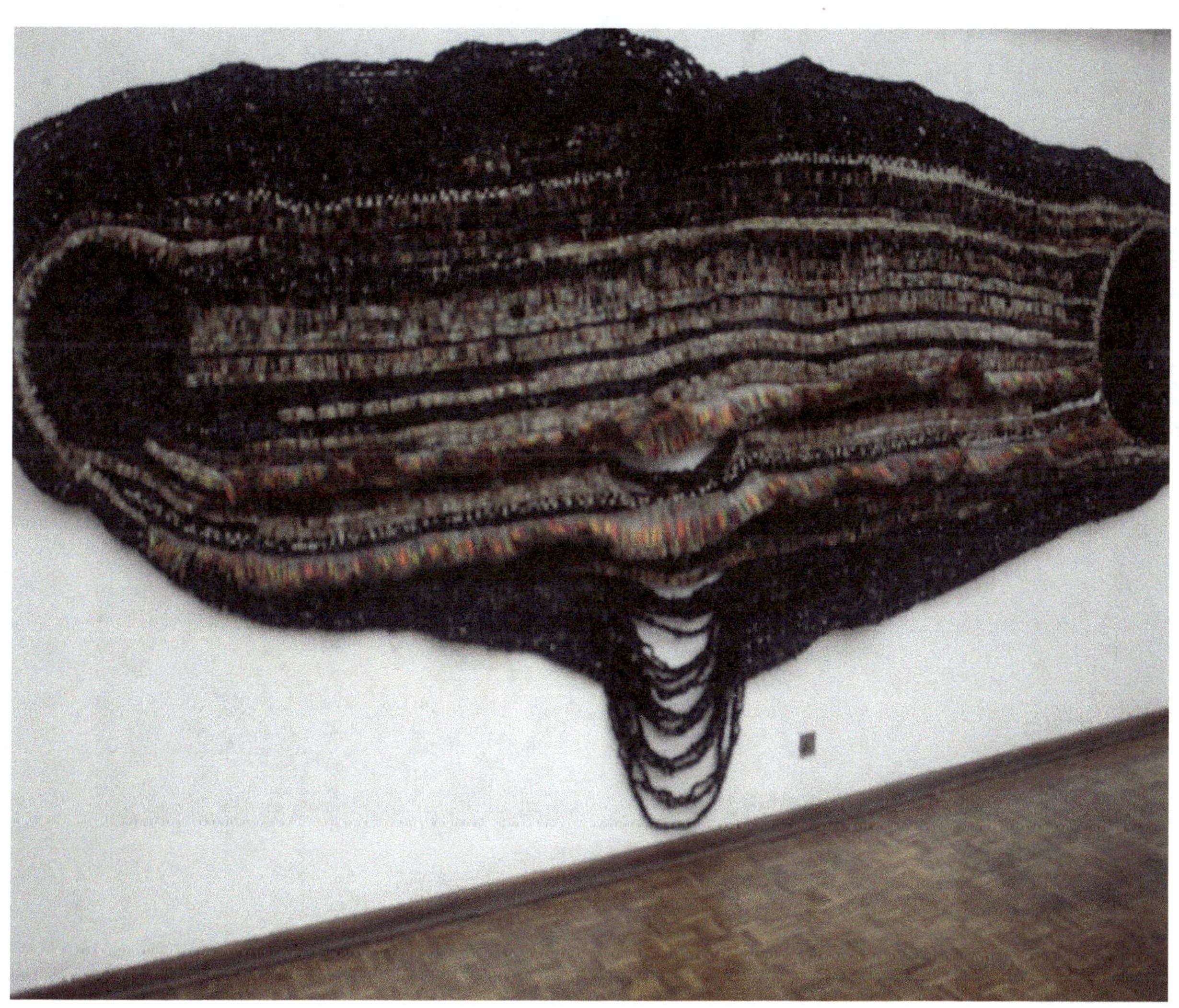

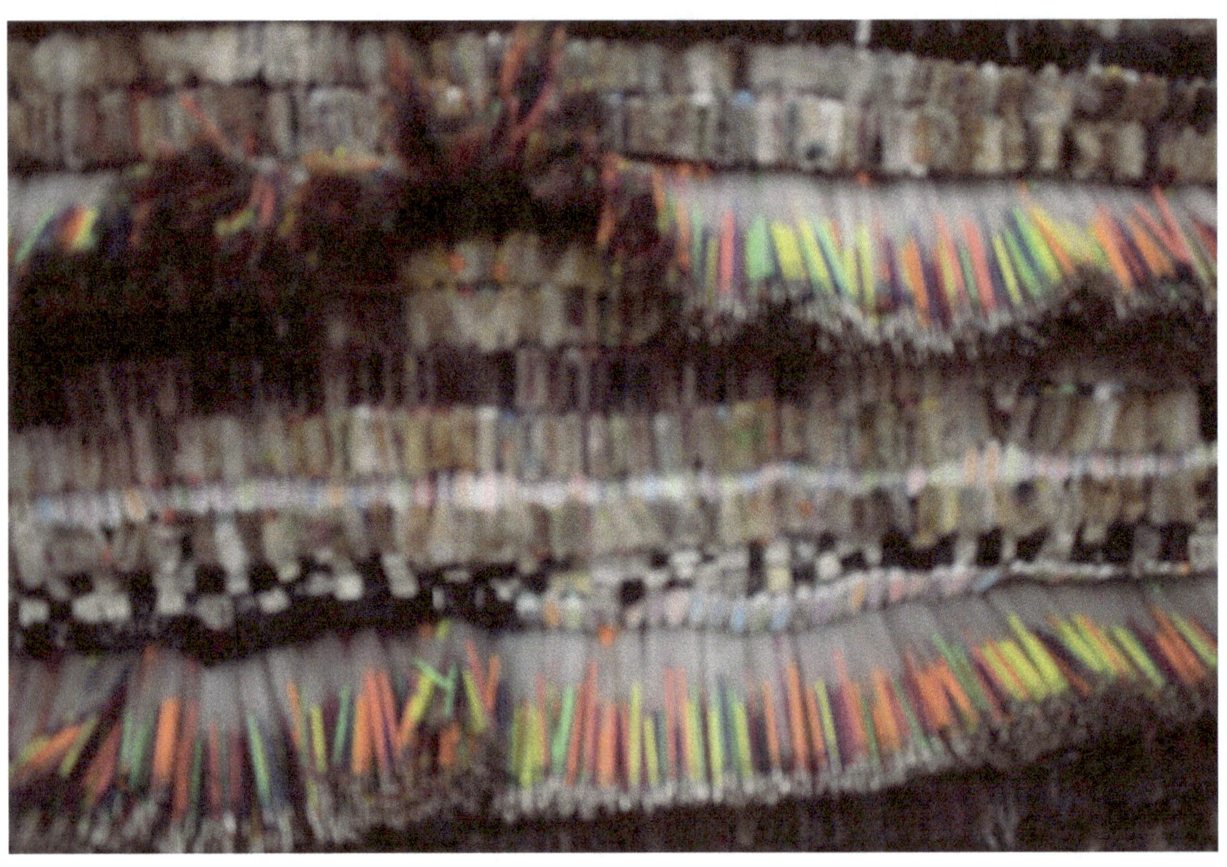

To escape or to overwhelm

Tendai Rinos Mwanaka

To escape or to overwhelm are two love's dangerous animals... I always uncannily choose not to cling to the shirtsleeves of a current. Aren't we most dangerous when we are in love? Imagine the people we have send to early graves through love, the ocean of tears we created, the anguish, the brokenness that's an ever-present fever, the fulcrum of passion whittling away at what was once us. They are a few instances I allowed love to overwhelm me, and I still nurse the wounds... frayed, scared, now closed and the only product are the memories. For none of my loves have grown to create offspring that I can look back on. It always dies a half moon. And we can't throw our arms around the half moon, warming upon the moon's heat. And I think all the memories that are worth writing about happen when you are young, for afterwards you start subtracting yourself.

I was at the edge of seventeen and totally in love, my first voyage into the treacle world of relationships. It's her mother I am writing about now.

Something greyish in the crows' voice, its crazy angry haunting cries at me, as if I had stood in its paths and blocked its sun in the open skies above my fields, makes me think about her, the mother. And the soft mourning of a hoe as I weed my veggies beds, low in the dark black soils of South East Harare. And the few wafts of white cotton clouds grace the western rim of the valley; I could hear the soft drones of vehicles passing through Seke Road on their way to Harare or Chitungwiza. It's a late autumn afternoon, the rains are fizzling out here and there. Summer is gone. These crow birds have been flying all over my paths to the fields too, as if they had a message they were trying to relay on to me, but I had been ignoring them.

Her mother's image as she turned dark with anger but held herself back from exploding seeing me with her daughter in a cozy intimate position beside the road to home never dies in my memories. We were on our way home, Friday afternoon's half-schooldays feeling and the overblown teenage hormones cursing through me as we steamed ourselves in Frenching it. I had her top shirt off, licking her two girls, the centre of my universe and then she was upon us like an evil spirit.

"Murikuitei vana imi", in a crowed voice full of anger she rattled me out of her cleavage. You don't wait to answer and tell her you were milking her. It felt like I was milking the mother. I took to my feet, bursting off into the fields instead of to home which was just hundreds of metres away. Going home was out of question as she could have followed me home and shamed me in front of my mother.

Let her tell her later, I thought as my feet get me beyond her fangled up anger. She shouted at her daughter and told her to go home, and she will deal with her later. It's obvious she will deal with her with sticks and stones.

She was on her way to the shops so she hurtled off to the South as we trundled off to the North. I catch up with my lover a hundred or so metres and tried to comfort her. She was quiet, troubled and I knew that was the end of it. The mother would make sure of it.

But the mother couldn't succeed in breaking Kresenzia and me apart though; it's me who later broke us apart. I escaped.

The crows continued their abuse of the surroundings with their throat corroded caterwauls as I thought of how much she had disguised her detest of me as I ran through girls who looked like her daughters like toilet paper. I was a shit teen, always seeking fleeting attention and backing off when it was too hot, always shitting on everything good I come across. In actual fact back then I just broke things; cups, plates, glasses, pens, books... it was one thing I knew would happen and that I was unbelievably good at, whether I consciously wanted to do it or not, I thought even my gaze could break things up.

I broke her grandma's heart when she saw me 3 months later in an intimate position with Kresenzia's sister, Karen; thereby ending that relationship. And I decided to break myself for a couple of years more trying to win Karen back. She trying to hurt me as much as possible to avenge for the hurt I had caused her and Kresenzia. And for years I was caught in the cycle of leaving and returning to Kresenzia and Karen. I loved both, the one who broke me and the one who made me. From that day onwards I knew how it hurts to lose someone you loved. And as I got older I have realized how the sister must have felt, why the mum detested me and the grandmother could barely answer my greetings ever afterwards, webbing us in unease silence for a lifetime. Love has come to mean escape for me. To escape all this shit I try to keep to myself, to avoid falling in love, to stench off this subtraction that is a constant ache upon us.

"I saw your father at the funeral of my departed Auntie and your father joked with my friend, my friend had told your father that I am his muroora."

"Kkkk," I laughed before I asked her,

"Who is this Auntie who died", and added, "how can you claim to be my wife when you haven't seen me for a year, haven't spoken to me for some time."

"It's Maiguru Mai Kresenzia who passed away", and I am like,

"You are not serious, she died..., when. Why. I can't believe this."

Of course I had been dating the cousin, off and on, but mostly off for 6 years. I can't seem to let her go. Is she the ghost shadow of my feelings for her cousins, for the one who made me and the one who broke me? It's the mother of these two old lovers who died right about the time the crows harassed me with their calls; were they telling me of her passing away. Is she still angry with me for making her girls unhappy? It is 30 years ago, a lifetime that stole the younger sister and the grandmother so many moons ago, and now it was the mother. All that had happened now was between me and Kresenzia. We were the two to outlast that angst and memories. So I asked after her.

"How is Kresenzia", I had lost touch with her decades ago in that period of young adult restlessness and doubt. The best grace a human could ever have is restlessness and sadness. Poets understand this easily, they learn grace by mourning and playing with words. Words are art. Grace is art, Sadness is art. Restlessness is art. Doubt is art. Being the artist here is developing the ability to deal with that which wants to eat you by letting it consume you whole.

"She is fine. She stayed behind home after the funeral, receiving guests; she must have left home just a day ago."

"Where is she now staying?"

"She is staying in South Africa."

Later that night I go to sleep wondering why I had decided to get in touch with the cousin when I had ended it over a year ago. Was it to learn about my first lover's mum- her passing away? I am sad, wounds I thought I had cased inside seem like they had happened yesterday. We never really heal, do we? We just face forward as we learn to live without them, even though we still fester silently.

I don't want to say sorry because I will be apologizing for being me. Who would I be if not me? It's hard to live everyday with who I am, but it's what I know. Of course I am sorry about her death, the pain it caused my first lover. She was my mother in her mother.

Mushona weMazino

Photography by Tendai Rinos Mwanaka

This group of installations in Takadiwa's Vestiges of Colonialism is entitled Mushonga weMazino (medicine for teeth). Those are hanging cavities made up of toothpaste tubes. He is alluding to how when we squeeze out the toothpaste, it's like the way a country extract and sells its resources, once sold its gone. What's left is the cavities

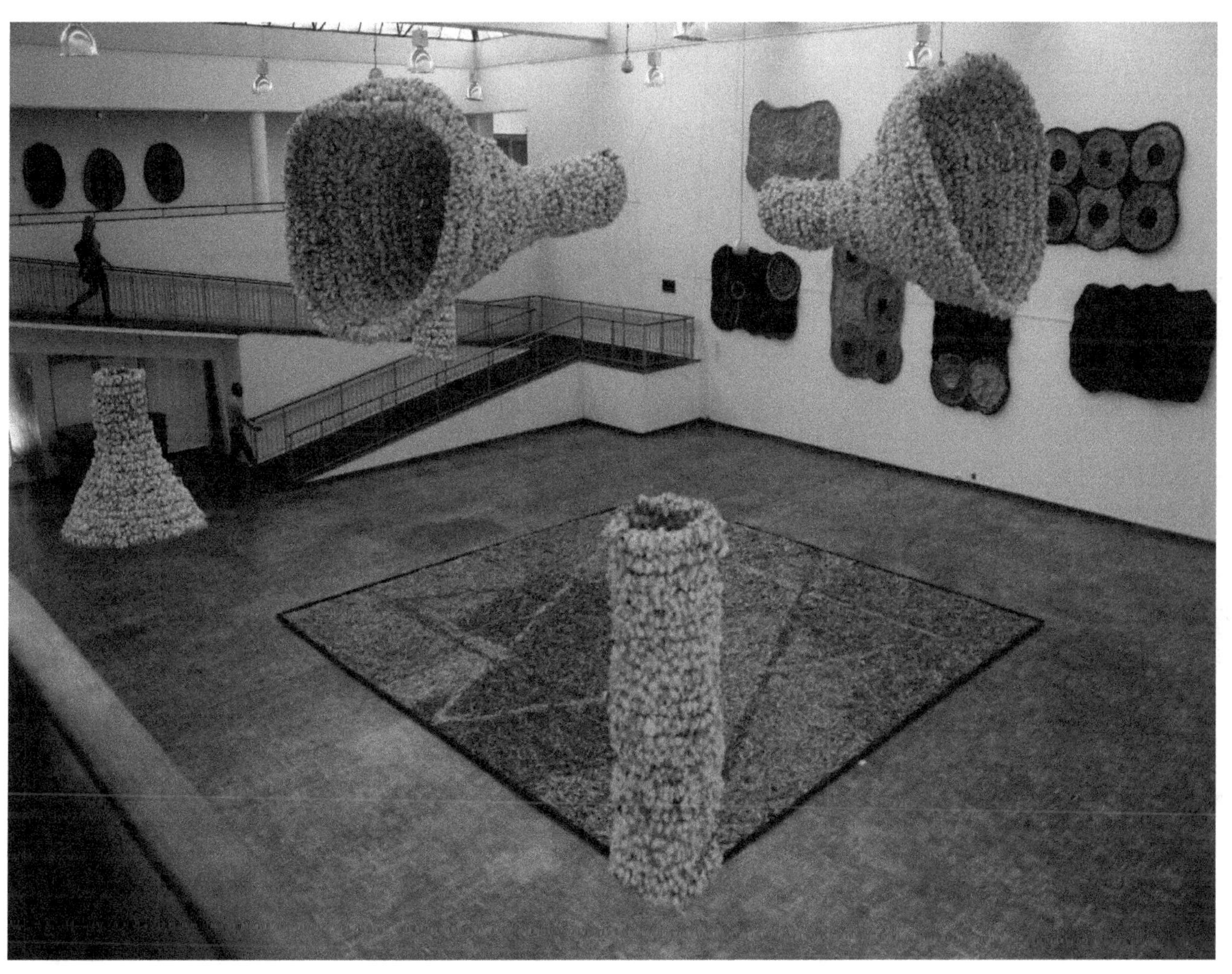

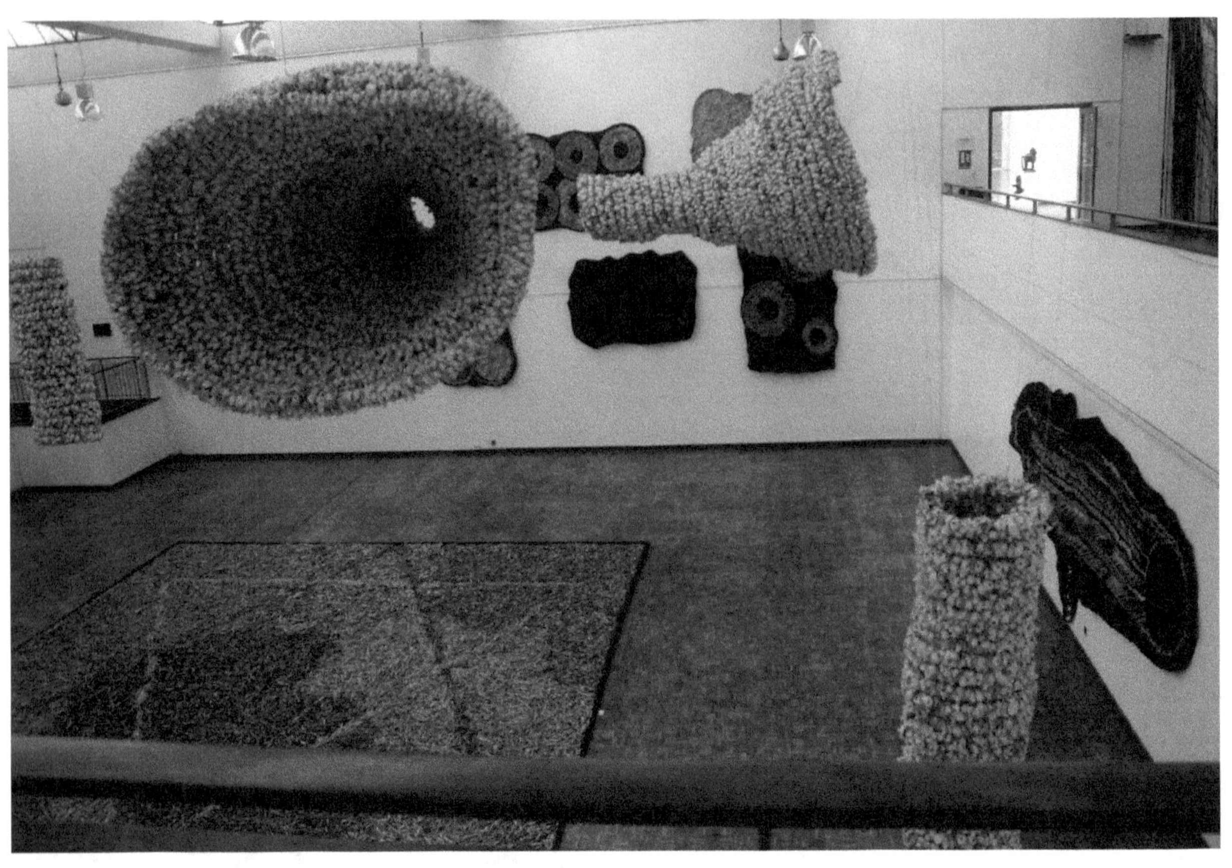

Tomb of the Unknown Soldier

David Chasumba

Tererai was kneeling and weeding the grass between the black granite gravestones at the Heroes Acre cemetery. It was a week before the Heroes Day celebrations and two weeks before the Presidential elections. He turned around and saw a man holding a wreath and standing in front of the tomb of the Unknown Soldier. The man gazed up at the statue and placed the wreath at the foot of the statue. He stepped back and saluted.

He stood up and approached the man. He cleared his throat.

The man jolted back to reality and turned around.

'Good morning, sir?' Tererai smiled at the tall, smartly dressed, middle-aged man.

The man smiled a friendly smile. 'I'm Moses. And you?'

'Tererai. I am a gardener and general hand here. Pleased to meet you, sir.' He shook Moses' hand.

'Pleased to meet you too, Tererai.'

'Do you live here, in Harare?'

'Yes and no. I have a home here in Harare, but I live in a small quiet town, Bexhill-on-sea in England.'

'I could tell from your fluent English accent that you come from the diaspora.'

'Thank you.'

'We don't normally see people from the diaspora, come here and lay a wreath at the tomb of the Unknown Soldier. I hope you don't mind me asking, but what brings you here, to this tomb of the Unknown Soldier?'

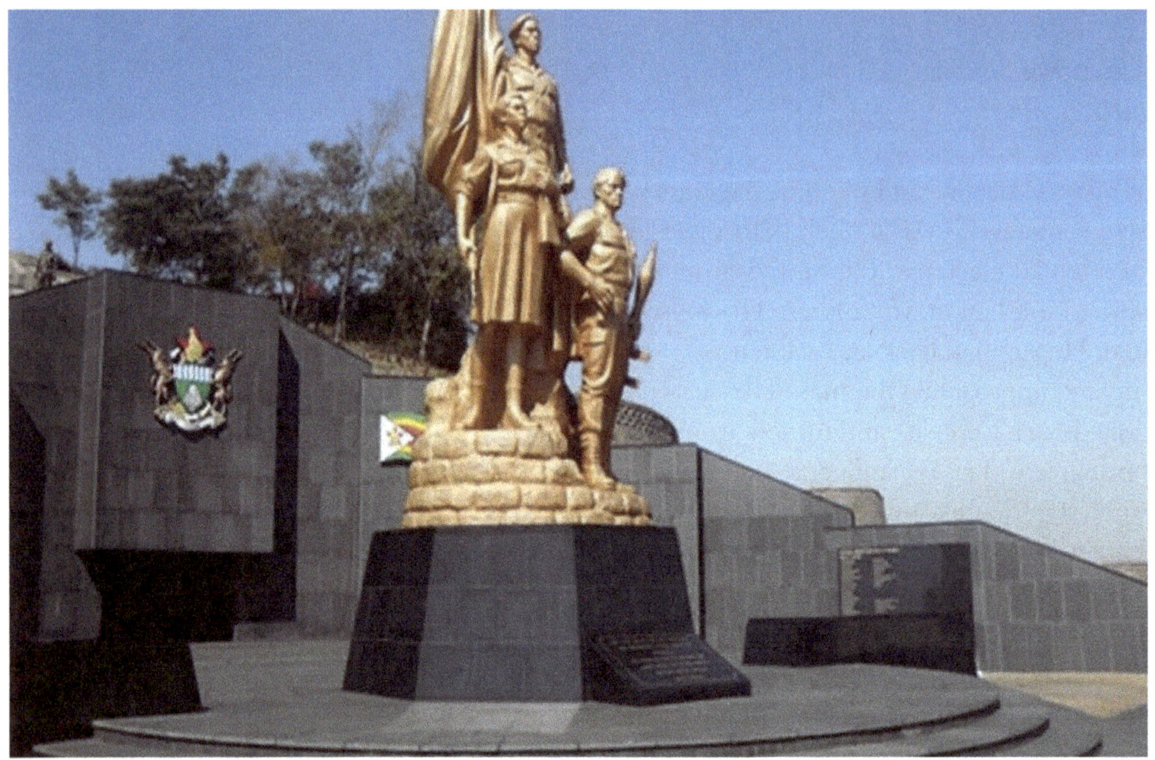

Figure 1: Tomb of the Unknown Soldier, The Herald Newspaper, ZW

'My Uncle Lovemore, the eldest son of my mother's brother, a ZANLA combatant died during the war of liberation, fighting for the freedom of the black people of this country.'

'When did he join the war?'

'1976.'

'Where did your uncle come from?'

'A village near Katiyo in Uzumba Maramba Pfungwe.'

'I heard that there were fierce battles between the ZANLA forces and the Rhodesian army there.'

'Yes. The ZANLA forces operated in my uncle's village with the support of the povo- people of various opinions. But the Rhodesian government responded by creating protected villages, Keeps, fenced and guarded villages to protect the villagers from feeding the 'terrorists', the ZANLA forces. The villagers lived under a 6pm curfew and had to show an ID to leave or return to the protected village before the curfew. One could easily be shot and killed if you didn't produce the ID. They were suspected of being 'terrorists'. The Ian Smith government didn't want the villagers supporting the terrorists.'

'How long did your uncle live in these protected villages?'

'Two years.'

'How did he end up being involved in the war then?'

'Uncle Lovemore was tortured by the Rhodesian forces when a sellout told them that he was still collaborating with the terrorists as a *Chimbwido.* After the torture, he fled with his family to our home in Sinoia, present day Chinhoyi.'

'Why did they flee to Sinoia?'

'The cities and towns were safer than rural villages and were refuge for displaced rural families.'

'What was your relationship with your uncle Lovemore like?'

'I loved him a lot. He was in his late teens. He loved to tell stories; folk tales, *Ngano* and other stories about living in the protected villages. He had seen villages bombed and razed to the ground, villagers killed, and dead combatants displayed in public to scare villagers from joining the terrorists. He produced model cars out of wire. I loved driving my wire model car on the dusty streets of the high-density township of Chitambo, Chinhoyi. Many times, Uncle Lovemore carried me on his back, and we went to the shops. He also liked courting girls. My dad owned a small grocery shop and was generous to his in-laws who were suffering from post-traumatic stress disorder.'

'And what happened next?'

'Unbeknown to my family, Uncle Lovemore began sneaking out of the house and hanging out with other teenagers at a certain house in Chitambo township. Black townships were recruitment centres for the freedom fighters.'

'Oh no!'

'Uncle Lovemore was radicalized to join the war and take arms to fight the Ian Smith government. He was noticeably quiet and was no longer as friendly. He no longer talked about girls. I wanted to ask what the matter was, but he had withdrawn into himself. One day, I followed him from a distance. I saw him shake hands with strange looking youths of his age and he disappeared behind a certain house. I wanted to call him back. I wish to this day that I should have told my mother what Uncle Lovemore was up to.'

'The following day, Uncle Lovemore took me to the shops as usual. He bought me a candy cake. He told me that he loved me a lot. He put a letter in my back pocket and told me to give my mother in the evening. He told me he was going somewhere, and he would be back soon. He left me by the gate and walked away. That was the last time I saw my dear Uncle Lovemore.'

Tears streamed out of Moses' eyes.

'Later in the evening, my worried mother asked me if I knew where Uncle Lovemore was. I said no. My mum went out looking for him in the houses of some of his friends in the township. My mum was distraught when she returned home and there was no sign of him. He was always home on time. Late at night I remembered the letter that he had put in my back pocket.'

Moses took out a discolored envelope and handed the worn-out letter to Tererai. 'This is the letter that he wrote 47 years ago.'

The letter was barely legible and read:

Dear Tete and family
I have decided to join the war of liberation and fight for the freedom of my black people. I have observed the way black people have been oppressed under the Smith regime. I hated living in the protected village, in Keep, like an animal in my own ancestral land. I couldn't just hide from the war in the sanctuary of the towns and cities. I made up my mind to fight for freedom. If it is God's wish that we should unite one day, in an independent country, so be it. But if I should die fighting to liberate my country, please don't mourn me forever. I gave my precious life for the freedom of future generations. I was not coerced into joining the war of liberation. I joined out of free will. I joined fellow comrades to free out mother land, Zimbabwe. I will always love you. Pass my warm regards to little Moses.
I will always love you,
Lovemore.

Moses smothered tears. 'My mother and the whole family cried for days and wished they had known what Uncle Lovemore was up to and stopped him. But there was nothing we could do. Many youths were recruited by ZANLA that way. The family at the home where Uncle Lovemore went said they had never seen him. I am sure they knew all about him, but they didn't want to admit it. It was an offence to not report that a family member had joined the war of liberation. The BSAP would have visited our home and arrested my parents. Everyone kept silent those days. You didn't know if your neighbour was a sellout.'

'Did he return from the war?'

'It's a long story. After the ceasefire and the ongoing Lancaster House talks, the combatants left the battlefield for the assembly points. It was a time of joy and sorrow. Families reunited with their loved ones who had been fighting in the bush. Some members grieved their loved ones that they had lost in the war. The assembly points were dangerous places where the war hardened combatants were suspicious of the ongoing talks and were itching to return to the bush to fight. My mum and her brother, Uncle Chirenje, Lovemore's father, visited different assembly points. They returned frustrated that they didn't see Uncle Lovemore. They held onto the thread of hope that one day Uncle Lovemore would walk back home. They asked everywhere but none of the combatants remembered Uncle Lovemore. The hope of finding him alive faded every day. He didn't return home. My family wanted closure.'

'So, what happened then?'

Moses looked up in the sky and sobbed. He avoided eye contact with Tererai. 'Then in 1981 a disabled stranger with crutches walked into the yard of our home in Sinoia, now renamed Chinhoyi. At first, I thought it was Uncle Lovemore but realized that this man looked older and shorter. I was disappointed. The stranger introduced himself to my mother and father as the commander of the section that Uncle Lovemore and other combatants belonged to. He described Uncle Lovemore as a brave freedom fighter. He narrated the tragic story of the section that he commanded.

* * *

The ZANLA freedom fighters had regularly raided remote grocery shops and looted for food, clothes, and other provisions. But on one fateful day, they raided a white owned rural grocery store. But unbeknown to them there was an observation point of Rhodesian forces on top of a nearby mountain. The observers had spotted them and radioed back up. The backup had responded quickly.

On the way out of the grocery shop with loot, the comrades were fired at from helicopters and quickly surrounded by ground troops parachuting from helicopters. There was a gunfire. The comrades were outnumbered and outgunned. Five of the nine comrades were killed on the scene. Uncle Lovemore had survived the shooting. He and four of his comrades were captured and taken away.

It was the routine for the triumphant Rhodesian forces to display the dead bodies of the comrades and warn the villagers that such fate would befall them if they joined the 'terrorists'. None of the villagers knew where the dead bodies were buried.

Uncle Lovemore was taken to hospital for treatment. He was guarded on his hospital bed. After he got better, he was taken to a detention camp where he was tortured for information. His interrogators wanted

to know where the freedom fighters' bases were located, the weapons that they had in their arsenal, their operations, and military tactics and how they received provisions from outside the country.
But Uncle Lovemore refused to talk and sell out his comrades. They continued to torture him and try to turn him. He saw the section commander during the torture. He told him about his torture. He gave him my mum's address in Sinoia. Uncle Lovemore had died during the torture and his body was dumped at an unknown location.
The section commander had feigned cooperation with the Rhodesian forces. He miraculously escaped captivity and rejoined the comrades. He had expected to reunite with Uncle Lovemore at the nearby assembly point, after the ceasefire. But they didn't meet. He said that Uncle Lovemore was a gallant freedom fighter.
My mum broke down and cried. I went inside the house. It was now filled with loud crying. It was a bittersweet closure for the family.
Weeks later my family went to our rural village to carry out the Shona cultural traditions and rituals to bring Uncle Lovemore's 'wandering spirit back home'. According to Shona tradition Uncle Lovemore's dead spirit was wandering in the jungle. It needed to be brought back home and be appeased. A grave for Uncle Lovemore was erected in his village.

***

'I am really sorry to hear about the tragic story of your Uncle Lovemore. I always wondered what the tomb of the Unknown Soldier really stood for.'

'It pays homage to the gallant freedom fighters, dead and alive, including my Uncle Lovemore, who paid the ultimate sacrifice to liberate this country.'

'Fair enough. I respect the ultimate sacrifices that your uncle Lovemore and many more freedom fighters made to free the country. But look at the current state of the country; high level of corruption, the high unemployment, the brain drain, the suppression of freedom of speech, and incarceration without trial of opposition party members like Job Sikhala, the looting of the nation's resources shown in the Gold Mafia documentary and many more problems bedeviling the country.'

'It is clear that the country is facing challenges that have also been worsened by the sanctions that affected economic development. What has this to do with my Uncle Lovemore?'

'He and other freedom fighters fought for freedom. But we are not eating the fruits of that freedom. Look I have a BA degree in Shona Language and work here at the Heroes Acre as a gardener and general hand. Don't I deserve a chance to get a good job, without paying someone corrupt, to get employment? Didn't your Uncle Lovemore die that we could live in a country full of milk and honey?'

'Yes. I have sympathy for you, Tererai, for the problems you are experiencing in the country. I don't have a right to lecture you on who you should vote for in the upcoming elections, when I live in the diaspora. That is your constitutional right.'

'I won't vote for these corrupt leaders. I will vote for change. It was high time there was change in this country.'

'You are entitled to hold your opinion and vote for anyone who you think brings the change that you want. But it doesn't take away the fact that my Uncle Lovemore and other gallant fighters, immortalized by this tomb of the Unknown Soldier, died so that you could exercise that constitutional right. It is up to you whether you want to vote to safeguard the sacrifices and gains of liberation or as you say, you want to vote for change.'

'I will definitely vote for change.'

'Good day, and good luck, Tererai.'

He watched Moses walk away. He felt sympathy for him. He lived abroad but carried the deep scars of a long-forgotten war. Maybe Moses was right that the younger generation must not take for granted the hard-won gains of independence. But what was there to celebrate in this wasteland, where his dreams are differed?

Tererai imagined that Moses' Uncle Lovemore might have been an old man with children and grandchildren now. He felt his pain. He realized that every generation has its own problems. The previous generation fought hard for independence. But his generation was fighting a different struggle against the liberators who had become repressive. All he wanted was to enter the voting booth and vote for change. But would the change that he craved for materialize? He wasn't sure. At least he had a better understanding why other people still voted for the ruling party, despite and still, the problems in the country. He returned to his weeding.

Korekore handwriting and mats
photography by Tendai Rinos Mwanaka

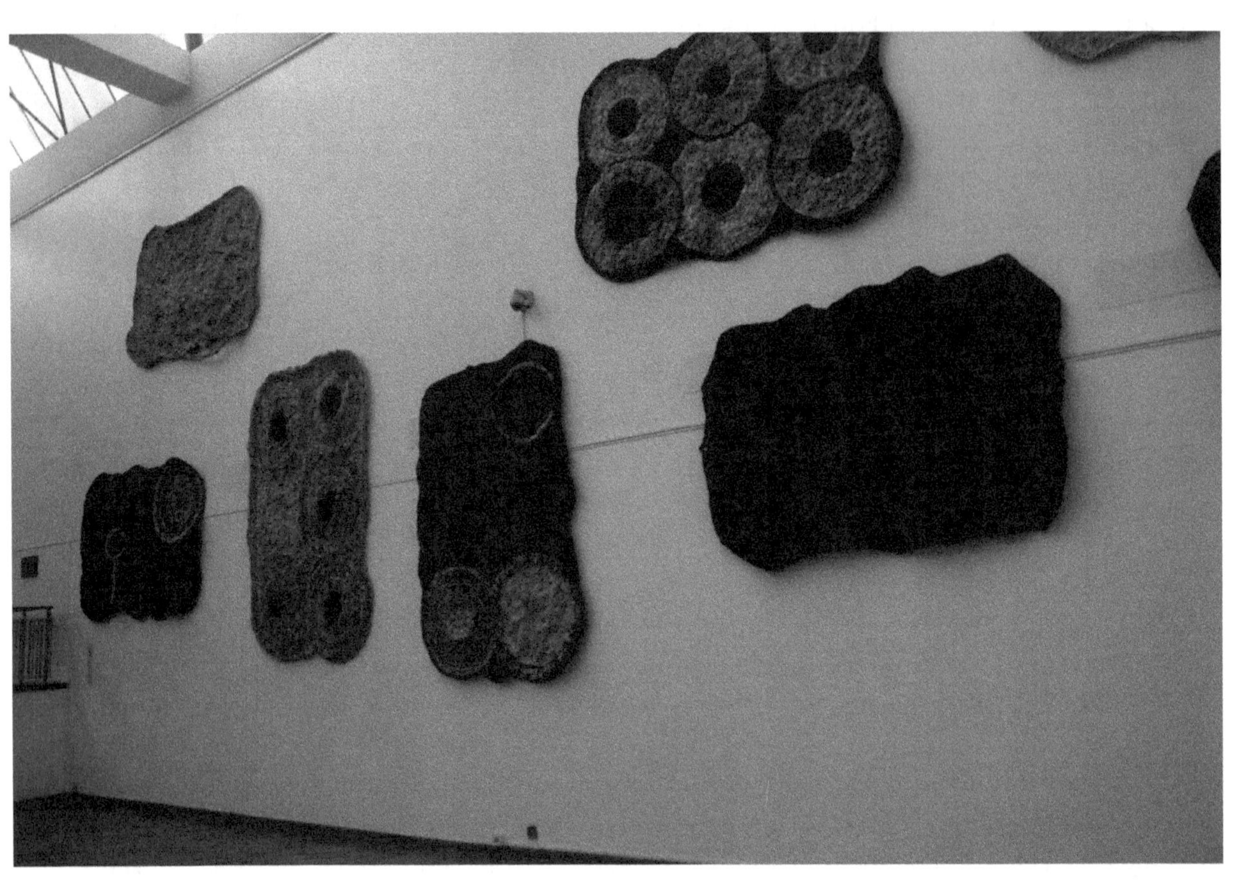

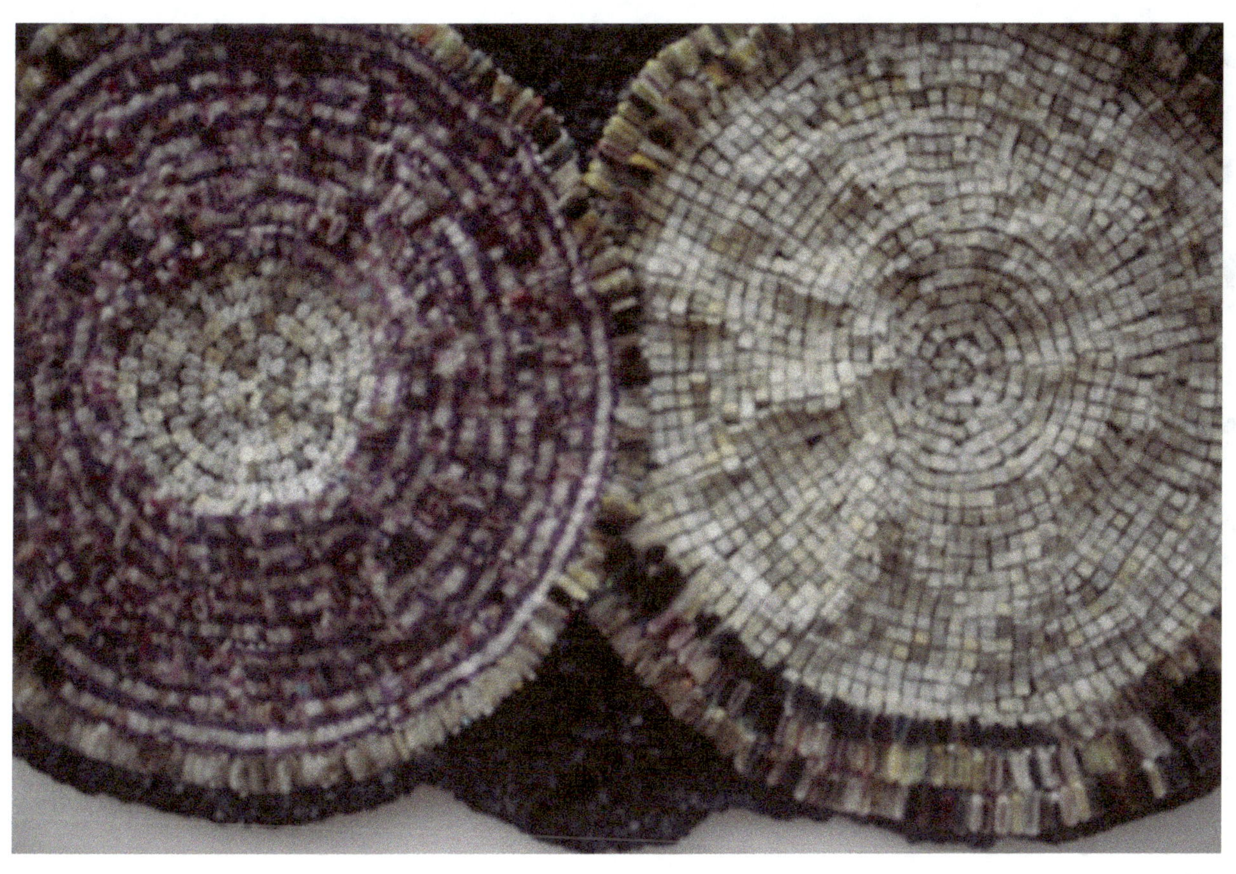

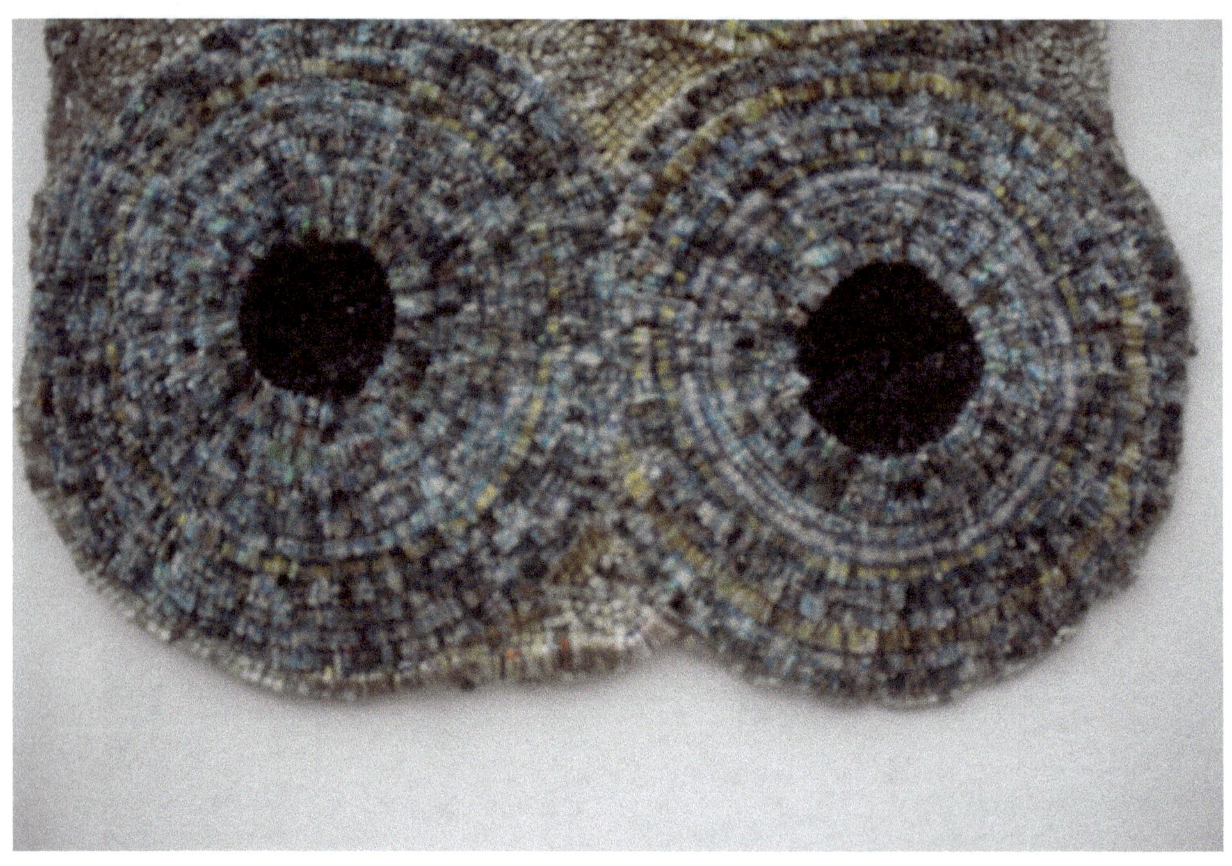

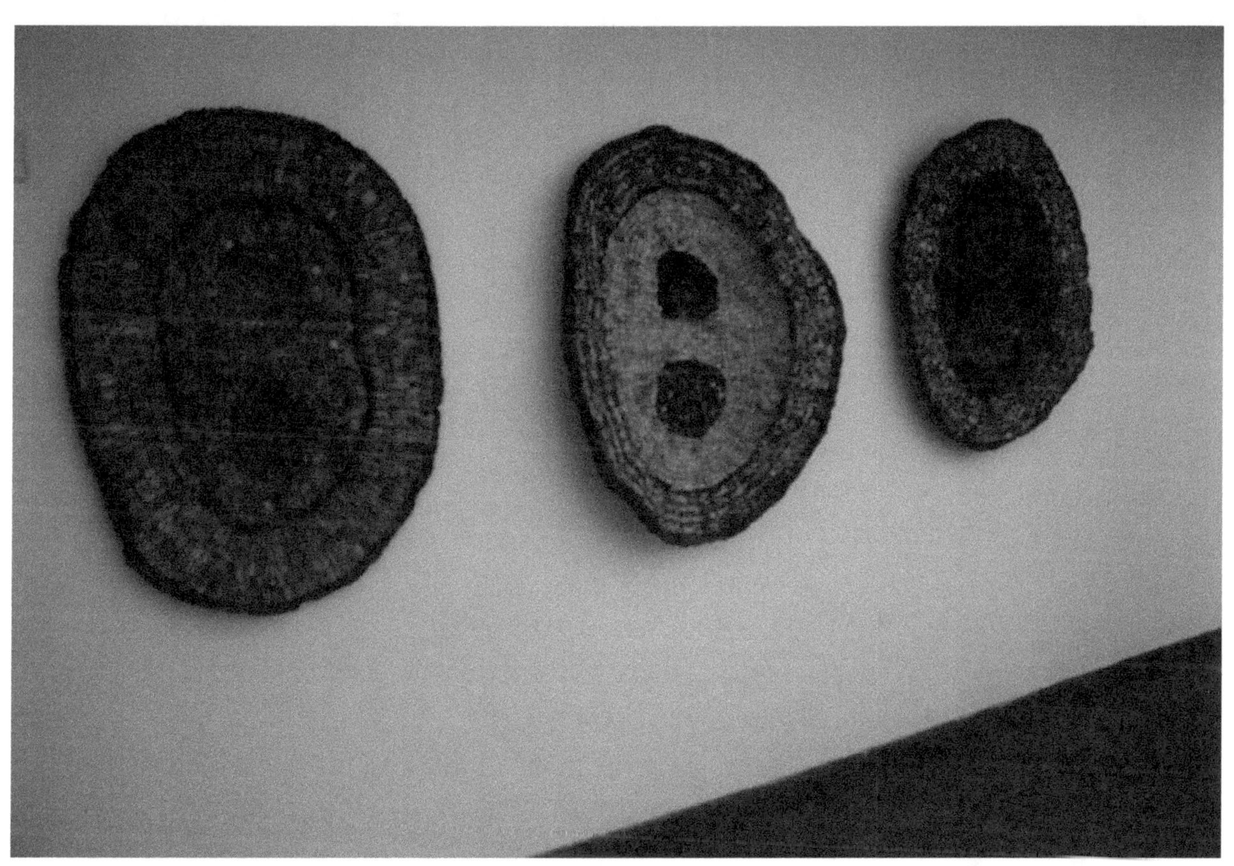

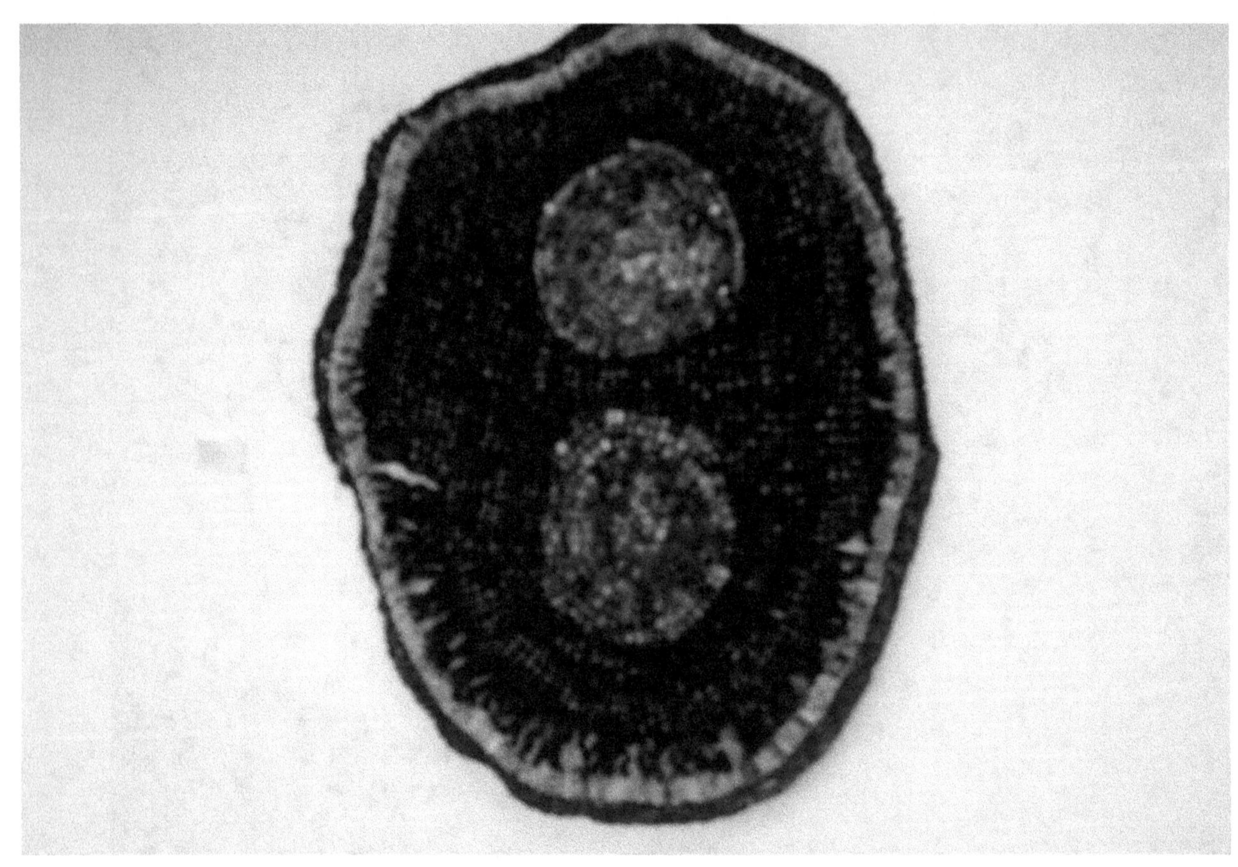

Fixable mistake

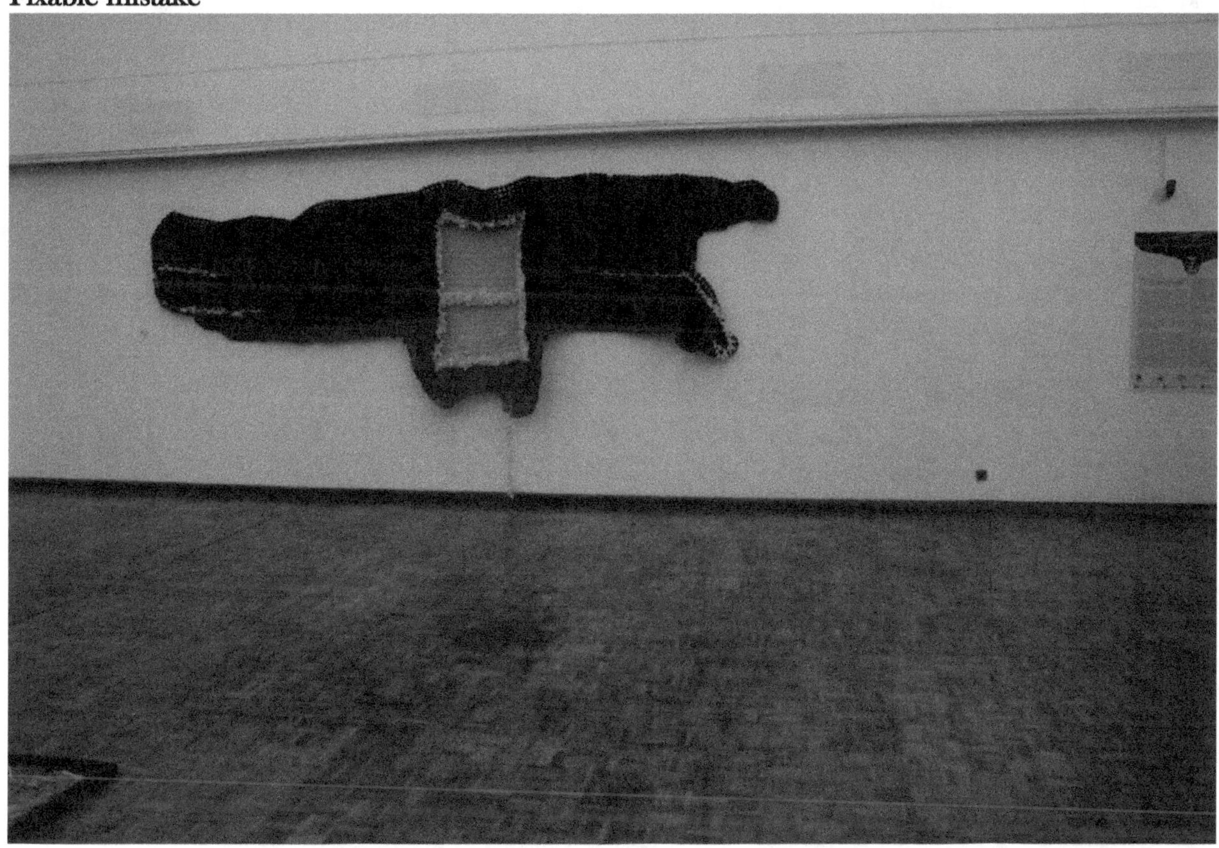

Mariva Enyika

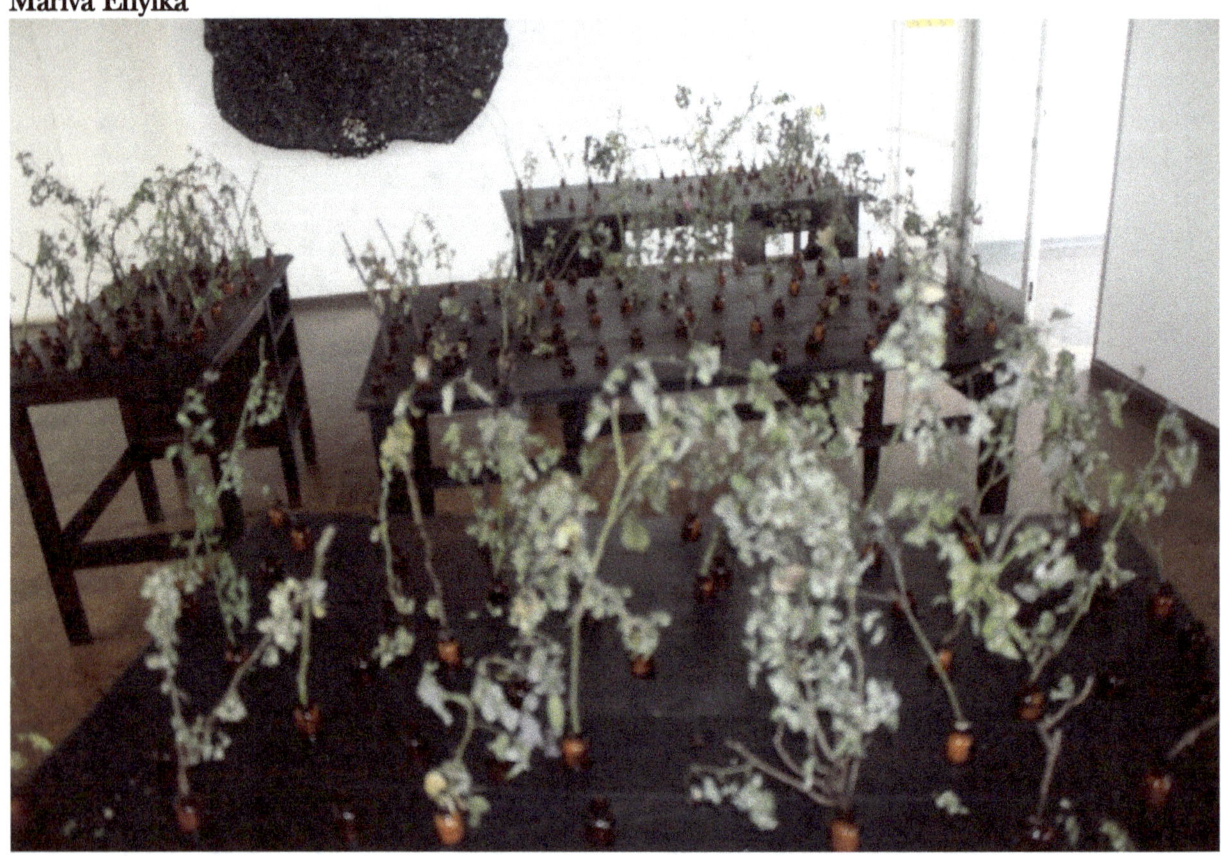

Rugare kwamuri

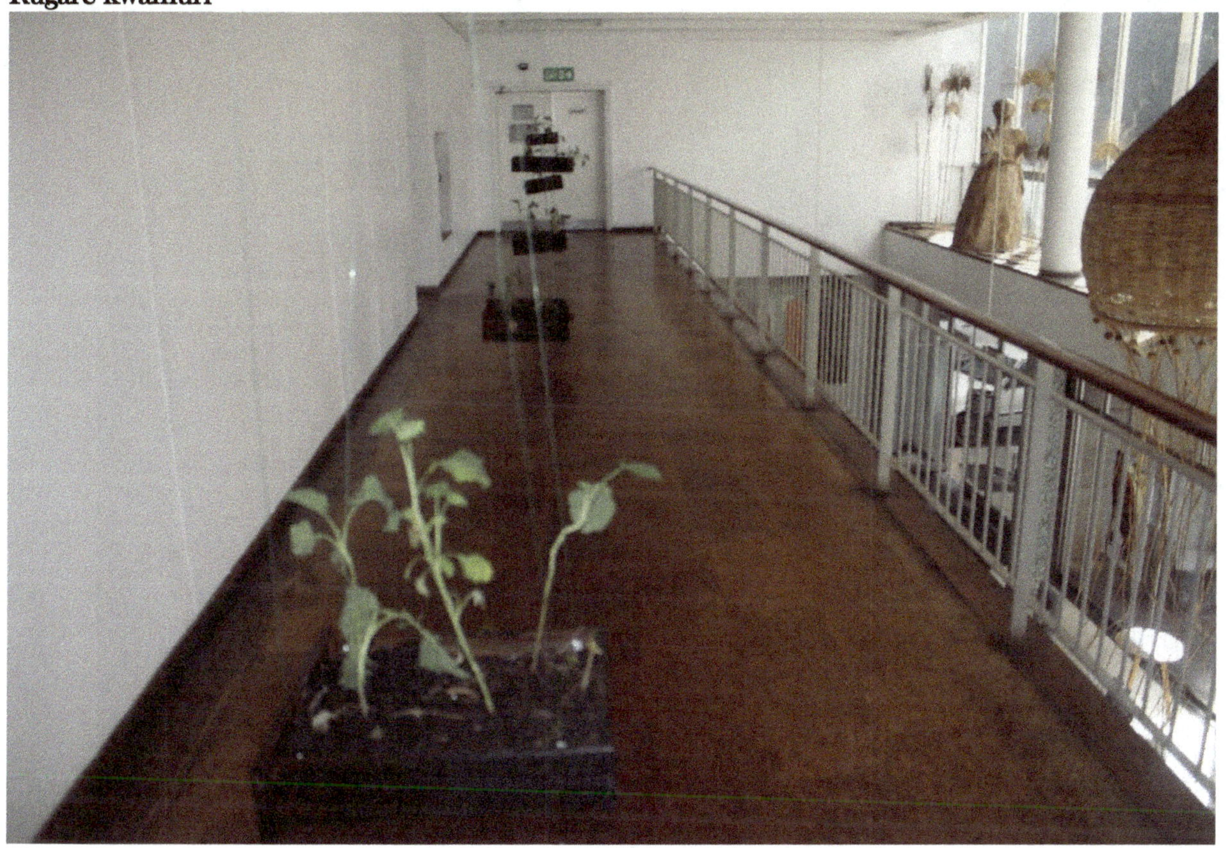

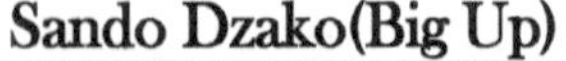

Sando Dzako(Big Up)

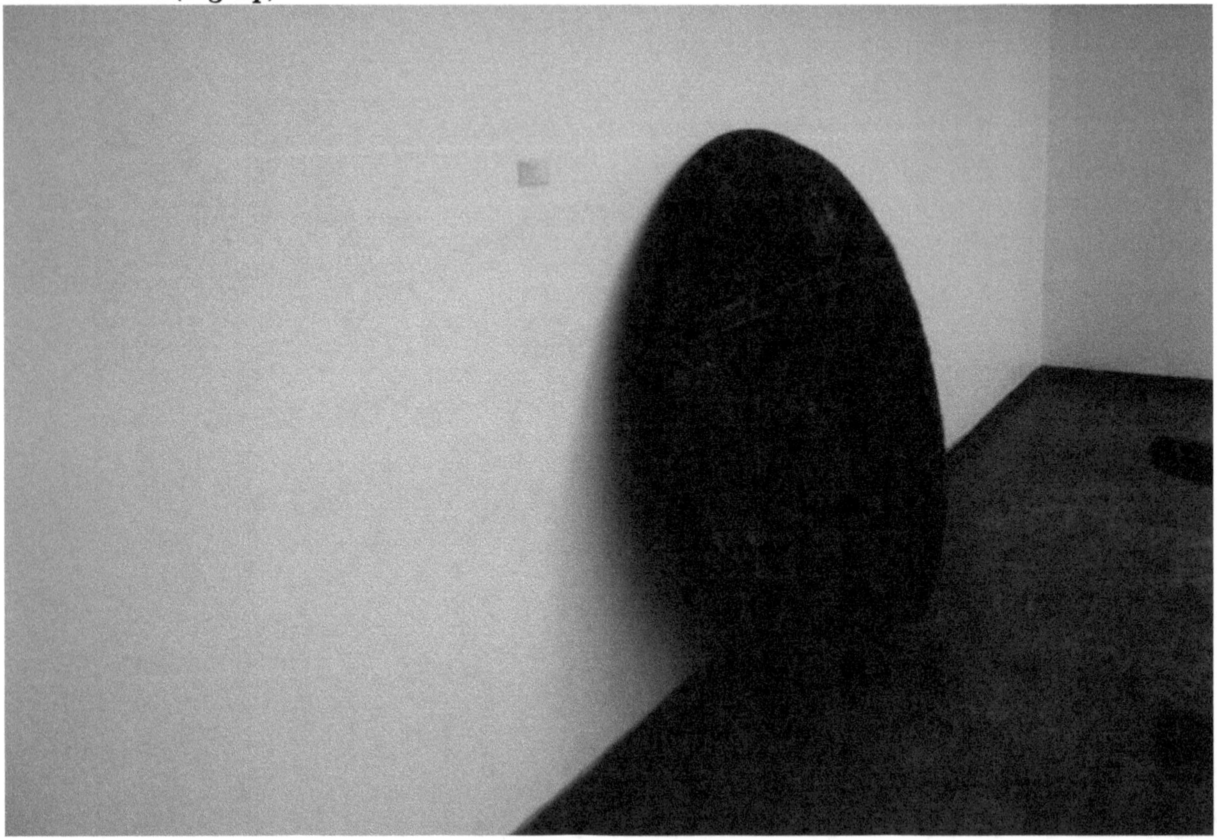

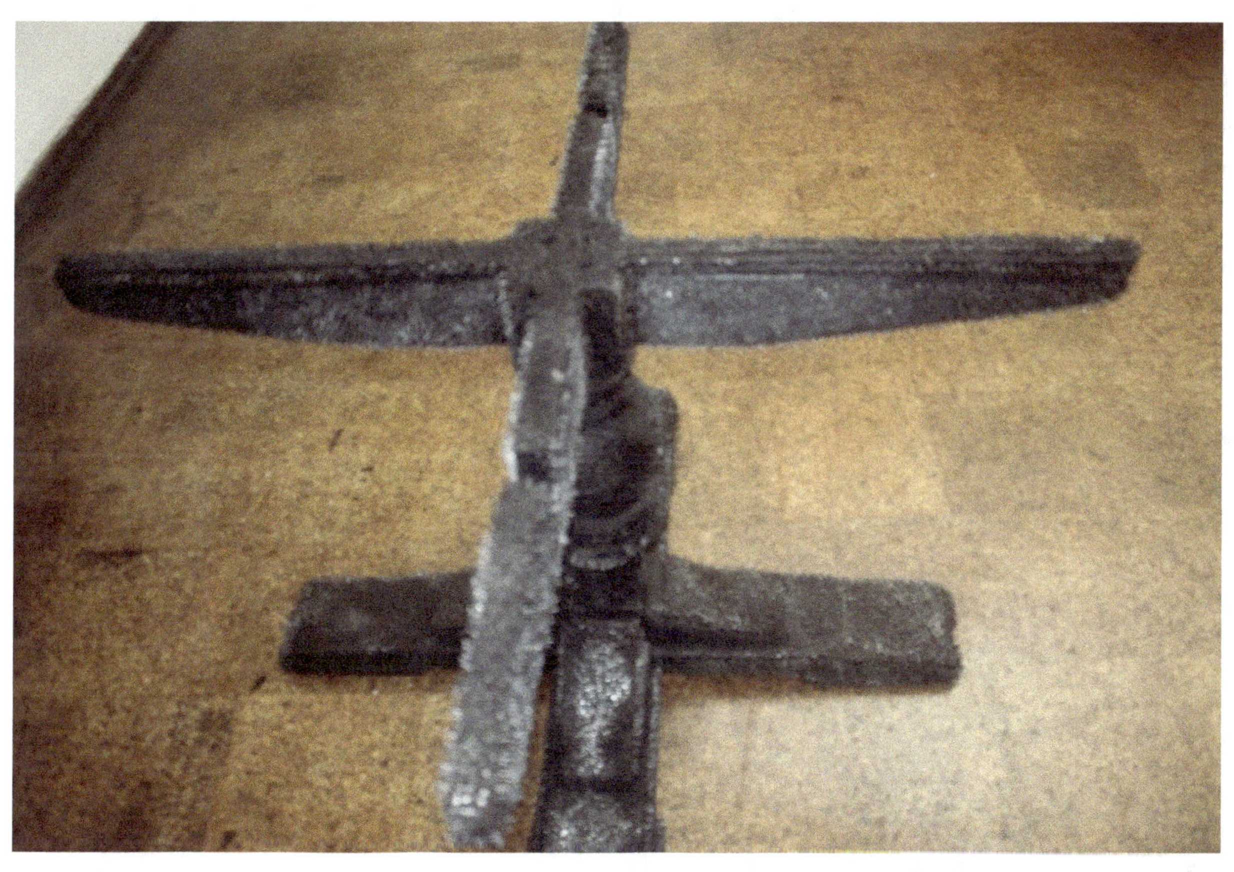

Same old song

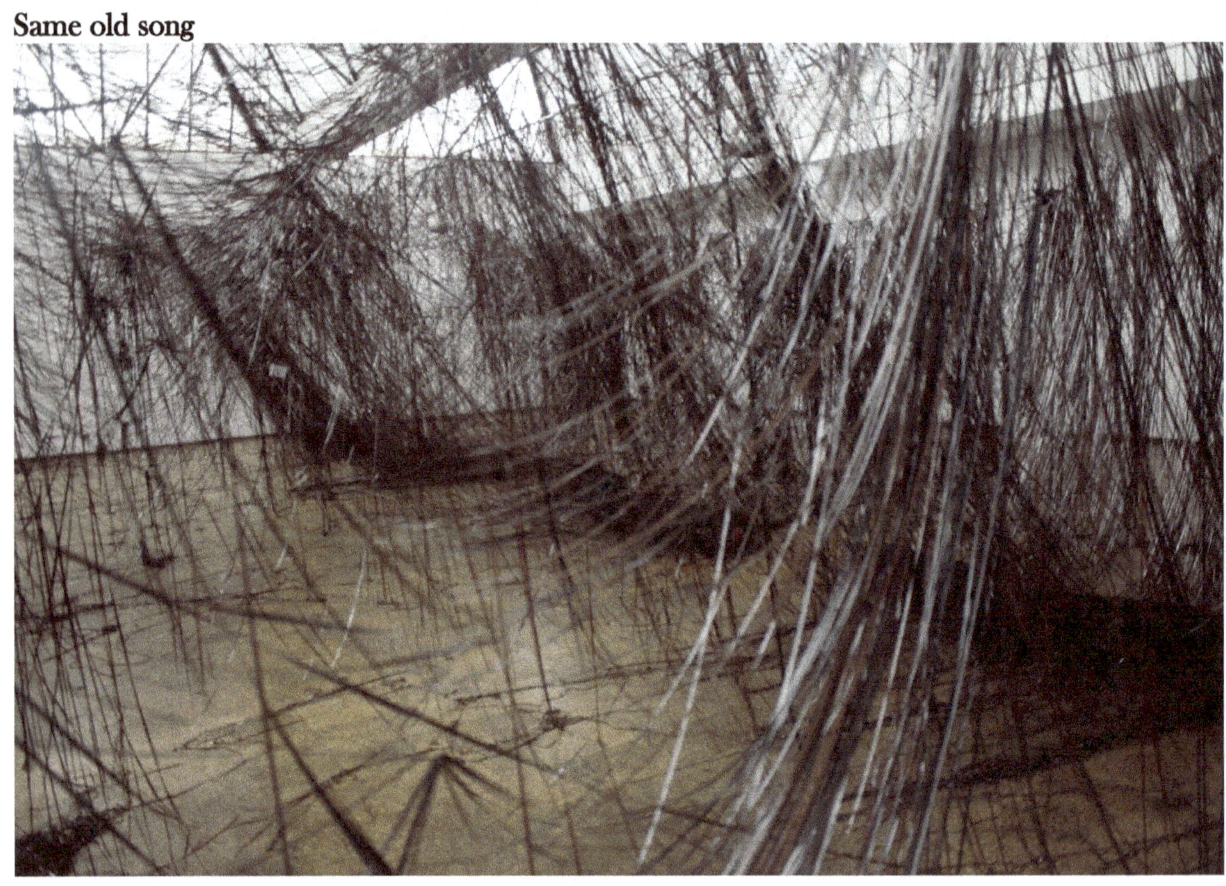

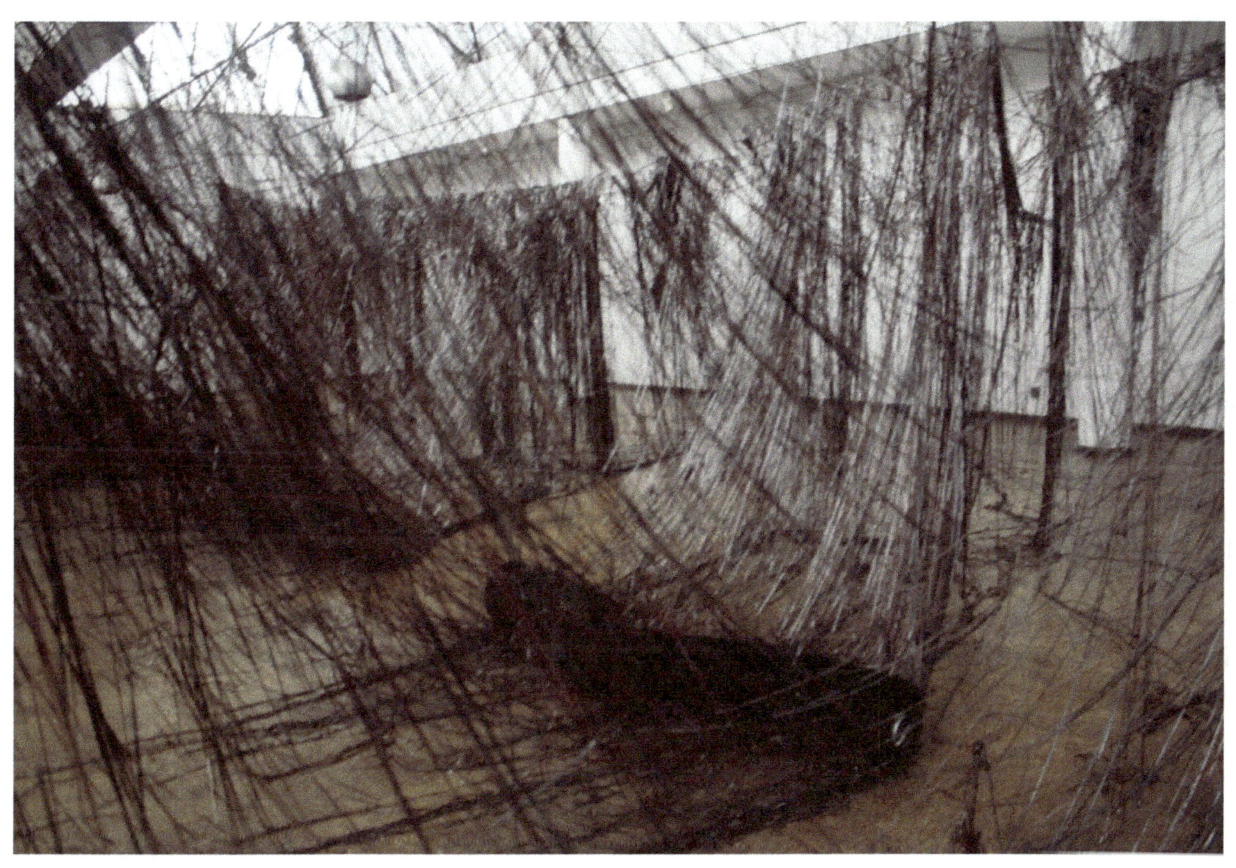

School Poetry

I never told anyone

Aisha Chikodzi

I never told anyone
I was just there alone, drowning in my thoughts
I thought it was my fault, that I never told anyone
I never told anyone
That when they asked how I am i would say I'm fine
But i wasn't fine I was hiding my true emotions behind a smile
I never told anyone
I felt like I was dying inside
That my heart was throbbing and nobody knew
Nobody knew how many times I sat and cried myself to sleep
Nobody knew how many times I just wanted to scream
Nobody knew how many times I focused on people's happiness instead of my own
All I wished was for someone to be there, someone to understand me
But nobody knew, nobody noticed because nobody cared

What is beauty?

Aisha Chikodzi

I thought I would look beautiful with makeup on my face
So I bought makeup and learnt how to apply it to my face
I thought beauty is what you see on the billboards with the models
So I searched beauty remedies on the internet
I thought beauty was when a person has clear skin, a symmetrical face,
The 'perfect' body,
I thought beauty is what you see, feel or easy to spot
But beautiful people do not have perfect skin, perfect bodies or a perfect face
Beautiful people are not perfect, their imperfections are their beauty
Beauty is something within, it is pure
and the beauty you see in anything is a reflection of the beauty in you
Beauty isn't defined by your looks
It is what's in your heart
But beauty is yours to decide what it is

Domboshava (Sacred hill)

Photography by Tendai Rinos Mwanaka

This is a photographic essay I took of one of Zimbabwe's Heritage sites under protection of Zimbabwe Museum and Heritage department, Domboshava. A group of hills 30km North of Harare that has several artifacts and evidence of settlement/occupation by an earlier civilization, thousands of years ago. I will be interspersing these photos with poetry by Zimbabwe's contemporary poets. The first group of photos is entitled Flowing Rock Rivers

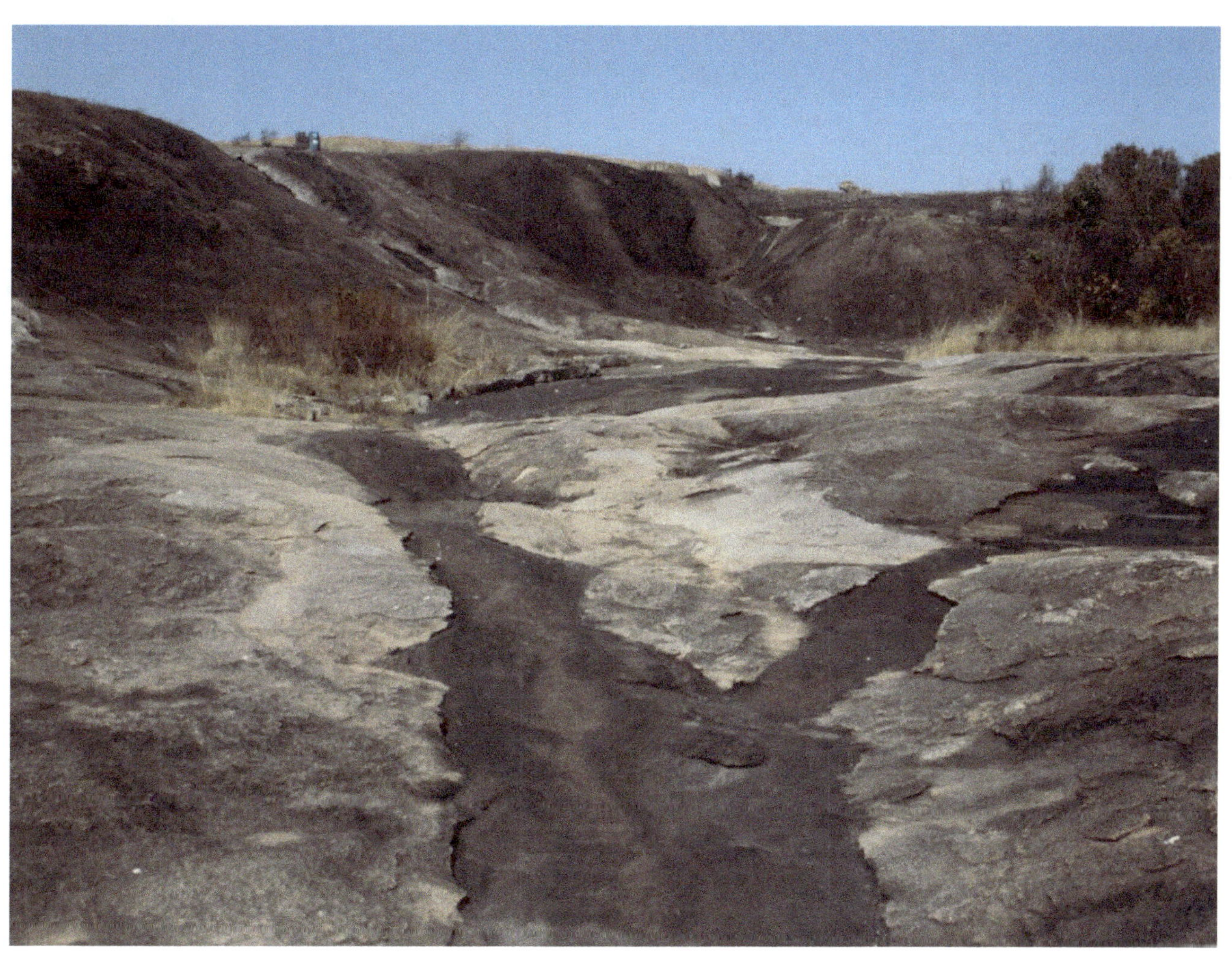

Birthday Blues

Gift Sakirai

Once again I partake begrudgingly
In this oxymoronic ritual
This celebration of my overwhelming impermanence
This ritual which reinforces my ephemeral nature:
A transitory happiness yearly celebrated.
Therein lies the source of my fears,
Which strange shores will this tide of life maroon me?
I'm overly sick of this existence where
I have grown old but failed to grow up.
Am I fated to be a juvenile in perpetuity?
I behold with a gaze nervous
Apparitions deemed old
Tethered to existence by a thread of regret and misery.
Apparitions of old folks
Whose overused bodies and hands
 overly bruised, have nothing to show for it.
Is it to be the fate of my generation?
Won't this boulder mockingly roll down
the mountain of my dreams akin to its yesteryear routine
If I with exertion great, haul it atop like cursed Sisyphus?

Nine lives

Gift Sakirai

I wish I had a life to spare which I would
without second thoughts wantonly put to waste
doing as I please to my heart's content.
I wish the same were true with these dreams
of mine where upon I would with hedonistic abandon
plunder chances that my way would come on a daily basis
for each sunrise would usher in a new carousel of dreams divine.
A pity it is that though I mightily strive for a tomorrow
glowingly bright, in the deepest recesses of
my nightmarish existence dwells demons,
genocidal maniacs who without remorse
murder my aspirations upon their birth.
Feline continuity is what I wish for day and night.
If I could start afresh nine times over,
I would perhaps master the art of deception
and finally bring to grief the vengeful demons which
with unrelenting hate and spite marshal my life
into a dark and desolate existence.

The Crossroads

Gift Sakirai

We find ourselves here once again comrades:
the dreaded forked thoroughfare whereupon
we know not which path to take.
Ours is a curse great which, time after time
leads us to this nowhere where both today
and tomorrow are forever strangers to us.
Like the yesterdays to which we bade farewell ages past,
we are caught in the grip of illusory promises
which never come to pass and a future which
apparently will never be ours to claim.
In between a raided past and a stolen future
are we caught, a standoff whose manifestation
is realized in these indifferent crossroads,
the spectres of our existential time loop.

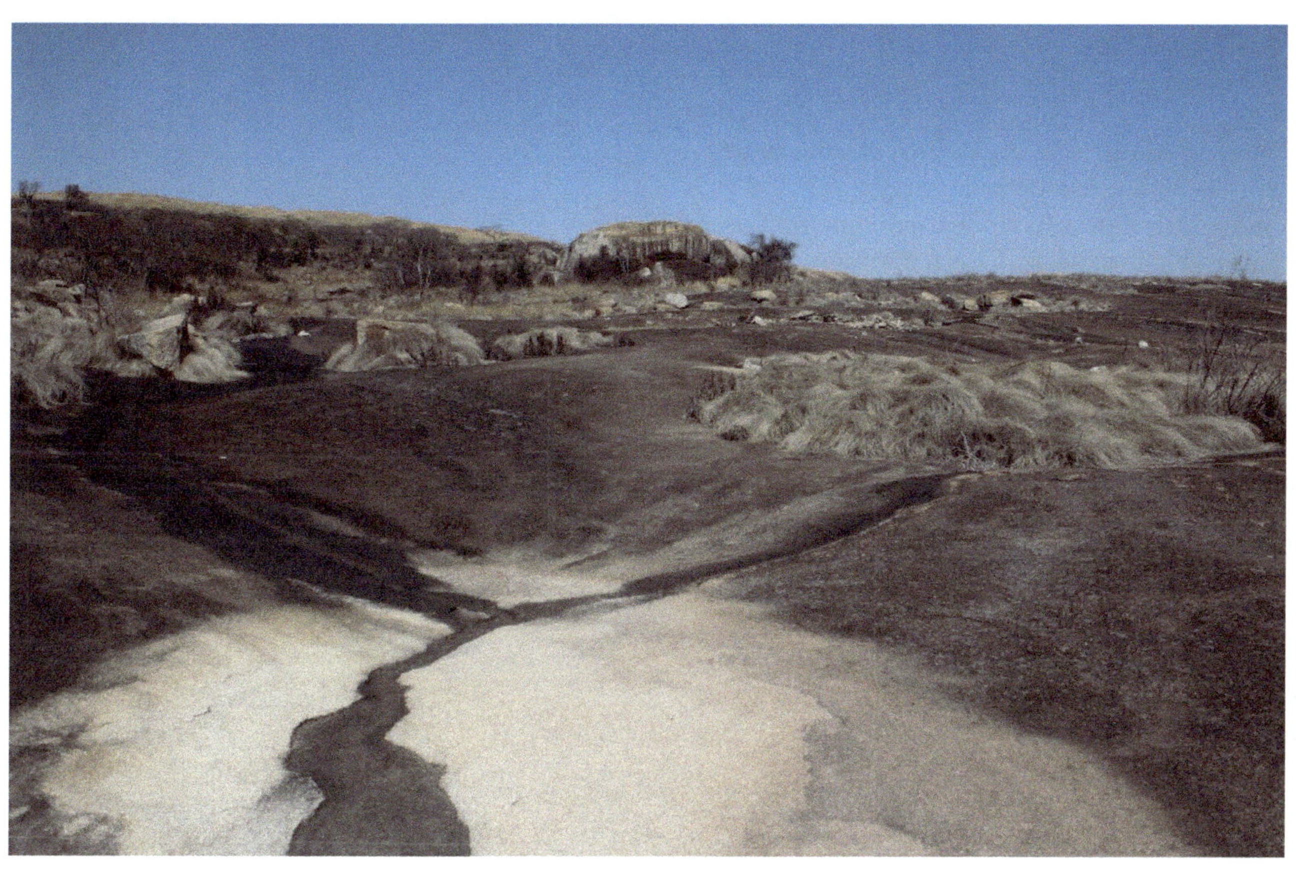

Promises and Lies
Gift Sakirai

They pointed out to us stars which like the sun
lit the sky and with unbound energy we chased
them towards horizons strange and hitherto unseen.
Fraught with an expectation acute we gave our all
for a touch of glory, however temporal.
With a will unshakable we snatched the stars with hands
overly eager only to realize with consternation
that they were just but feeble fireflies.
All spent and way past fifty we no longer
can give chase to dreams which may perchance
be what proved elusive in early adulthood.
We are thus condemned to forever exist
on shoestring budgets for which our children
curse us for not trying in a world
heavily populated by the well to do.
A pity it is that they will never know
how like marks we were conned
into pursuing useless quarry while
our so called friends and their ilk
amassed a wealth abundant at our expense.

Cliches

Gift Sakirai

Within the dreary existence of the ghetto was born,
dreams which like the bald eagle soured sky high; a sight unseen.
Hopes like a thunderous downpour fell
drenching our juvenile minds to the core.
We dared to dream Happy, Patience, Kevin, David and I
in a dispensation where like dew in the morning,
aspirations fizzled into nothing.

Like a latter day Pele, Happy captivated the neighborhood
with his extraordinary soccer skills : a soccer star-to-be,
whilst I blazed through novels and poems:
a pseudo-artist whose career was in progress.
Like little Einsteins come to life, David, Kevin and Patience
amazed everyone with their mathematical ingenuity: futuristic scientists.

Within our dreams we dared to soar sky high,
but within such endeavours we recalled to mind Icarus.
We chased the sun all the same whilst the ever distant horizon
beckoned to us over the humongous vista of time.
Like Lot we vowed to escape the lot
that had been assigned to us with our lot.

Patience, like Lot's wife, stumbled, fell pregnant
and got stuck to a 34 year old beau at a tender fourteen.
How could a girl so bright, be caught up in a trap so deadly?

We soldiered on though, David, Kevin, Happy and I.
At twenty Kevin passed away, a victim of a mining accident
in the Chiadzwa diamond fields, which was a tragic epilogue
to a life which had subsisted in an amaranthine pitch black dispensation.

Like a heavily pummeled boxer, Happy reeled
in the wake of his widowed mother's death.
Sorrow rained on him like an incessant hailstorm
until he sheltered in the arms of his pregnant sixteen-year old girlfriend.

His thoughts ablaze with recriminations of an education
dearly acquired but absolutely worthless, David fled to South Africa where
alcohol claimed him, body and soul.

I lived in a virtual wreckage of dreams but somehow
I got by-barely. I tried to try and I loved being loved
and I tried to claim still what once was mine:
that amorphous imagination but twenty years
down the line I'm still sitting, pen in hand,
summoning an artistic flow that just won't come.

Patience, the erstwhile academic genius cowers
in the kitchen where like a soldier under siege
she evades blows from her domineering monster
of her husband whilst her six terror-stricken children
huddle around her tenaciously clutching her tattered dress.

David, the would-be engineer drowns himself
in drink and subsists in a parallel universe where
he can be the self-proclaimed king that he once was.

Happy, the yesteryear soccer star is now a destitute
who is being played by life in a league of sorrow and strife
where each score is made apparent by every tear that falls down
his shrunken cheeks and here I sit, contemplating these tattered clothes;
the emblematic mainstays of our lives.

We are fast becoming cliches, Happy, Patience, David and I,
textbook cases of the ghetto tragedy and our dreams of yesteryear

will forever hang above us; amorphous and still born,
stifling us just as they did Johane, Mildred, Reketai and Lucky twenty years ago.

Patchwork Quilt
Photography by Tendai Rinos Mwanaka

This seems to be the entry into the most important part of these people dwelling and religious connection. As you see in the second photo it overlooks the half circle of large boulders of rocks flanking a circular path. There is something religious about half circles in all the religions in the world. Something not finished or closed, something that has the power of allowing, mutating...

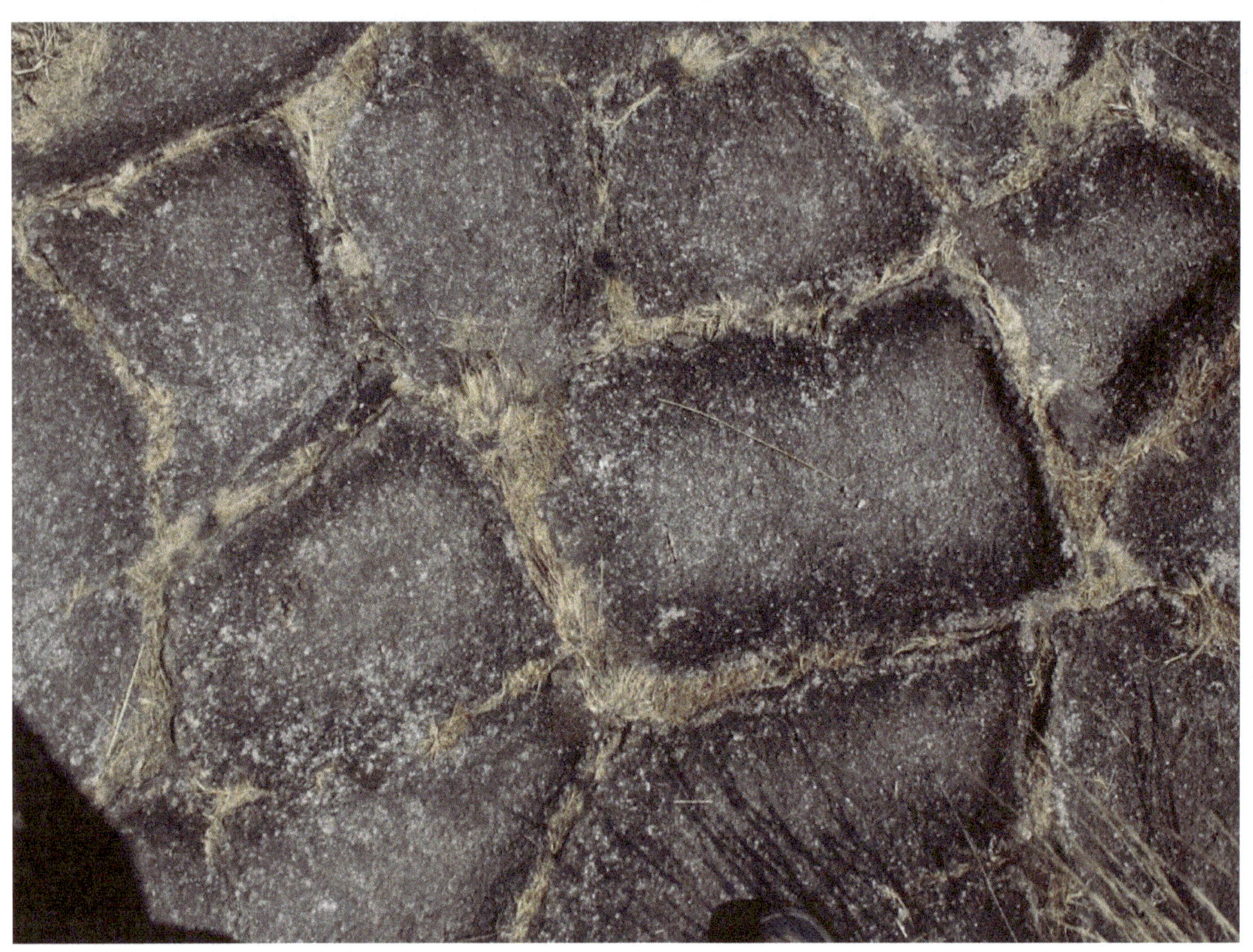

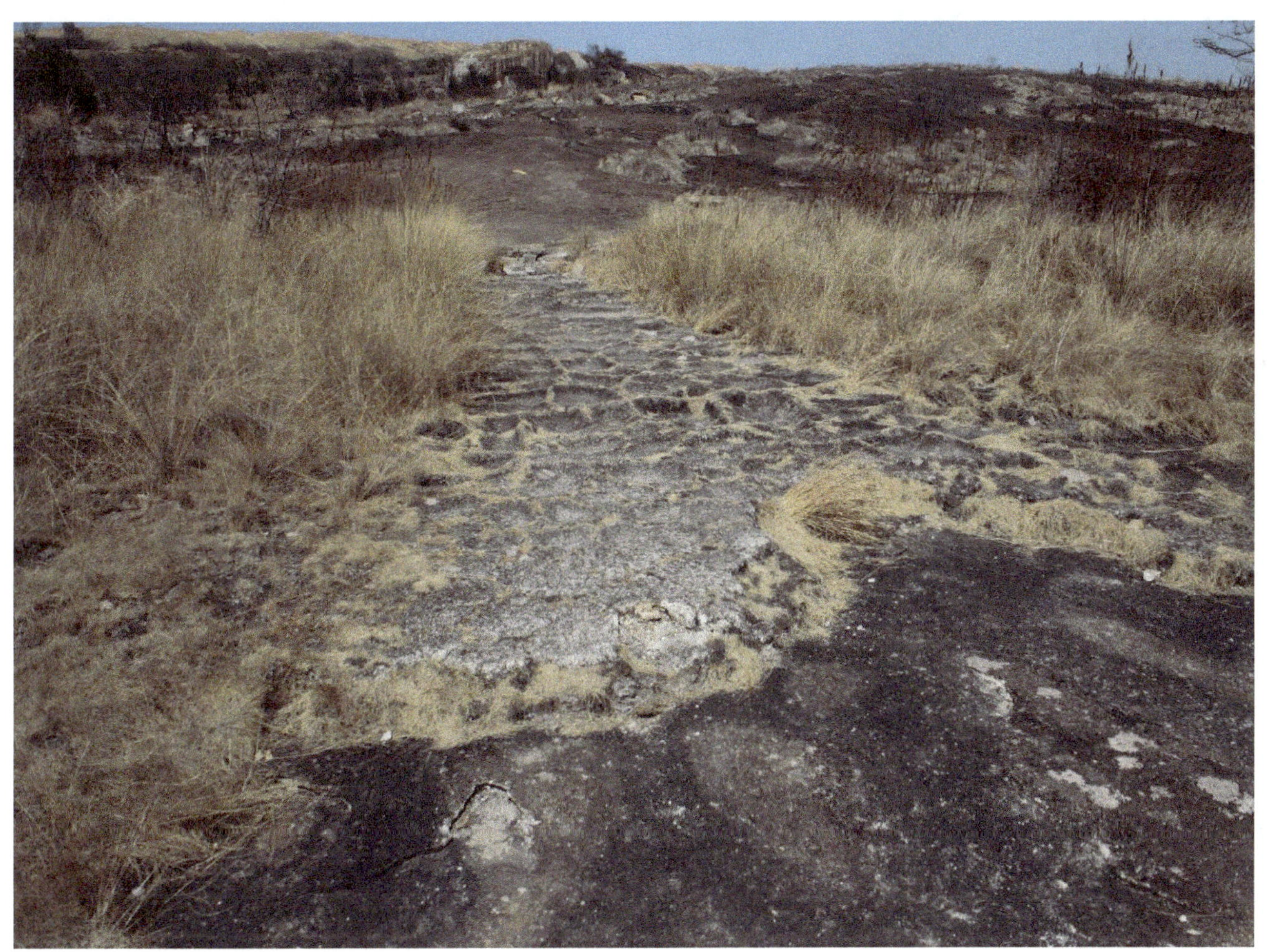

Filling the blank

Edward Dzonze

The spook of Ame
knocked on my pillow-
A ball of fire
to consume the ground
beneath my bed,
-flipping through pages
to where beauty is a taste
beyond the brick walls
Dragging me through galleries
to pick the debris beyond the Depth of Diamonds.
When she asked for a cigarette,
My life went ablaze; up in smoke
The dream chokes, the dreamer gropes
She kissed my mind
With the vigour of a Catholic nun in a secular pun
A dream is never lost
Where the dreamer is found
I took off my pants;
Time was nigh to wear Marechera for a write walk
When I set my lips for more
She banged and whispered through the key hole-
'Pick up the call -
Blank pages to fill
When the new sun is up

Wreckage
Edward Dzonze

(To Kupakwashe and Stacey)

Echoes
Of words said and things done
Like a snake, the past slithers into the future
Moments of regret, moments to pride
The truth can only slip, it cannot hide
Where is the spark in the embrace of darkness
Memories to confront, reality to contend
Every meal is it's taste
beyond what it looks
Walking the road, the rider bends with the curves
Lonely nights are cheap, only a moment to weep
Beyond the taste of this life
the cigarette goes out to divorce the burden
And the maze is born anew in mind
Where is the light in a man's life
When a son is gone,
Whereforth is the bloom of it
When a besotted flower wilts before the eye
The measure is gone when the treasure is gone
Life is no taste without those two

Resurrection
Edward Dzonze

One lie is a sensible truth
Caught between the lies
The truth is a shadow of more
what is desired than what fares
Every season
awaits the right tock of the clock
Heaven is this poetry page
Proclaiming the resurrection of verse
Missing rhymes found beyond the Cemetery of Mind
Passion is this cell in a literary membrane
No wonder why we live the jail with the pen
The Hararean maze wields the same-
Stinking skid rows to
every passionate of art
Profound verse no worse than
a rancid fart
One thing said, many things yearned for
A beat of everything sensible
throbbing from their pen stroke
It takes Marechera's write foot to walk the terrain
The Black Sunlight shines upon me
to revive The Portrait of a Black Artist in London
All shades undone; to depict the triangulation of the dead and the living
A chunk of wisdom
to keep the House of Hunger lit
The truth thus fares
as a shadow of what is desired

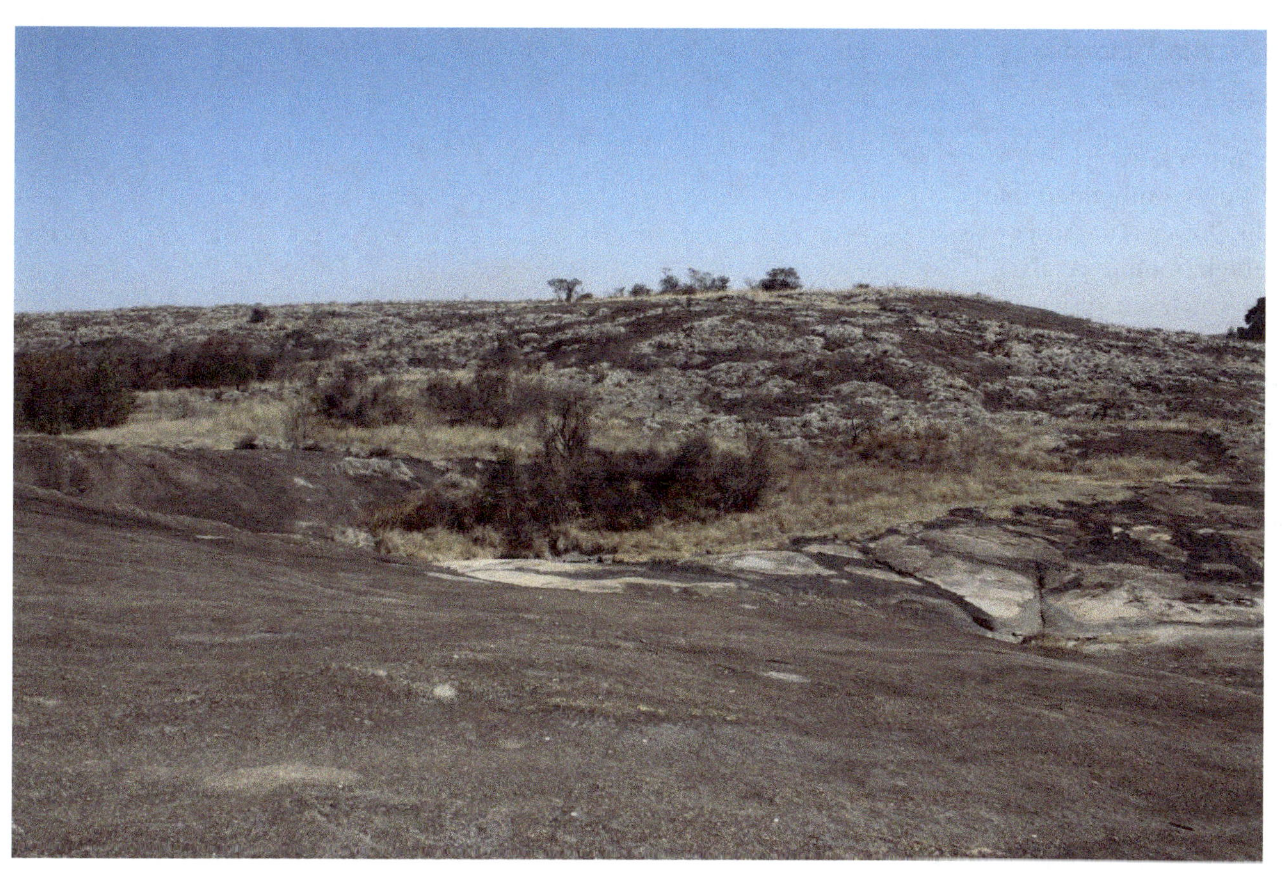

The African Panorama

Edward Dzonze

Freedom is here
the essence embedded there;
All the flower is to Africa
Are the blooming petals
Upon which our resilience glows
Beneath the mask,
Beneath the borrowed vest
The clever bees of Britannia
Mocked the rose;
To suck the pollen for the queen's ambrosia
Because African freedom is defined to taste
From the outside political tongue
The drumbeats of African virtue
Are shushed by the gunshots in the African ghetto
Where Mandela and Lumumba walked barefooted for freedom to sail

Every gunshot is a wakeup call for Africa to slip;
Jihadists and the Militia
Blow the horn of Africa
From a patronised political fart
Beyond the melanin mask,
We are a shattered civilization
Pitied inside our own beauteous dimples
Because corruption and xenophobia is all your valor-
Because terror and brutality is now your color-
Flood the turf with all your bloody tears
The Mighty Nile River will replenish
The spilt blood in qualms of regret
Swallow all the dignity
To spell a name upon the black jacket
Because Africa assumes the morning sun for Europe to bask and see the day

There will be a celebration
To the virtue of African dignity
When the wailing in Sudan secedes political madness

Sing not the valour of Nyerere and Biko
In revolutionary hymns
There is more to denounce before we could dance to freedom;
Nobody needs the spectacles of Mugabe to see the mineral loot across the turf
Because your Zuma knows how to fool his mates
While Gaddafi holds on to the oil tit
Freedom on the board-
Buhari knows the whole chess is a gambit
As long as the African president keeps the shortgun beneath his stinking armpits
Nowonder why the gold in our hands cannot paint our homes golden

Grime

Edward Dzonze

Everything said, nothing given
A sweet line is cast
To sell the slogan fast
The vile brews where a ballot is cast
The freedom train sails on colonial rails
Everything to see-
Where the blind leads the deaf and dumb
A bullet is shown to one without a vest
Between the bullet and the ballot
A sure death is served in an empty plate
Parallel to every path we tread
Bread and butter is vulgar
To what the face of Nehanda have come to witness on a dollar bill
Condoms and cigarettes trending in university corridors
Where sex is a means nearer the poverty end of the jungle we tread,
No better than the beast we dread

Tapestry

Photography by Tendai Rinos Mwanaka

Just like in the previous group of photos, this group stays on the slopes to see that artwork small vegetation and burnt up slopes creates. When I posted the first photo on my fb page some people called it Trumpville, mocking the uncanny semblance of these dried grasses to Donald Trump's mop of hair

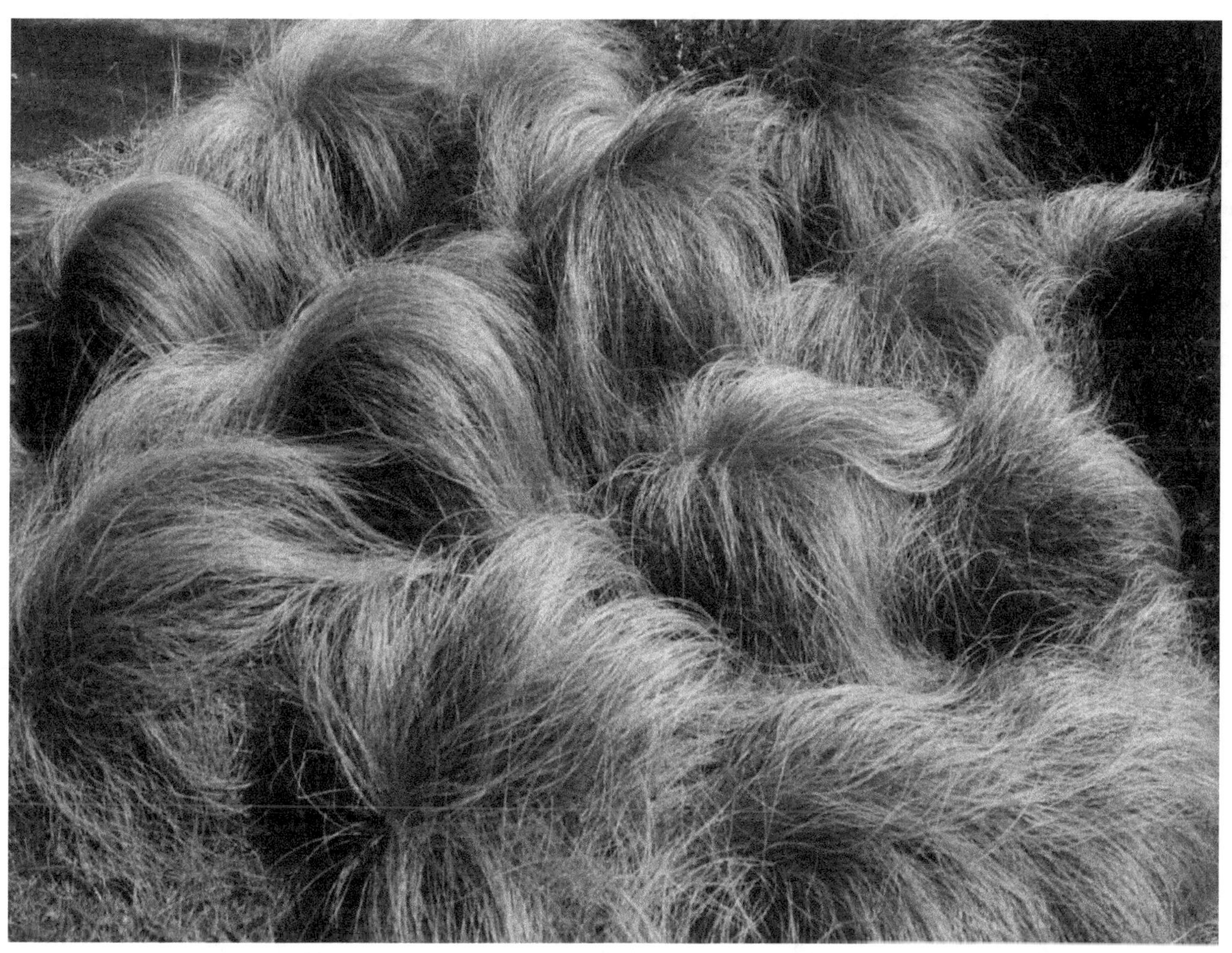

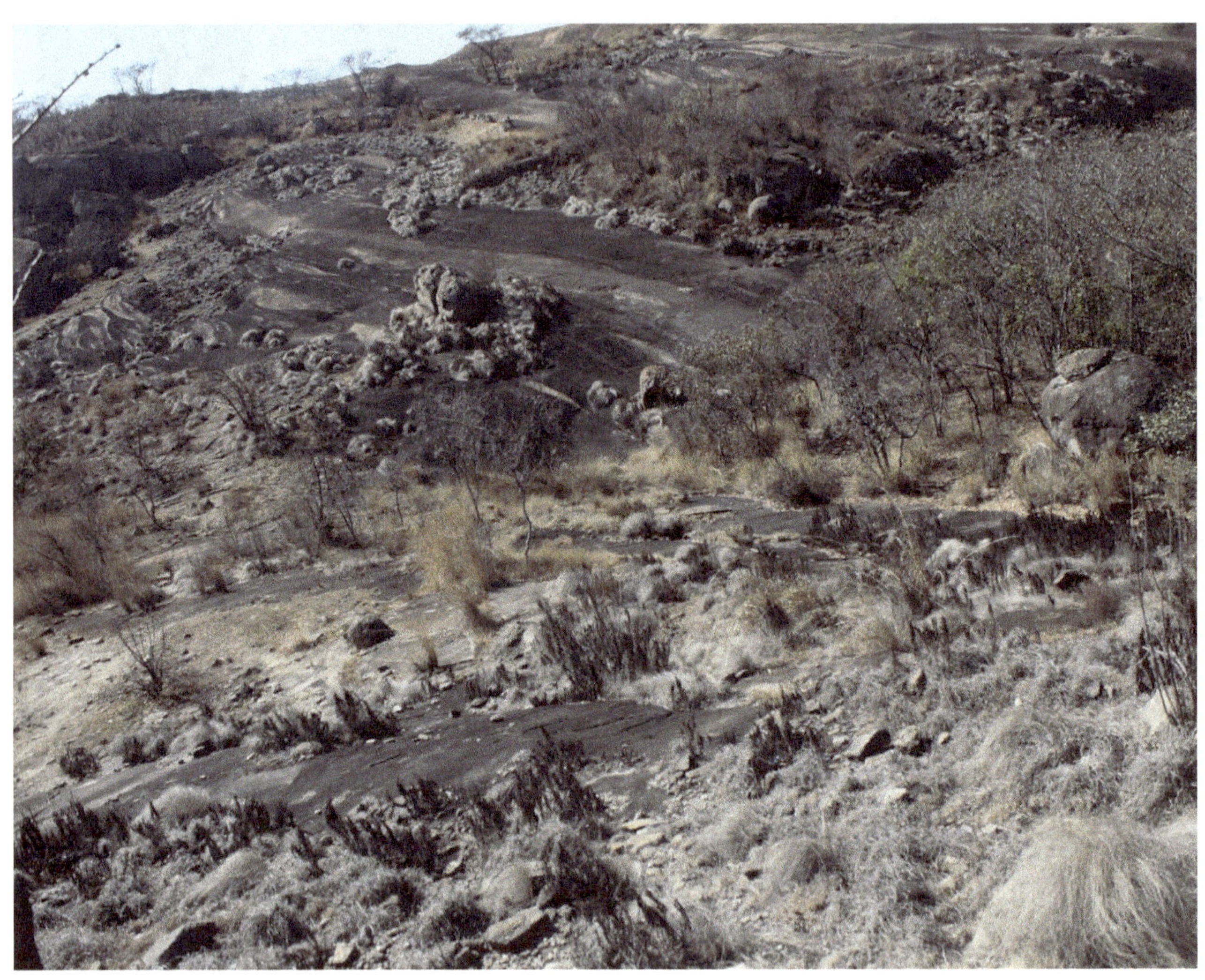

Colours Of Our Time

Handson Chirefu

Inexplicable experiences hound me
Dreams have summered and wintered
Only to spring a cycle of ugly colours
And in a night morass I am knighted
With blighted pride beaming brightly

Yet employment is gnawing dream
In my forty-eight-houred day
Whose minutes starched in shades of blue
A new letter ignites hollow hopes
Yet each day ploughs back a mountain anxiety
And when replies run wintry dry
All hope, all confidence stinky stunt

Alas, colours of time coldly scald
Alas, counterfeit life crisply crushes
Alas, iridescence of time tersely irritates
Alas, mischievous life measly maddens
Alas, where is the world of substance?
Where has the probity of time gone?
When time, when life, glows glum colours!
These colours of colour are deceitful
Indeed, they strangle the progress of salient time

But I am building a mansion of hope
A mountain of resistance
A stone immunity to the viral life
To crash the stinking graft life
Decolourise the steadfast colours
Time to coin new narratives

YESTERDAY

Handson Chirefu

Adieu yesterday
Hello today
It is exhilarating to break free
From strangling yesterday
Yesterday was mouthful
And thoroughly talkative

I love this day, this today
He is comprehensively inspiring
I hate the ugly yesterday
For I have no power to alter the system
But today this very day is in my hands
I can possess skin lightening creams
To tan the face of today
But yesterday is history and intangible
It is a deserved past
I have had enough of yesterday
It feels good he will never ever be here again!
Sure, yesterday, is gone
Disappeared with all the acute hardships

Today smells aromatically fresh and amorous
But I can handle its arousal
The suffocating yesterday is disposed
I am elated this yesterday is biodegradable
And thus its recycling is out of question
Yes its ululating time and dance
For I was a minor, now a man
I was a lodger, now a landlord
I was a driver, now I am driven
Yes go yesterday, I know your frigid face

Great, I will never see another you again
You were frugal with your ideas
You were crappy and floozy!
A world of ominous odds
Go, go out of my sight forever

LIFE OF A HOUSE GIRL

Handson Chirefu

It all begins in the rural area
In an obscure village of Kuchakanya
When father withdraws her from school
Citing lack of school fees
Yet the cattle pen is overcrowded
And creamy milk outpours from clay pots
This misguided undertaking
Marks the beginning of her endless
Journeys and huge uncertainties

A relative comes to take her to town
The first few nervous months
She minds the relative's naughty children
And yet the reward is random and meagre
Then a woman from another city comes for her
Once in another city life turns full circle
She becomes a seasoned house *technician*
No more kind gloves treatment
The lady of the house has firm grip on her
She is the master's dirty hand
There is no chore she cannot offer
No place is unreachable on foot

Come rain come cold
A maid is a MAID
No feelings or privacy
No errand is unfulfilled
No distance is too long
No food is too little
She stands from dawn to midnight
And she does not really need to
Be beautiful to attract abusers

Meanwhile her adorable adolescent growth
Her East West breasts and round outline
Win her unwanted returns
From adventurous male tourists
Who desire exploring her *Zambezi Valley*
The adolescent girl is dilemma driven
The father of the house
Itches to explore her beautiful
Scenic hills and youthful valleys
The eldest boy of the house
Drools at the house girl's perky hills
The girl is overwhelmed with praises
From both the boy and the father
Father and son compete for her attention
The young girl becomes a ball of nerves
She burns clothes and food simultaneously
The lady of the house puts an axe on her neck
In utter shame and sorrow heads to her friend

After a few days at the friend's work place
Another city woman employs her
But she continues to swim in slavery
History resurrects to torment her
Because of her rare body endowment

Vultures swarm around her body
Every man is smitten by her unique curves
They have wide eyes for her virgin valley
But they only want her for breakfast
No man is ever going to be serious
Because she is poor and maid
Yet every man sees value in her valley
Sees it worthy to play and bath in it
Someone should knock sense in men
Before single-motherhood
Becomes her dependable husband
And give a thorough talk to other women
For blame is the intersection of the two sets

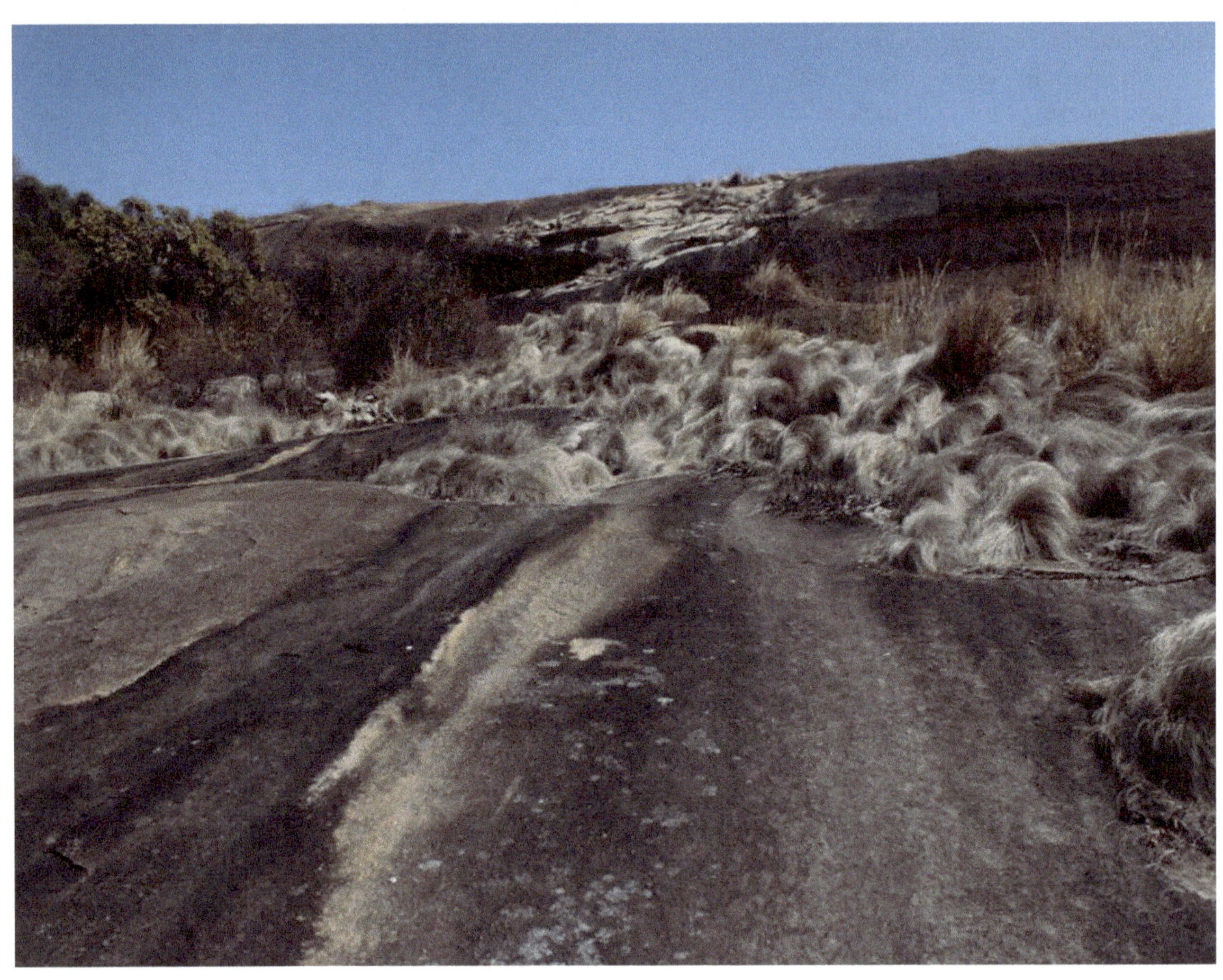

TOUCHING THE WORLD'S HAND

Handson Chirefu

With my insignificant life
I want to do a great
Oh yes, that is a true
I want to do peace
I want to do love
I want to do honour
I want to do benevolent
Most importantly
I want to do a Mandela!

I want to do a wake up
A worth wakeup call
To the world's conscience

In my own small way
Using my own humble hand
To touch the world's hand
And with all the power vested in me
Heave it up with what is left in me
And lift the falling world up
I want to sustain its standing
I don't want to see its falling
I detest its falling
I want to emulate someone
An exceptional someone
Who lived for the other
And less for himself

I am wearing the Madiba spirit
A rock of determination
A dwala of resistance

A *freedom-phile*
A lion of conscience
A world of worthy awareness
The world whose hand I am silently
Touching this watershed moment

Yes with this weak strong hand
I want to touch the world's heart
To arrest the heart's tearing
Yes my hand is weak for its one!
But its strength is its probity

I sing the world heart's happiness
A life-changing mantra
Coining a new narrative
I want the heart to be free
To drive Lorries of happiness
To live in honeyed harmony

Where the free heart shouts
"No to racism
No to tribalism
No to regionalism
No to nepotism
No to individualism"

But to cling to the togetherness
Of the spirit of true Africaness

It's not the leaves or the flowers
But the roots that dig deep into earth
For the nutrients of the whole plant
But the leaves make food for the plant
The veins carry food, water and nutrients

To all the living parts of the plant
It's a collective effort for survival

The other fingers need a thumb
To make a working hand
We need each other in this ecosystem
We are all people with distinct roles
We are each important in our own way
No one is more than each of us

Yes with my limping limbs
I want to touch the world's feet
Yes, those cracked feet
Those disabled feet
Those feet dripping blood
It is time to heal the crying feet

Yes I am a clarion call
This world must be a world
Of genuine free freedom
Of happy hearts
Of one peaceful spirit
A world of genuine probity

I hail the touching of the world's hand
It is my burning desire
My blazing hope
My unending aspiration
My unceasing breath
To see this dear world on peace feet
At peace with itself

Touch the world's hand
With a kind and loving heart

Be a Mandela of this world
And arrest arrant wickedness
Apprehend autocracy
Be that magic hand
Conceive a rare moment
And give birth to this unique baby

Oh yes be famous
Be well known for a touching hand
Yes I do not want to let go
Let go of wanting to
Do good for the other
Be defined by benevolence
Finance the goodness in us
To mature and lead this world
To a new narrative

NEXUS NARRATIVES

Handson Chirefu

A diabolical call it is
The action being lived
But this is a clarion call
This world, this motherland
Must be aptly advised

Dejected

I watch from the broken bridge
Tired and teary eyed
A decrepit diviner eloping
With a pitiable teen bride
A green orange
No resistance from her
No remonstration from the kid
But her languid deportment
Draws a million poignant pictures
Curves contours of continual cruelty
Writes a thousand depressing tales of deprivation
Her demeanor pleads for clemency
In this lopsided affair
Her clumsy eyes cry for deserved compassion

Depressed

I watch from the lab window
Far away from the rest of the world
A Sir using a bulging tongue
To test for the mouth pH
Of an enthusiastic female learner
Then like a true professional
Uses a fleshy thermometer
To check the girl's rising body warmth

Between the hungry tan limbs
Yearning and yearning for more
Disgusting yelping, sickening whimpering

Disheartened
I observe with a heavy heart
From a reddish brown gigantic anthill
A libidinous youthful blue-jeaned man
Wrestling and overpowering a village girl
Tearing another unripe fruit
And claiming a hollow conquest
Without the poor woman's consent
His action tattered and blooded her one underwear
He dusted his blue jeans and left devoid of feelings
The poor girl stunned and clutched the torn underwear
With her chastity violently cracked
But there won't be any court case
To arraign her lover-cum-attacker
Because the two exist in decadent relationship
She is not going to report him anywhere
He takes advantage of her vulnerable love
The monster's action finances emptiness
In the village girl's heart and soul
For he has usurped all her wealth
But she sticks to the rapist
For she knows no option
Since he claims to love her dearly
In this impolite transient world

Flabbergasted
I witnessed a free African movie
From the church entrance
An elderly blue-suited pastor
Praying vigorously for a youthful woman

Practically infected with a whole-clan evil spirits
But this church film was interestingly distressing
The revered pastor was talking in tongues---in trance
Passing his holy spirit directly to the frantic woman's tongue
Their wrestling of tongues was disappointingly pleasant
They were both speaking in live tongues
Here was an articulate and a dexterous pastor
Casting demons of love away from the young woman
A conscious shepherd of the flock
A pious one too, yet a salty Lot's wife
While in tongues, his aged deft fingers played *marimba*
On the heaving woman's perky nipples
The youthful woman whimpered a hymn while the hem
Of her tight red skirt moved up slowly exposing tan thighs
Right close to the pulpit marked *keep praying*
Or was it *keep preying?*
Hallelujah! Pastors of our prophetic time
No movie could surpass the holy action

Disconsolate

I peeped through the faded blue curtains
And stared at a grey-suited lawyer
In a very cozy room assisting
In undressing a curvaceous young lady
It was quite a lengthy battle for
The navy blue mini skirt was stuck on the great curves
But it surrendered to the power of the lascivious lawyer
And immediately the dog-dance commenced
She held on to the table edge with dancing fingers
He danced, danced and she twisted up, down, left and right
But my ears strained big time to get the sweet melody
The kind-hearted lawyer was giving legal help
To the needy divorcing young woman
The revered lawyer was blessing the divorce

Through the discolored cloth
I seriously hoped the woman was not vulnerable
And that the energetic lawyer had his latex glove on
For the learned lawyer was good at his dance
But are we not misrepresenting our constituencies?

Deprecating
I observe a flabby sugar-mummy
Sucking life out of an early teen
Like an African python licking its prey
The boy wriggled endlessly gasping for air
But luck for him was elusive
Soon his tender groin was buried in the soft valley
With kinky black and white grass
And then the lascivious mummy gashed waters
Flooding the sacrosanct valley
The boy mourned contentedly then drowned
Is this the way to teach our boys to swim?

From the dry Matize River bank I saw
A famous Headman on the river sand
Digging up water on a soft valley
Of his humble subordinate's wife
And she was walking on air
What an eye-sore!
But is this the way to teach our women morals?

From the shed of a leafy mopane tree
I could see a bearded councillor
Charging widows ten US dollars each
For them to receive a bucket of maize
From Social Welfare
In which cupboard should we pack
The clergy?

The leaders?
The greedy?
The immoral?
They have overgrown
This house is overburdened
Is littered with decadent leaders
Who change wives and husbands like clothes?
We all know acute blemish about them
Here and elsewhere in this world
But do nothing ... NOTHING!
Is this your love for humanity?
To let evil flow and choke the rivers
The many and helpless rivers of this world
It is time to re-define narratives
To download new solid values and save them

Down faced I walked away from the decay
I wished my eyes and ears were padlocked
These events cast a pall over our tomorrow
The narrative is not a page-turner

Disgraced
I look at all the events of life
They form a contemporary universal set
They are the core of the people's problems
They are the nucleus of humanity tribulations
Yes a solid intersection of all our problems
Common problems... the core worries
The greed and vice of today
The central issues ...
The unending difficulties of the disadvantaged
The new definition of humanity
The societal challenges put in one story
In their explicit diversity

Form the nexus narratives
Common narratives of the day
The mantras of the new millennium
People should lose hair because of these
Sad events of this world

Domboshava cave and paintings
Photography by Tendai Rinos Mwanaka

A couple of days after returning from Domboshava photo tour, my neighbor asked me where I had gone with the camera. I told her Domboshava. She said she had been meaning to go there, that her church goes there for prayers. I asked her why, she said there is a lake inside the cave where the water is sacred so she had been meaning to get the water for spiritual washing. It reminded me when I was taking the photos of the cave, there was definitely signs people were entering the cave. But it's a protected site, with a little barbed wire barricade around the cave opening. I wondered why these people weren't afraid of, say snakes. It's a long thin cave that goes up to the top of the hill. As you can see from the pic of the cave there are paintings of all sort of animals, buffaloes, rhino, elephant, giraffe..., drawn thousands years ago by civilizations before us. Imagine what life was like for this civilization before us, the intelligent life we see in the paintings, how the cave is structured such that in times of war they can easily evade their enemies and disappear down the other side of the hill. The cave mouth is shaped like a shade or veranda where they could hide when it rains or it's windy or even sleep under...

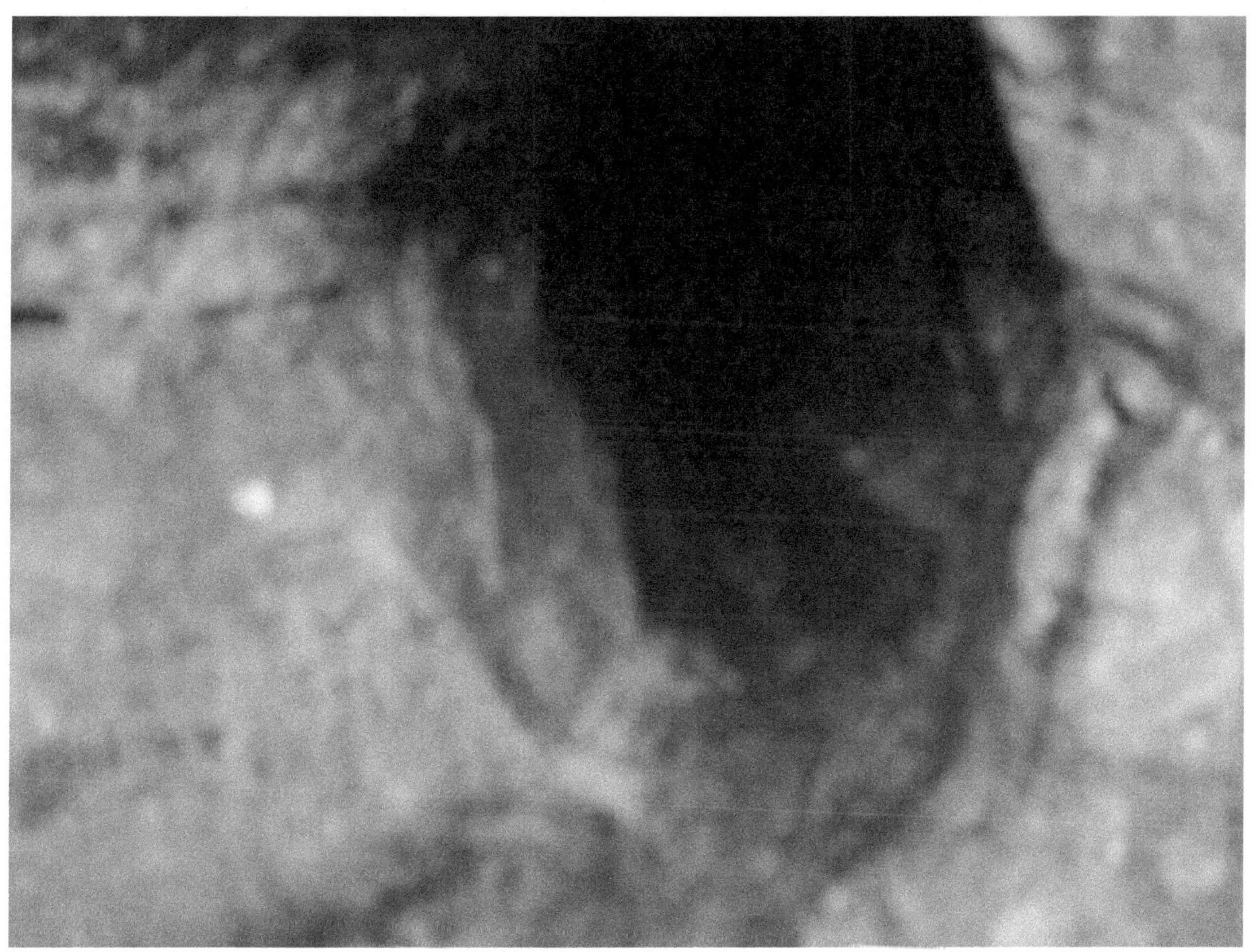

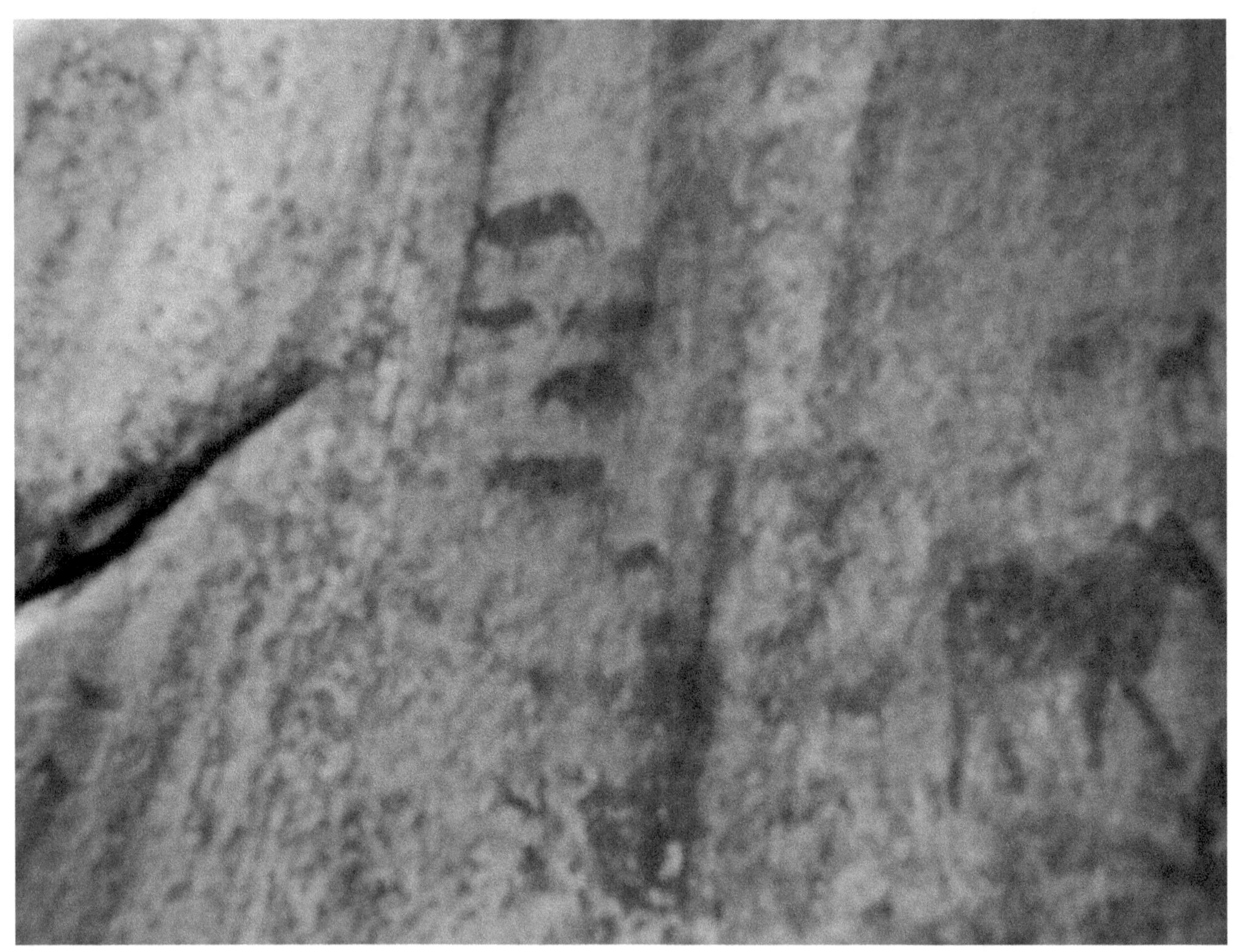

The Man on the Lone Shore

Tafadzwa Chiwanza

I saw a man, dear brother Matt,
That crawled to that lone shore,
Where the wind lays all to waste,
With his hand clung to his chest.
His shadow trembled when he crawled
As the wind lashed at him with its claws
But he to all that pain seemed numb
As the wind chopped at his lanky limb.

I stared as his shadow forsook him
Like he was a rusty penny in the street.
To my own chest, my hand tumbled
As the scene before my eyes unravelled.

In my misery I called out to the man,
Who for a while seemed not to hear
But when an angry storm drew nigh,
The man in the storm did disappear
But not before he winked at me, and I froze with fear.

Like a camera, I could only focus,
Not sure what my eyes had beheld,
I dared not wonder if it could be,
That the forlorn man was me!

A Child in an Old Man's Body

Tafadzwa Chiwanza

Last night I went to bed
Young, happy and free
And woke up old as the sea. Tell me how this could be!

Reality
Hurtles me to the present, My skin besmirched to find
With scattered wrinkles
And my chin a wheat field.

Not entirely sure
How this change came about, Into the mirror I dare stare
To find terror as my reflection

Terror
When in the mirror I stare
And can't find myself.

I could swear a while ago,
Upon mama's breasts I climbed
To gaze lovingly into her eyes
As their warmth upon my face
Like a flood of sunshine on a budding flower poured.

At last I stare at the scars,
To trace the path to a past I can't find,
Yet I don't recognise places I've been,
And the faces all smiling around me
Claiming to be the children I left behind.

How could it be,
That I a while ago was as little as they
Yet now they sprout around me,
Calling me their father!

My father yesterday,
With me did sing songs sweet and gay
As he on his rocky shoulders carried me
But you dare jest that for twenty years
In the cold earth his body has been.

Father! Mother!
At these graves I stand and shout
If you're in there please come out
For my hands I've stretched out:
Your little boy in an old man's body!

All I know is that
Last night I went to bed, Young, happy and free
And woke up old as the sea
Tell me how could this be?

Fragments of Emptiness

Tafadzwa Chiwanza

Footsteps echo in her hallow mind
Naming the fragments of emptiness
That chew at her mind's filthy walls
Where dirty underwear hung out to dry
Whispers in a silent fart, strange tales
That drown in the void her walls surround,
And her mind becomes the dirty underwear.

Her mind is under a serious siege –
Menelaus has come to claim Helen of Troy
But Helen is a wet toilet paper on the shivering walls
And the fortifications are a flood of diarrhoea
Reaching out to the toilet paper for an embrace
But then, the walls and the diarrhoea are her mind
Kissing the void and loathing rescue.

Like Judas' kiss at the night of betrayal
The cannons thundering against her barriers
Tremble with the confusion of a fire burning under water
Before disintegrating into fragments of emptiness
Heaped at the toes of her walls, worshipping,
The threads of her tattered long skirts,
At dawn her mind and the rubbles become one,
As her hazy mind begins to siege its own sanity.

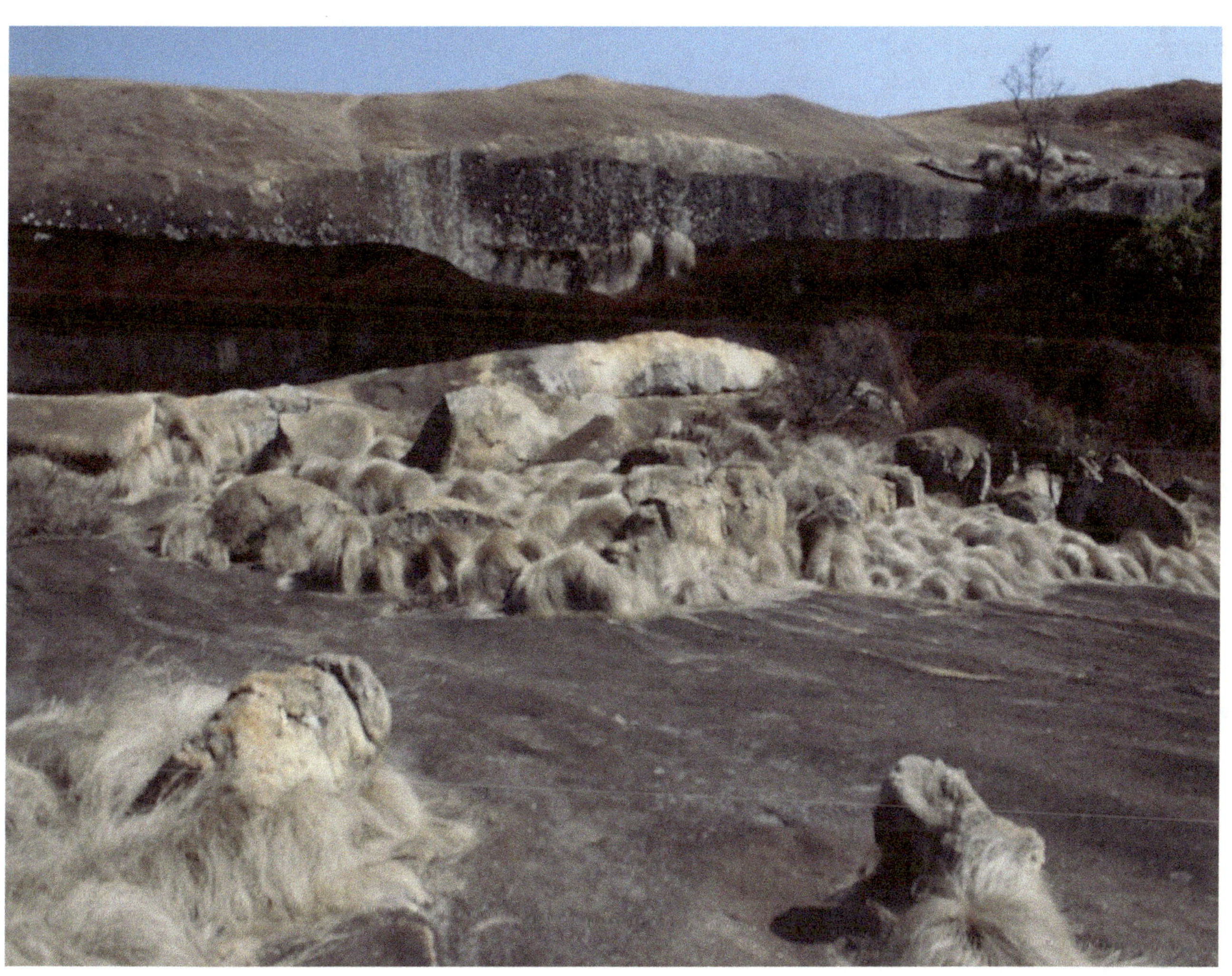

Emerge

Moira Marangwanda-Chipanda

Flutter by, butterfly
Don't be afraid to soar through the garden of life
Clad your wings with the armour of resilience
For it's your season for resurgence.
Your past morphed you to this
Enabling you to break your limits.
Just like how blooming flowers do not compete,
They bloom when their season arrives,
This is your season to emerge
So, flutter by, butterfly
Because now,
not even the sky is the limit.

Poetic Justice
Moira Marangwanda-Chipanda

Criminal justice
Infinite justice
Concept of justice
Department of justice
Court of justice
Symbol of justice
Chief justice

Even with all these justices and more
There's still not enough justice in the world

Patriotic me

Moira Marangwanda-Chipanda

Being Zimbabwean is like a boil right in the armpit
It stubbornly exists inside so nobody can see it.
In spasms of reality, the pain increases
Unable to hide the pain, you embrace yourself
By walking with your armpits wide open

Being Zimbabwean is like a Christian prostitute
Self-righteous by day, a Jezebel of all sorts by night
You blame the system for putting you in that position
Yet day in day out, you wake up and choose where and when to wear your faith

Being Zimbabwean is like an epidemic rash
Uninvited it arrives and unexpected it spreads real fast
All over your skin so much that it gets under your skin
Leaving you scrubbing, puffing and shrieking.

Being Zimbabwean is like the life of a hen
You live on handouts and food is readily available
Unaware that its availability is only preparing you for your slaughter.

Being Zimbabwean is like a beautiful rose
Borne from prickly, thorny bushes
Many love the end product but are not bothered by the process that brings about the beauty.

Vantage point

Photography by Tendai Rinos Mwanaka

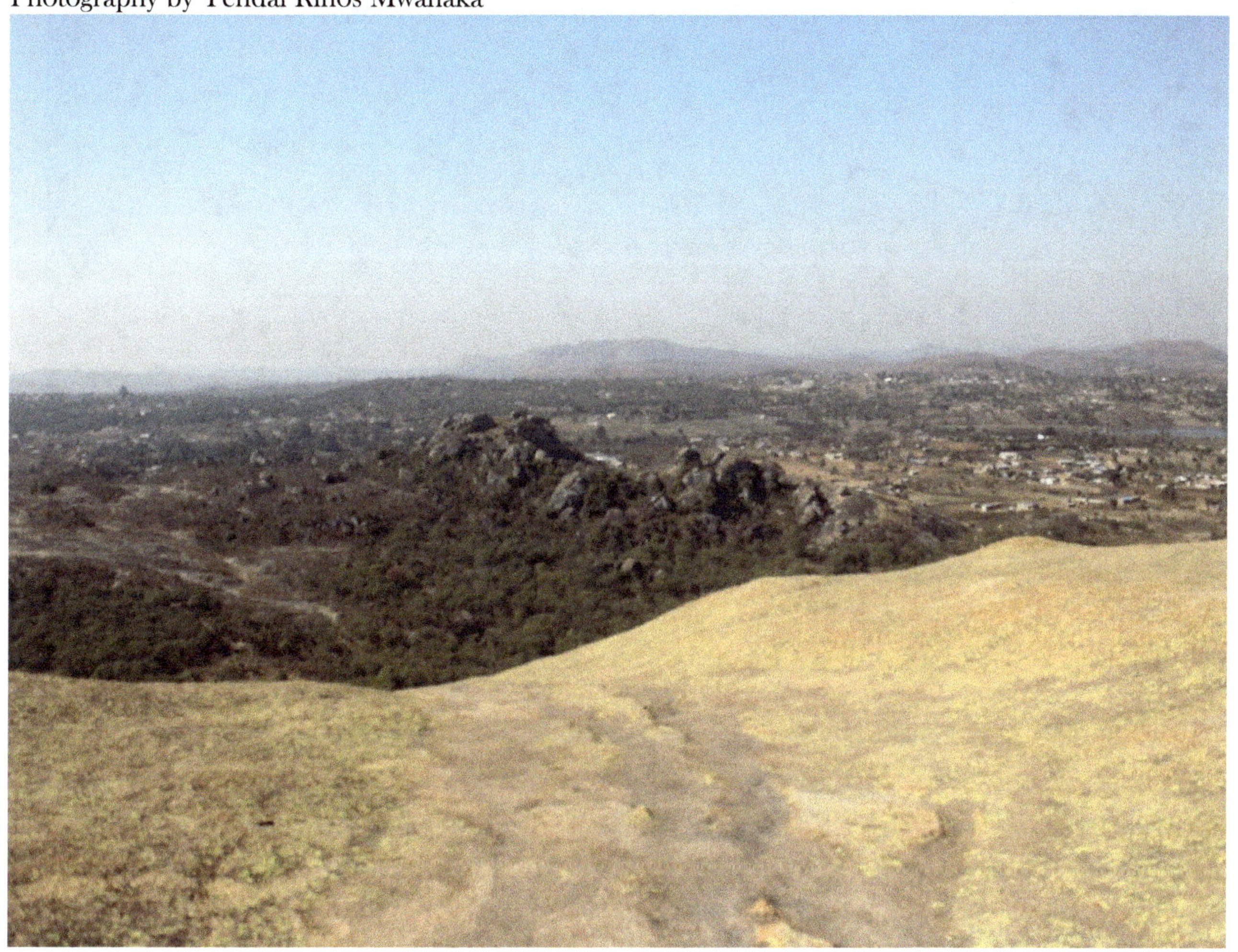

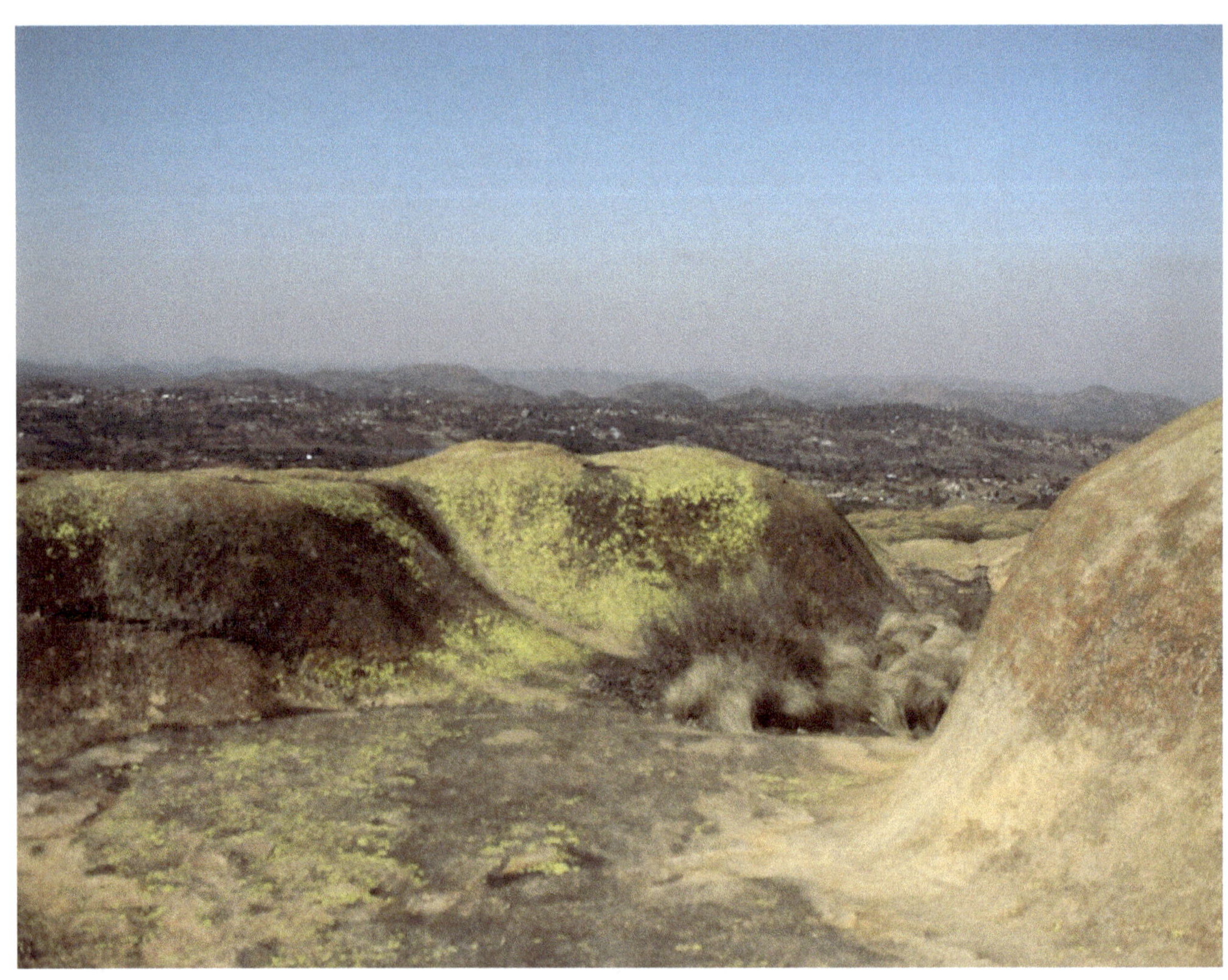

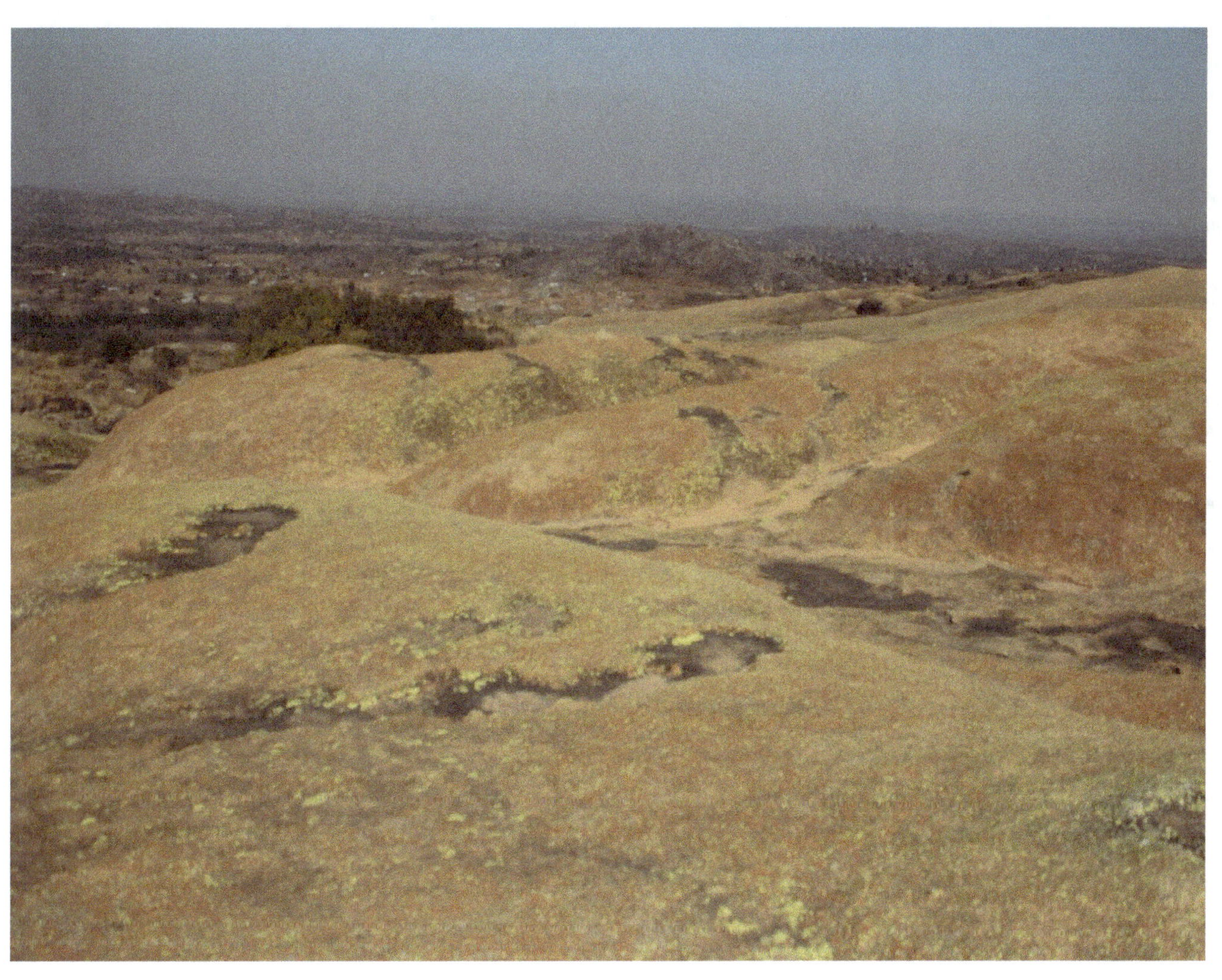

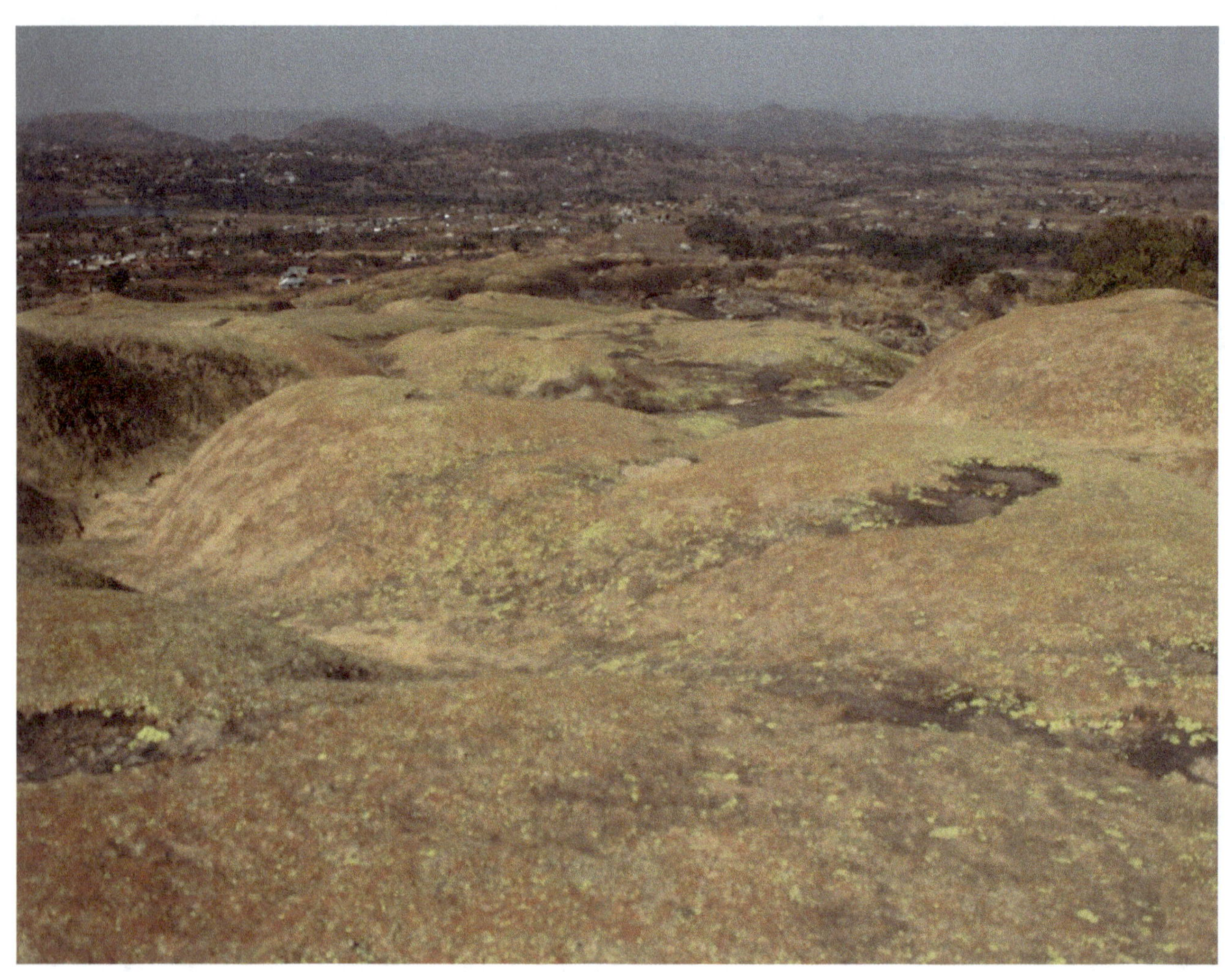

A LONG PAUSE

Hasan Simani

I USED TO SMELL THE COLOGNE OF BROTHERHOOD AND SISTERHOOD
BUT NOW IT STINKS WITH MISERY, POVERTY AND DOUBT
A LONG PAUSE IN THE WAYS WE MAINTAIN OURSLEVES
NOW WE FORTIFY OURSELVES WITH NOTHING
I USED TO HEAR PEOPLE FASTING AND PRAYING
IN EARNEST INQUIRY OF THE TRUTH BUT NOW WE ARE LIVING A LIE
WORLD POLITICAL TURMOUIL, MORAL LANDSLIDE
AND WHEN I READ THE QURAN, I SEE THAT THE EVIDENCE POINTS TO ME
I'M GUILTY AS CHARGED
GUILTY OF IGNORANCE, CORRUPTION
ROBBERY, LUST THE LIST I CAN'T EXHAUST
SHAITAN IS SEEING THIS AS AN OPPORTUNITY COST
LEVERAGING ON OUR BAD HABITS
THE WORDS HAVE BEEN WRITTEN, PREACHED, WELL- SAID SOMEBODY LISTENED
SOMEBODY CHOSE TO FORGET, ALL WAS FORGOTTEN
A LONG PAUSE IN THE WAY WE WORSHIP
A LONG PAUSE IN THE WAY WE DISPLAY OURSELVES
WE ARE LIKE USED CLOTHES THAT NEED EXTRA-EXTREME IRONING
THE CONSEQUENCES IS LOW PROFIT AND HIGH LOSS
WE HAVE SUBSTITUTED ALLAH SUBHANA WA TA ALA WITH EARTHLY PLEASURES
THE WORLD IN SHAMBLES FIGHTING LIKE A PURE ROYAL RUMBLE
YOUNG FLOWERS NO LONGER PETALS OF THE WORLD
BUT TO BE USED LIKE TOILET TISSUES
OLDER FOLK STAND IN DESPAIR
THINKING THE YOUTH CAN'T BE REPAIRED BROKEN BEYOND REPAIR
WE ARE POUTING IN FAILURE, STUCK IN THE MUD
BROTHERS AND SISTERS IT HAS BEEN A LONG PAUSE
NOW WE NEED TO GIVE THE WORD OF ALLAH SUBHAANA WA TA ALA A
ROMANTIC SPACE IN OUR SOULS
LET'S TREAT THIS GIVEN TIME AS A LOAN AND ACT WISELY

Poetry without hesitation

Hasan Simani

Forgive me for my mouth is like a loaded gun always ready to explode
I could lose my teeth for spitting out the truth but my spoken word is meant to correct and rectify
I'm a human too who make mistakes too but I don't take pride to become the shadow of Satan
I'm a poem trembling with anger not deaf and dumb
I'm a poem with a burning sensation to see my generation turning away from immorality
Embrace the divinity world pleasures all vanity read the ancient scrolls you'll get the clarity
I'm a poem with a road to redemption where silence is not an option
The lord didn't create you to be pedestal of evil, treachery
I'm a poem disheartened my sisters no longer pearls to beatify the world
Her body a body laptop where everybody logs in and out
She forgets to read the scriptures all lost with sweet temptations of the world
Her mom weeping pouting in failure daughter no longer daughter of valour
Not well-groomed like, MARYAM AND AISHA
My brother drinking sobbing bottles and puffing noxious vapours
Confined in fiction-false lifestyle
I'm a poem exorcising demon extending knowledge beyond the self
I'm a poem inculcating wisdom not over speeding youth to vanity
My words are for free my advice to you is charity
I wish to see my brother of peace uplifting small brothers' flowers to bloom
How can they know the right when normality is misconstrued with abnormality?
Then it becomes casualty of abnormal normality
A well-groomed youth will never desire to do things which are uncouth
Or do things they later loathe

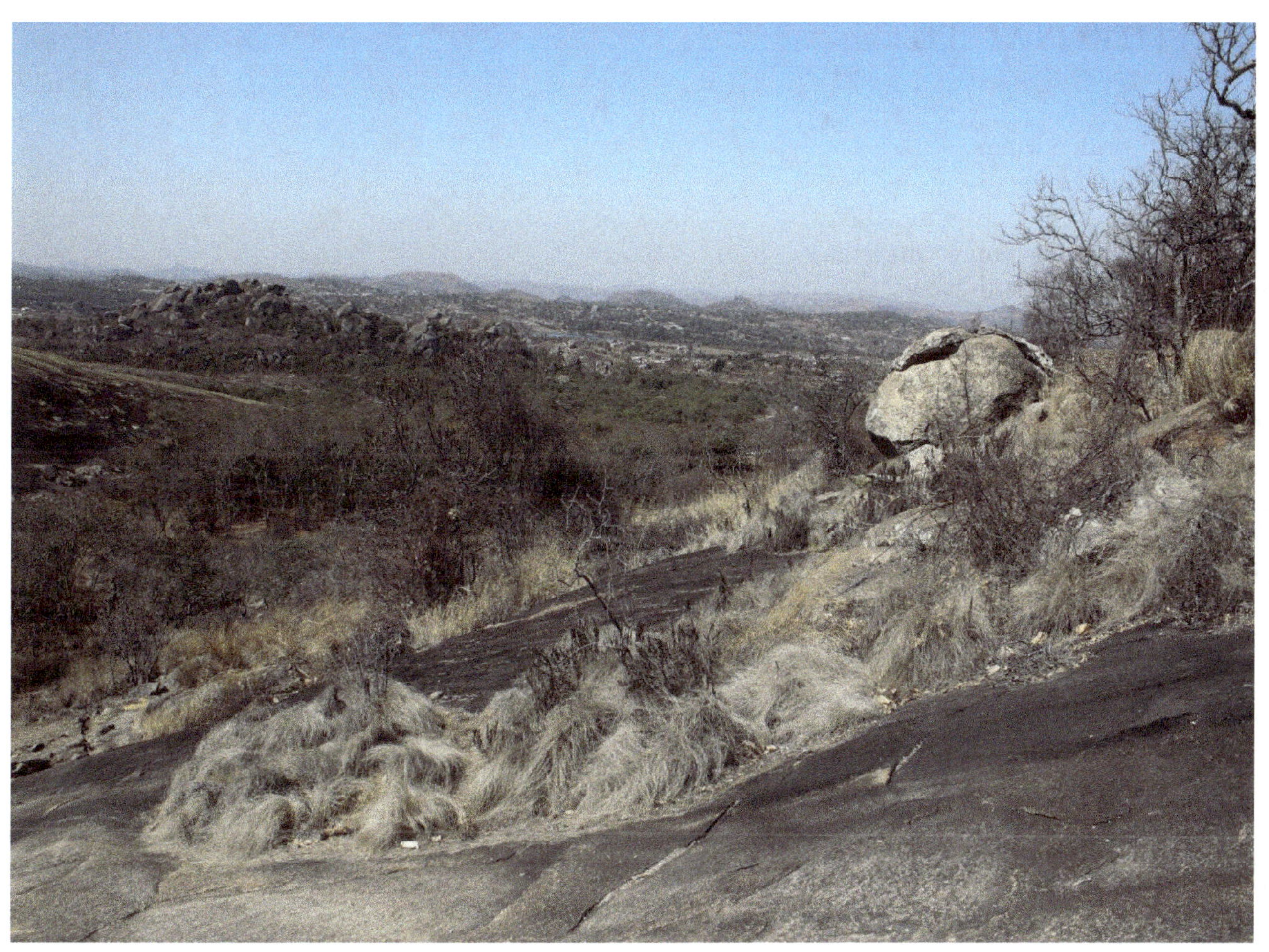

THE LETTERS IN A LETTER

Pardon J. Simango

We are like written letters,
Meant to be read later,
We were told we came from the Maker,
The one who has been until Omega....
But this earth is filled with haters,
People who scrounge for our wings and feathers.
Always alert to take us into dismay and further.

Mama said never back down,
But I see the wind howling and turning sand brown.
It's a mist of disaster in our town,
The crippled are stretched and turned down,
The hungry being fed to the sitting crowns.
As the world sells them a strange frown.
The unnecessary is the inevitable....
Our today is indeed a cloud,
In which the poor has become the crowd.

Pull out, push in, is the talk of tales,
Pulling out to separate from the dark days,
Pushing in to fit in the little we have,
Breaths of struggles are the panting of the choir,
Mysterious uprisings of the rich in a delta of slowdowns,
Devices capture less of nature,
Revise your life and you get the pressure,
Everyone is always looking and lurking,
In the thought that tomorrow will,
Turn the moon into a shiny sun.....
I wonder what the kids will read.
For we are a letter to be read later.
We want to climb the train of progress,

But our hearts are stuck in being restless......

SPEAKER
Pardon J. Simango

What I was, she wanted....
We couldn't say it out,
But we felt the cold weather added.
It was like the gene of the cold had chanted....
But still we had clatters of persuasion....
Until reason made an emersion......
She twisted my angle of sight,
Suddenly I did the thud of a sigh.....
My mood was all up and high.....
What if I drew her close and died.....?
She still wanted me for the ride......
But in me was this sense of pointless pride....
I panted, I panted but our paths could no longer be parted.....

A closed session with destiny..........
A CLOSED SESSION WITH DESTINY
Pardon J. Simango
THE SPEAKER

The electrocution of the mind is a mess,
Leaving the victim in distress,
No point, no go at all.
To everything they seem to take the fall,
If they ever live to tell the tale.....
As their breath starts to be heavier than a wale's.....
Sitting on the front page

I can't even go downstairs,
Everything is just not clear,
It’s like I'm drunk from the doses of bronclair.
We hesitate when it’s so dear.
Thinking of how much we can hear,
Or even what our hearts can't bear.
I’m trying to be the one sitting and so real.

The operators of the rock drill,
Are going deep with no bills
Everything they plan has no deal,
And their hearts have this feel,
Of maybe a lot of what they feel,
Or maybe they need the chill pill,
For tomorrow will be another hill.

So, speaking of that till,
The one that hits so much of the dollar bills,
It’s like the land we didn't till,
Even when we needed to make things so real.
I want a moment to go real......

Rice from underground Gods
Photography by Tendai Rinos Mwanaka

Legend says way back these rock mounds would every morning be filled with rice. Like the bible Manna from heaven story, here it was rice from the gods below. People would collect the rice for nourishment. Now it's covered with lichen and moss...have the gods given up on us?

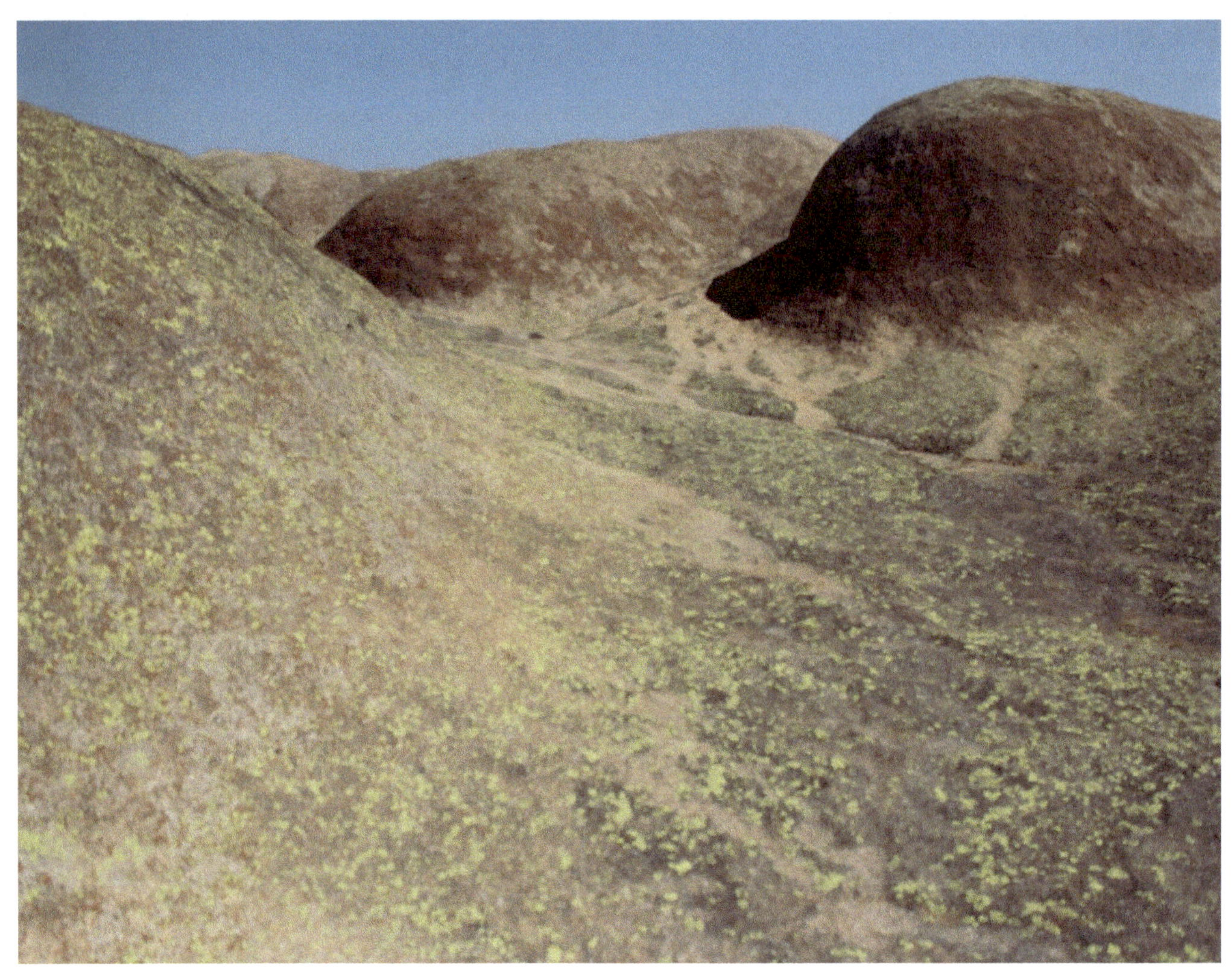

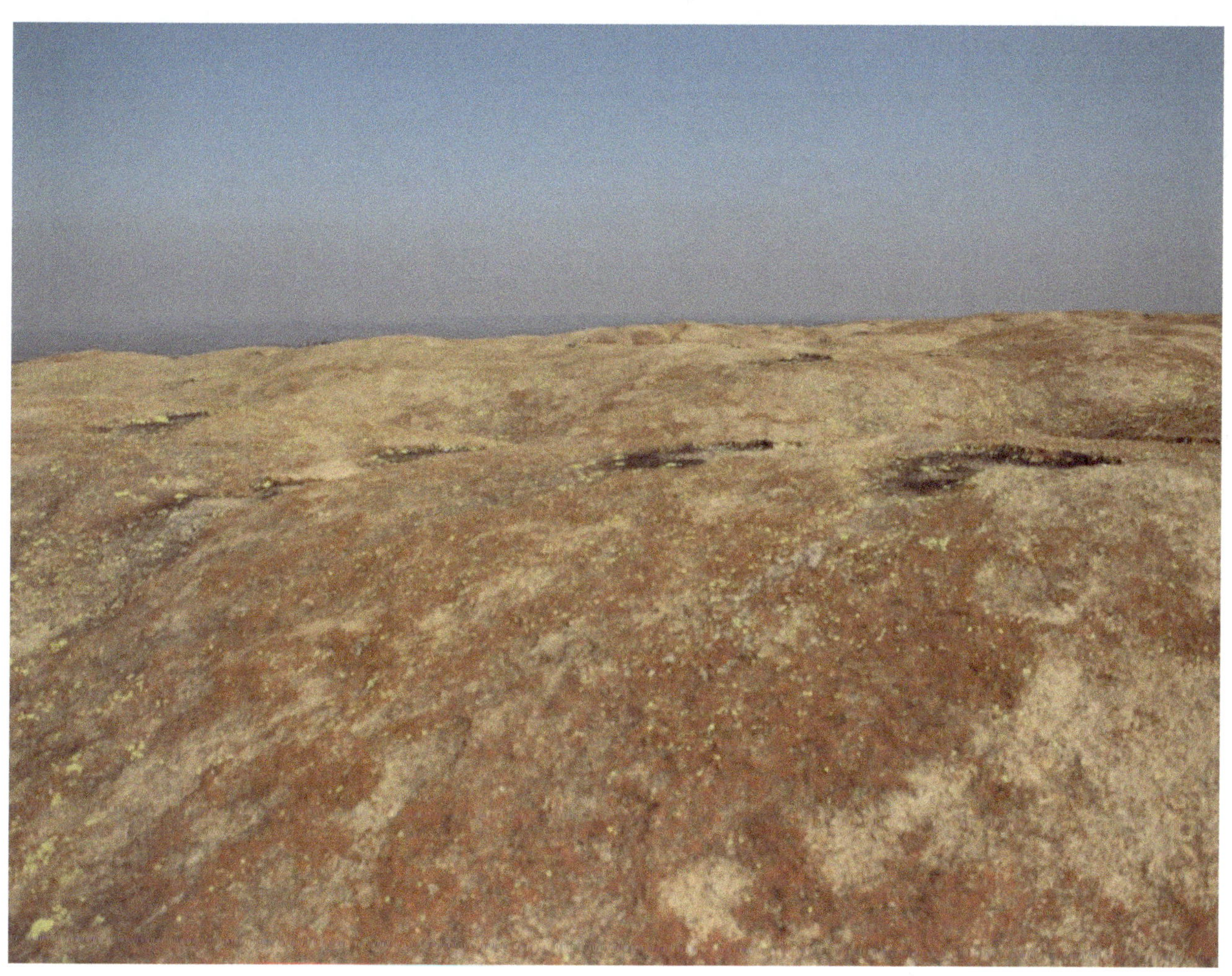

Thoughts of a sterile woman

Nelia Nkazimulo Mutema

Lifeless
Loveless
Childless
Everything seems to become less
The world seems to be closing her in
Every breath she takes seems to be a mockery
As it reminds her of her failure
To fulfil a simple task
To give life and to nature a soul
A lump in the throat
Tear drops
A river of tears
Thoughts of a pained woman

Of what used to be a lover
Should the heart stop functioning?
I hope you will live in peace
With no reminder of once a perfect person
Sorry for not being perfect

How are you

Nelia Nkazimulo Mutema

Hy, how are you?
Am good and you
I will be ouky if you didn't lie
The pain in your eyes is visible
Even a blind man can see it
In a single glance
The fake smile plastered on your face
Can crack into a sad smile
The sorrowful look you have on your
Face doesn't say you good
Stop trying to be strong
Be strong enough to show your pain
Half circles and gods' heads

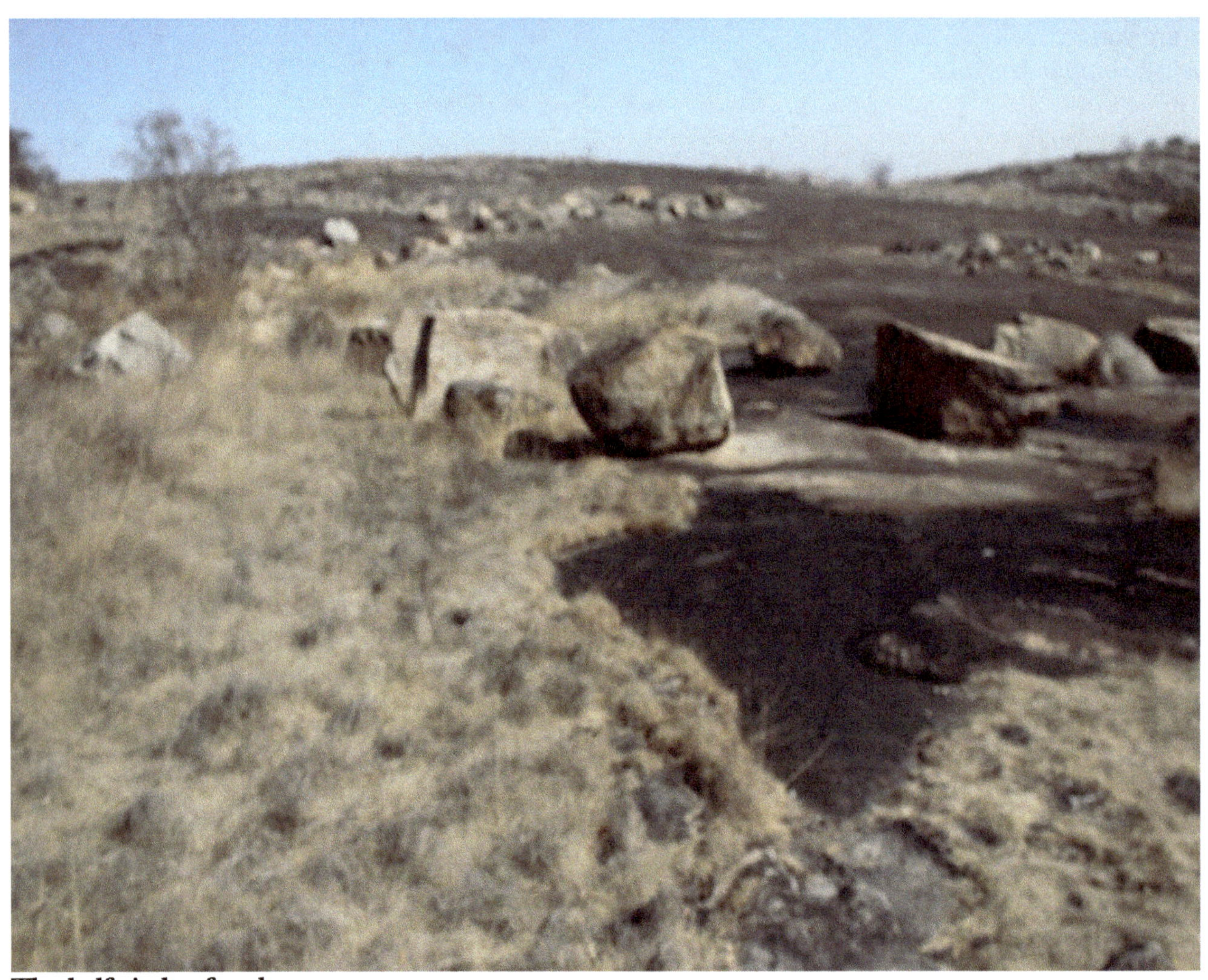

The half circle of rocks

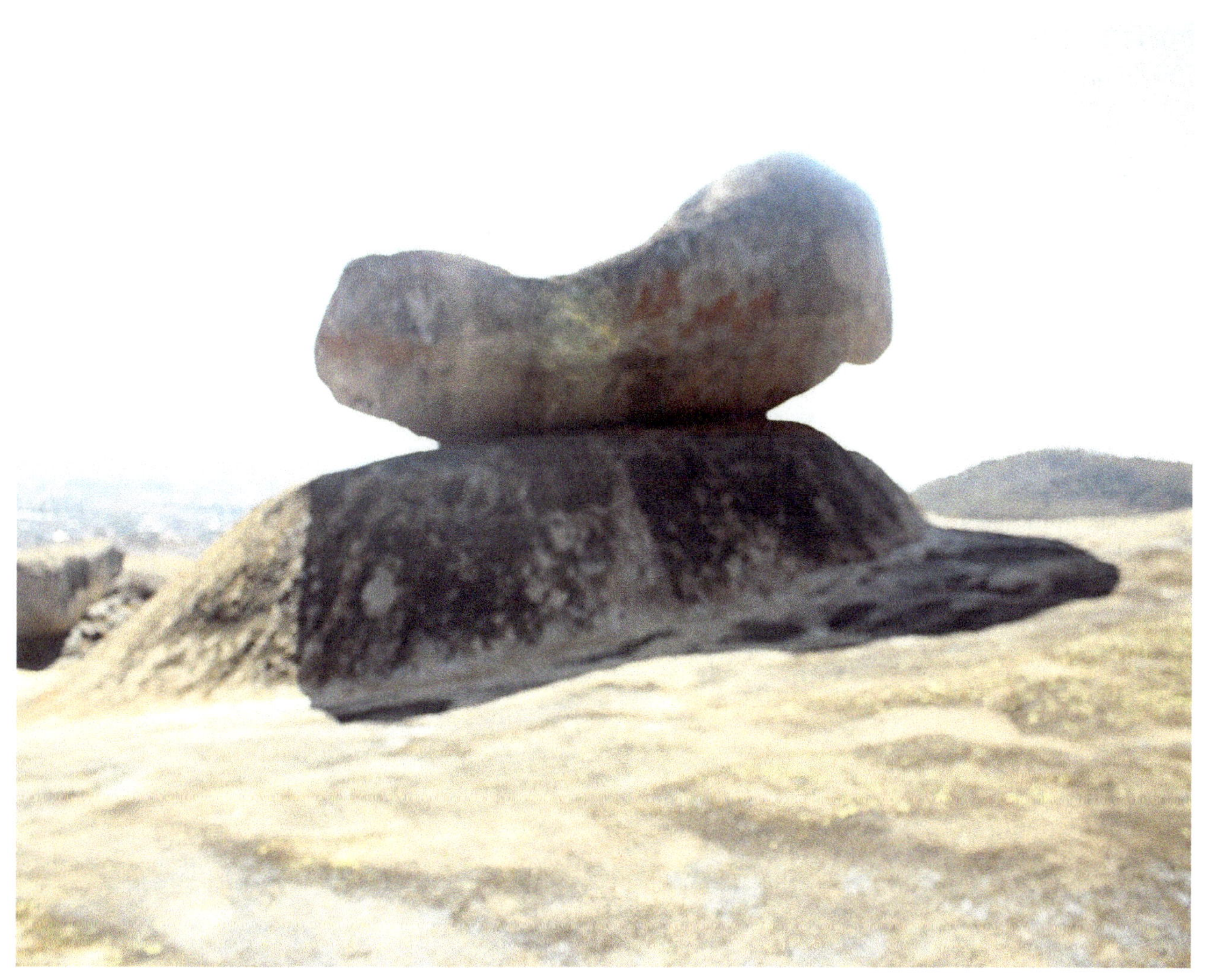

SCRIPTURAL TRUTH

Fabian Choto

Did you know
That there is that light
Light of scriptural truth?

It all depends
On the fact that
What kind of life principles
Do you embrace?

Are you one that follows
Or sticks to biblical truth?
Do you walk in the light
Or in darkness?
For some live their lives
In a thick
Very thick
Cloud of darkness.

There's that integrity
Servanthood,
And being a servant.
Following God's command
And hosting His presence
In you
With a truthful heart.

Never abandon the biblical truth
For ignorance is not a defence
Trust in God.

CULTURAL DIVERSITY

Fabian Choto

It is the quality of diverse
Or different cultures
As opposed to monoculture.

As Africans
We are there to respect
Each other's differences.
Having different cultures
Depending on where we come from
Our roots
And our origin.

It is the variety of human societies
Or different cultures
Of a specific region
Africa,
Our home,
Our motherland.
At large
Different cultures
Of the world.

I am an African
A truc African
The black person
Of the black skin
As Africans
Let's adopt
The inclusion
Of different
Cultural perspectives

In our society
Of various cultures
And different tribes.

Afrika Unite
For a common cause
And for a peaceful Zimbabwe.

MY PRINCESS

Fabian Choto

Arise my love
My beautiful one
And come away.
Let me see your face
For your face is lovely
Let me hear your voice
For your voice is sweet.

Oh my dove
My beloved one
You're mine
And I am yours.
My beautiful African
Whom my heart loves.

Behold my love
You're beautiful
I tell you certainly
By the look of your eyes.
Your lips are like a scarlet thread
Your mouth tender
Your cheeks lovely
And your neck upright.
Your body from head to toe
You're altogether gorgeous
Your outlook matching the inward.

Come with me
My bride
Your eyes have held interest
And my attention

And have persuaded and aroused
My admiration like magic power.
I tell you,
Many waters cannot quench love
Neither can floods drown it
Never.

Scripture Ref : Song of Solomon 8: 7

Humans connecting with the past
Photography by Tendai Rinos Mwanaka

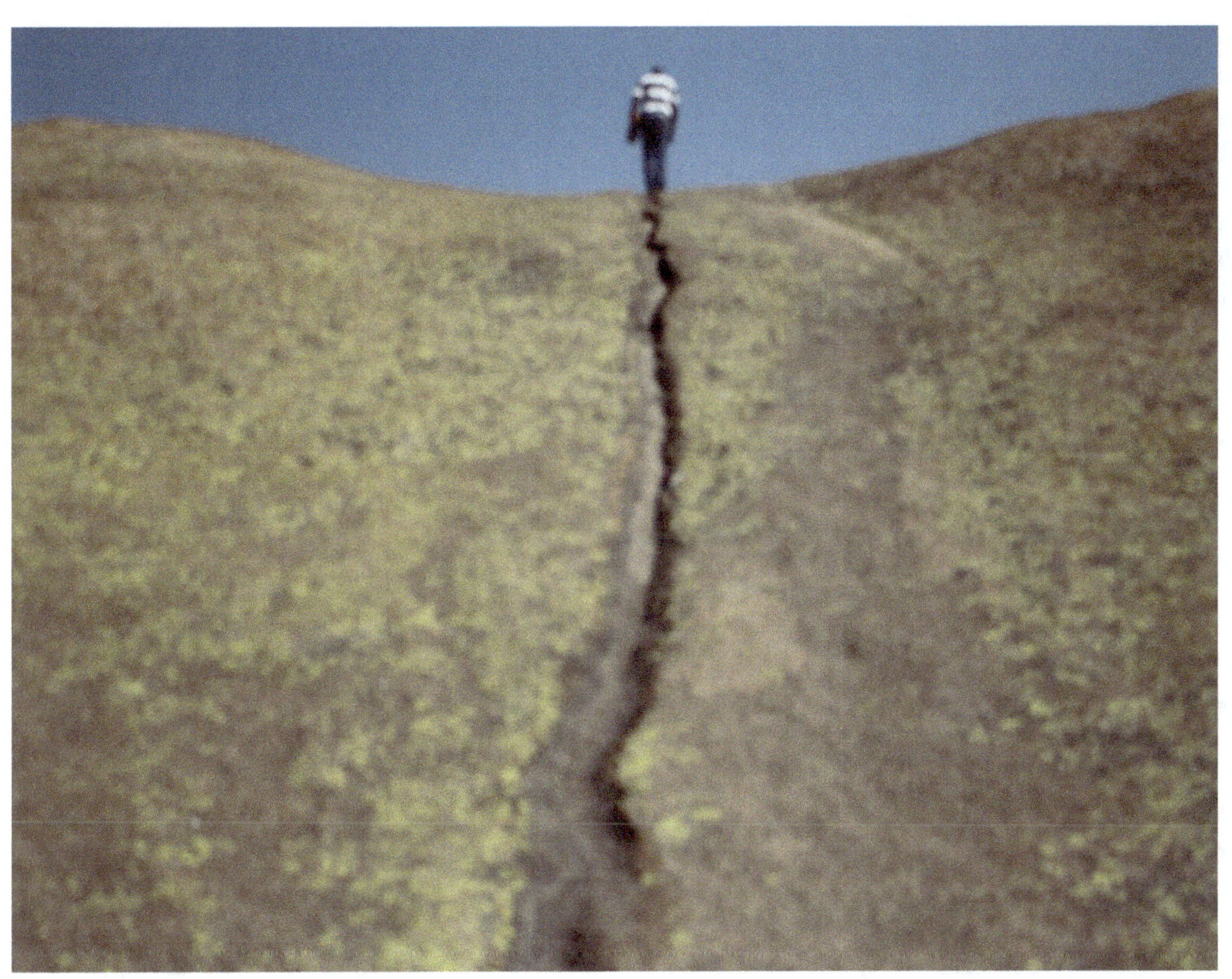

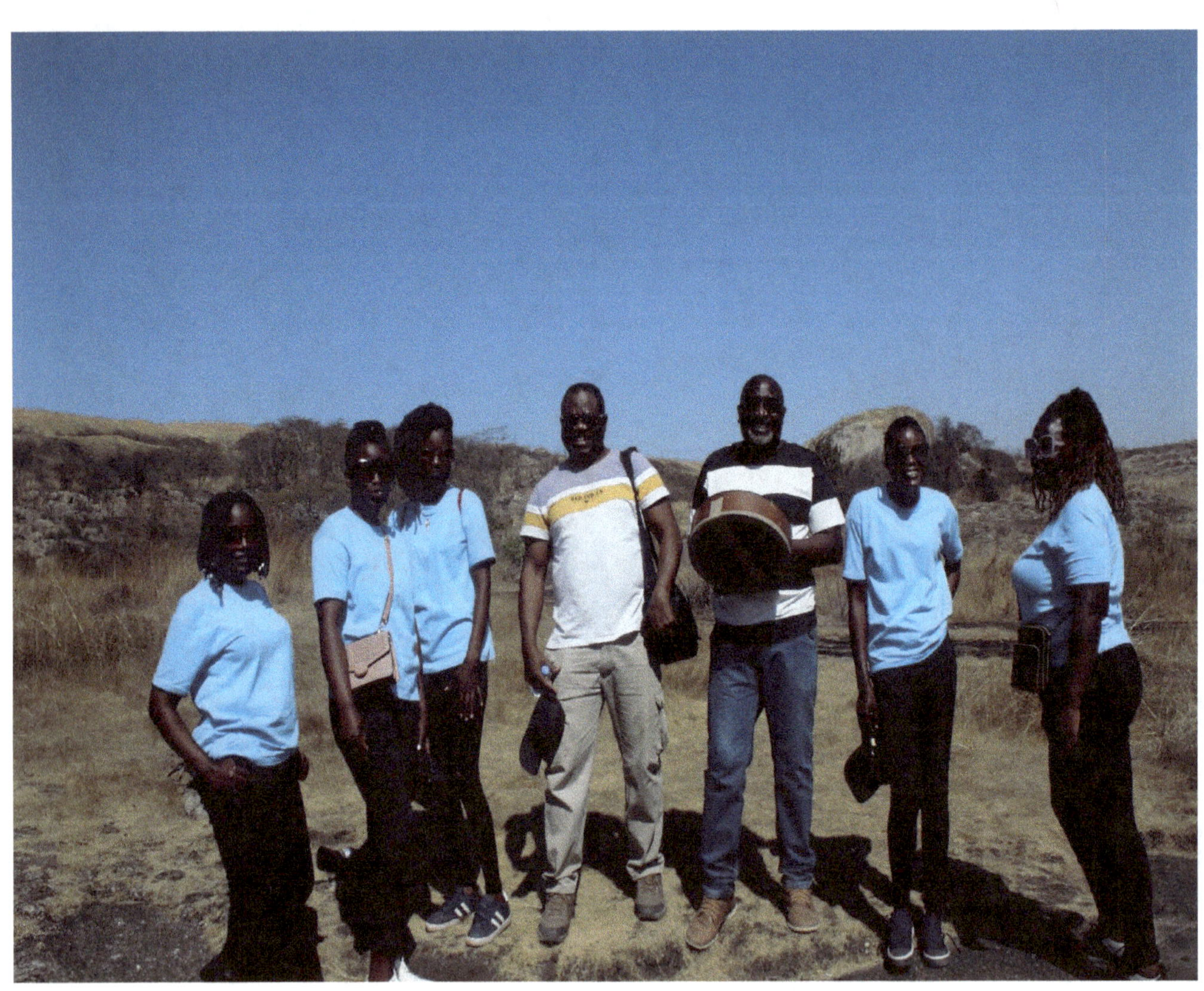

Teach me, not to sin!
Kudakwashe P. Simbi

Dear Father!
I've evolved a wanderer in the land of the living dead,
like a sheep without a shepherd,
I'm lost in my ways,
teach me, to sin not!

I lost my ways, a long ago,
Lust got me carried away and ran away from your truth,
I pushed you away,
all the love you gushed on me, like the morning rains of winter,
I threw it away & lost it,
I forgot all the heavenly rememberings,
My passions led me astray,
Like a prodigal son, I moved towards your mercy and cried wholeheartedly,
Teach me, to sin not!

Hakuna musha usina gonzo
Kudakwashe P. Simbi

Zvinoyera kushaya chan'en'ena dhirezi rambuya,
Husiku itswiki tswiki kugudubura mapoto,
Kungoti ubatidze magetsi
Ndiyee ziii semvura yemuchechetere.
Achapedza musarinya uyu ndiani?

Dzimwe nguwa Bhobhi anenge achitambisa hake muswe seasingadyi makonzo izvo akazvimbirwa nemakoko aanokandirwa
Mbatya dzopera takatarisa here?
Kuti uise mushonga oita seafemerwa
Hakuna musha usina zvawo
Asi zvangu zvandikandisa mapfumo pasi
Angowa mabiribobi kutarisana kwevakarambana.
Asi handingakande mapfumo pasi musha wangu ungaparare ndakatarisa
Ndafunga kukwira gomo nditsvage chiii chingauraye gonzo ranetsa mumba mangu
Kungosiya maoko mangwana unomuka wakan'en'ena ruoko rwese apa richifuridzira.
Ndafunga kuFirita makonzo pamwe musha ungachengeteke tikasununguka nekupembera,
Ndaneta nekungoti ndikadzima mwenje mumaziso ndoona Mbatya dzichipera nekudyiwa nekurumwa rumwa hweNyoka inoruma chaisingadyi.

Ndakaona rufu
Kudakwashe P. Simbi

Ndakaona Rufu achiuya kwandiri ndirere,
Kuhope akanga akafanana nedutu remhepo, yakanga iri pwititi pwititi,
Achiyevedza semavara eshato,
Pakuonekwa kwake akanga akaita semutumwa wechiedza,
Pameso aiyevedza semazamu emhandara,
Akandifudza semhuru,
Akandinyemwerera zvakandikatyamadza,
Akandisvesva semukomana anosvesva musikana,
Chimiro chake chakanga charongedzwa semhandara isina kumboziva mukomana.

Ndakaona ananyanduri vachibaiwa nepfumo rakatesva vakarivara,
Akauya semombe yakasisa nomukaka Kuda kukwezva mhuru,
Kuuya segondo kuhukwana.
Ndakamuona ndikazvibaya neshungu kwazvo.

Mukoma, munin'ina, mbuya nasekuru akangotora kuti nyamu segondo rinotora zvitiyo,
Moyo wangu vakati shutu nehasha,
Muviri kusara vakati rabada semufi,
Ndakasara ndangoti surududu,
Auya hake rufu akandiruma kuti n'a sechikwekwe, kusara ndava ndonda.
Dai asiri rufu akatonga tingadai tiripo tese.

The lake
Photography by Tendai Rinos Mwanaka

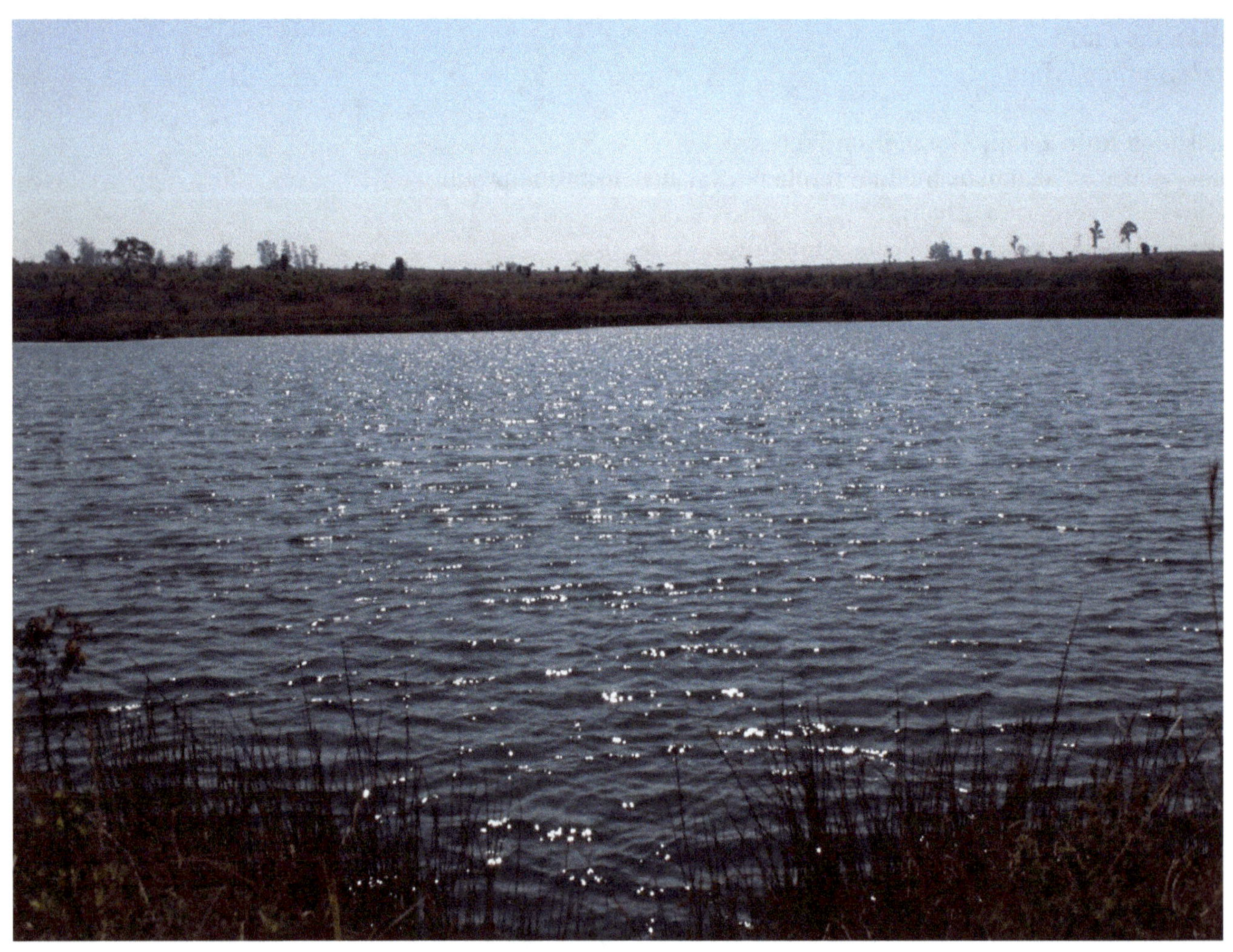

RODS OF CONFUSION

Ayanda Valeria Sithole

I habituate in two planets,
The supernatural is so dark and gloomy,
But it shines bright like a diamond.
I fight the unknown,
Perhaps the one in me performs the magic.
Blood spillers l have stared
Pretenders l have ironed
Fake love, sweet danger, spears, doom
But the repent bell rung,
Death assigned, confusion created,
Demons poured, But all failed
Drenching in His blood l am,
This physic I'm wearing is nothing but vanity.

SKYCLAD

Ayanda Valeria Sithole

I gaze at her now and again
No roust can bind the chain.

I watch her closely,
Short temper intriguing instantly
Bearing suicidal thoughts,
But closed off carefully.

Her none vocal expressions are amusing
Her brown forever teary eyes contemplating.

The window she carefully closed,
Shatter in the roaring midst of the wind.
For a shallow lace, fear is emancipated,
Neutral response is flattened.

She is alive but cold and warm.
Till today, the reason behind the darkness is unknown.

THE OBSCENE

Ayanda Valeria Sithole

Asphyxiation on its way,
Found me in the streets of panicky.
I flinched in prayer until angel helper's arrival.
Tears failed the pain and embarrassed my sweet rapid voice.
Rudeness and African flavor endorsed by a man stung in my carnal mind,
But his help was a blessing in an evil paradise.
His cocky bold voice and questions bruised my sanity,
Only if this typical man knew how l hate being helped had no choice but to be humble.

My final destination was a queue to say thank you,
But the mongrel did the unknown and left me at the gates of calmness.
I crawl to independence daily,
When l reach my destination l will make a call,
Just to remind you that I'm still humble.

RAYS OF SPARKLING SHADOWS

Ayanda Valeria Sithole

They say love is my weakness,
I never envision to be a mistress.
Sleepless nights my mind and soul invading in the darkness,
Rolling in a pool of misery wandering in your wickedness.

My heart, you bruised,
My mind you killed,
Can't say much about self-esteem that you butchered,
Cut my muscular organ complimenting women in my face.

You spewed ugly lame excuses like a curse,
But I embraced myself like a lace,
And drenched in solace,
Only to find myself let go scot-free with no case.

I wail in my dark shadow,
Scream in my naked hallow.
Continue with your game thriller,
The thread between love and hate is just thinner.

Home

Photography by Tendai Rinos Mwanaka

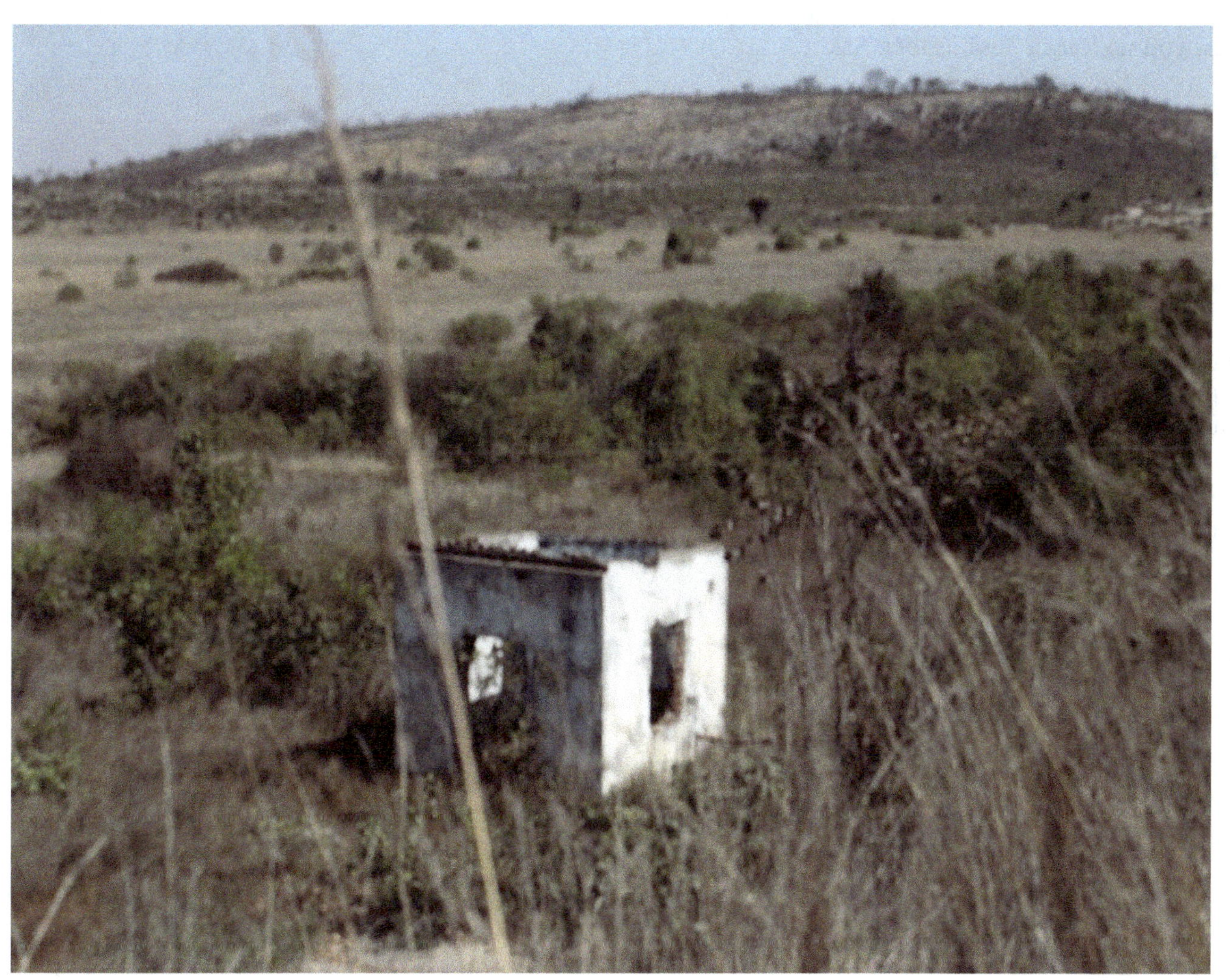

why you no longer Visit us they Ask
Blessing Barnet Chiniko

In the tapestry of family, woven through time,
Lies a tale of struggle, not always sublime.
Politics and power, like a tangled skein,
In the dance of relations, love and pain.

Whispers of witchcraft, like a shadow's kiss,
Juju and charm, in the abyss.
Inheritance wars, greed's cruel game,
In the family hearth, a flickering flame.

Gossip and rumors, a poisonous vine,
In the garden of trust, they intertwine.
Old men acting foolish, lost in their pride,
In the corridors of respect, they no longer reside.

Relatives, like crows, claiming their due,
Believing they own you, through and through.
Yet, bonds of blood, are not chains to bear,
In the theater of family, all should be fair.

Then there are those, you never visit,
Lost in time, in memory's limit.
The ones you don't communicate, a silent call,
In the gallery of relations, portraits on the wall.

In this labyrinth of faces, known and strange,
Comes the struggle, of finding one's range.
The quest for identity, a journey deep,
In the heart of family, secrets we keep.

Yet, amidst the chaos, the conflict, the noise,

There lies a choice, and it's yours to voice.
To rise above, the politics and the greed,
In the field of family, to plant a new seed.

A seed of respect, of understanding, of love,
To soar above the turmoil, like a peaceful dove.
To remember that family, in all its hues,
Is not about owning, but about the clues.

Clues to our past, our roots, our core,
In the family tapestry, there's always more.
So, choose to see, not just the strife,
But the love and lessons, in the book of life.

For in every old fool, there's a tale to tell,
In every greedy heart, a wish to quell.
In every gossip, a cry to be heard,
In every silence, a longing word.

So here's to the struggle, the search, the way,
May you find your identity, come what may.
In the family saga, may you find your part,
Not just in your name, but in your heart.

Soldiers that are not spoken about

Blessing Barnet Chiniko

In lands of tales and memories,
Where valor and strife intertwine,
There dwells a father, strong and wise,
Elias Chiniko, a name divine.

A soldier by heart, his spirit unbowed,
From Cuba's shores to Mozambique's ground,
He bore the weight of battles fought,
And emerged, a survivor, renowned.

Through the Chimoio massacre's grim affair,
He faced the tempest, the horrors deep,
His kin, in sorrow, mourned despair,
For they believed he'd forever sleep.

A funeral held, with tears that flowed,
In somber dirges, their grief displayed,
Yet destiny's hand had other plans,
As Elias returned, their fears betrayed.

Amidst the anguish and disbelief,
Relatives scattered, their hearts undone,
For in the presence of life's relief,
They saw the father, the prodigal son.

A Presidential Guard, his post held high,
Intelligent, sober, a beacon of might,
With hopes soaring for his beloved child,
Guiding him towards a future bright.

Disciplined and stern, yet love held sway,

A father's wishes, his son to excel,
To forge a path, with honor's array,
And in his footsteps, to proudly dwell.

A passion for music stirred his soul,
Lucky Dube's voice, reggae's sweet embrace,
Melodies weaving dreams untold,
A rhythm that painted his vibrant space.

Awards adorned his life's grand stage,
Recognition for his vision's flight,
His dreams alight, like stars engaged,
Illuminating the darkest night.

Elias Chiniko, a man revered,
A soldier, a father, a legend whole,
His legacy etched, forever endeared,
In the annals of triumph and soul.

So let us honor this valiant man,
Whose spirit soared, undeterred by strife,
With grateful hearts, we understand,
Elias Chiniko, a beacon of life.

Extraction
Photography by Tendai Rinos Mwanaka

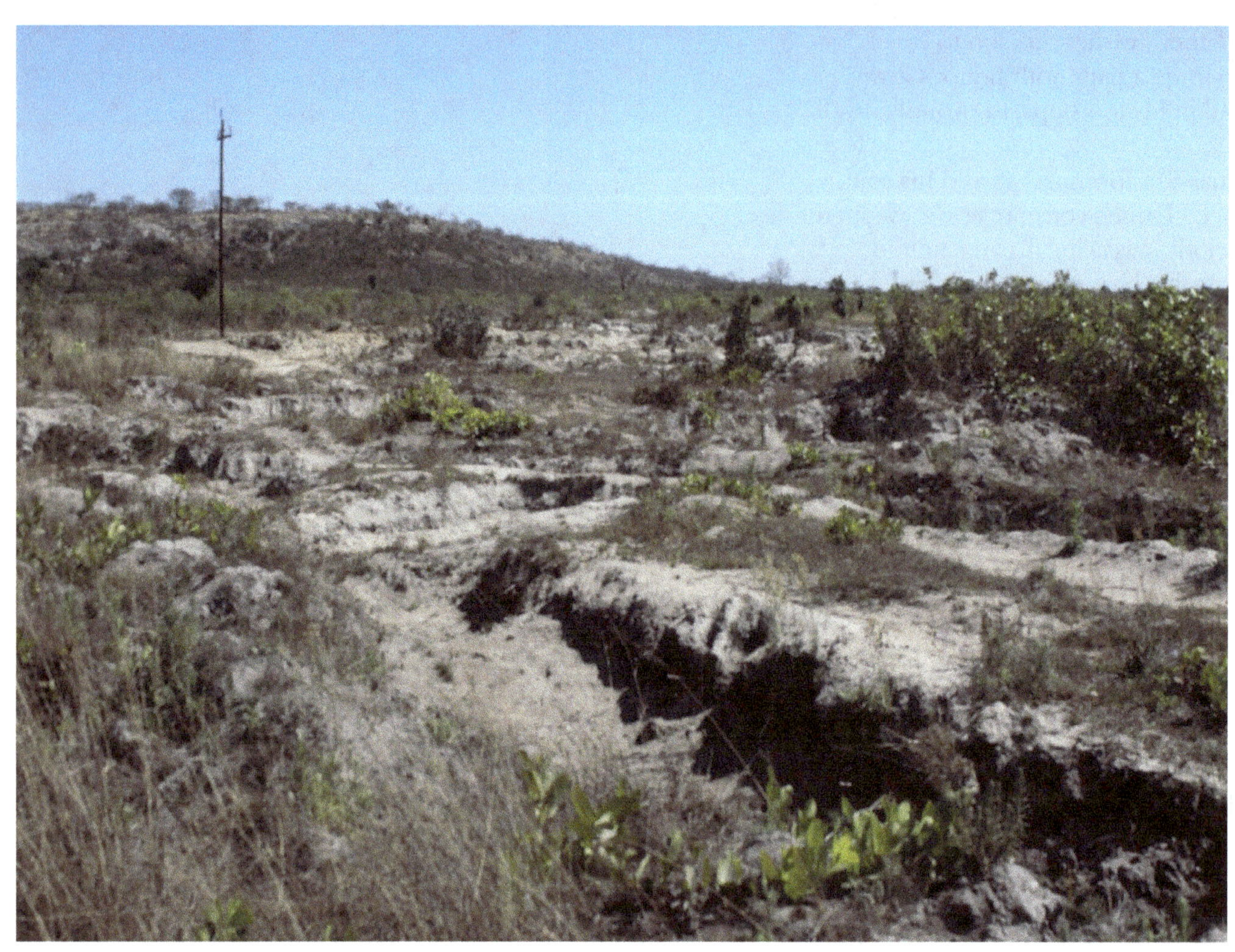

DUST UPON MANKIND

Ranganai Chikwara

When it heaves upon us
It's the journey's end
Dust to dust
A Handful of dust
Rituals of dust
Upon this measured shelter
Drips in laps
And dust shoveled
Sealing me in freshness
Of my journey's end
When I no longer see, breathe and walk
A statue forever
Grandma it was too soon!
Friend gone
Is this the bridge to dreams!
I will forever
Miss the dances in the dust
Celebration of life
Dance to remember me,
All the virtues of dust
Here I am
I am yet to find
If there is peace here!

CONFESSIONS

Ranganai Chikwara

I have no words of my own
I confess
Neither I am closer
Fashioning this diction
Fashioning this rhyming words
To paint words in their meaning
Nor have I sat in a kiln of language
To manifest an alien language
In perfection and sound in meaning
For the words are rare nowadays
These decades have lapsed
But now trickle in this season
In bursts of wonder and confusion
Some early mornings shine
With some new stock of words!
I see,
I read,
I write,
I hear,
I confess.

BEYOND THE EYE

Ranganai Chikwara

On a rock at the edge
of the lake comfortably, I sit
Dangling feet seemingly enjoying, the environs
long I stare and contemplate
At the vast carpet of waters
A grandeur of life
Although I can't see where it ends!
I feel its grandeur migrate silently
Into my whole being, a silent mystery!
ceases all the fury boggling my mind
I feel a bolt of lightness, a fresh breeze cooling!
'Am part of this wonder', I say quietly!
A momentary healing cascade up the terrains of my mind
The loneliness and quietness
Sails me on a fictitious ride, yet real
We see today, yet not all!
A beyond there is, but we can't see!
Perhaps a prayer
Maybe this stillness
Can take us there!

BEFITTING TUG

Ranganai Chikwara

Blunt heart-rending errands
I can see its winding trail
Craving for a journey's end!
Sweat soaked face
In a maze of what if's
If you weren't...
From this befitting tug
Here is a beacon of hope
Liberate your soul
Here is your siesta
Let the clogging pass
soul wrenching softens
If herein
Give it a chance
You will look back with a sigh!
Of how chance
Cleansed all fury
drown your distress in such
To cool yourself
In cold waters
And seal
the what ifs for a while
In a concrete cage
Here is your paradise!

MIRAGE IN THE SAVANNA

Ranganai Chikwara

The base of their feet is hot
Yet the lone travellers couldn't rest
Meandering in the sandy soils'
Heavily weathered and leached landscape
Yet it somehow sustains a livelihood
Still they engage in its coarse ground
Echoes of a new pathway within
Bang on their ears!
Keeps them along
Till mirages loom large in the grassland
Echoes of a new pathway
Still ferment
For they realise
They had been travelling in this road
For a long, long time
It's the mirages of the dry Savanah.

Sculptures by Fair Makunde

Photography by Tendai Rinos Mwanaka

He works with his father, Rangarirai Makunde at their home sculpture park near Domboshava hills and Caves monument. He is mostly interested in abstracts, especially flowers

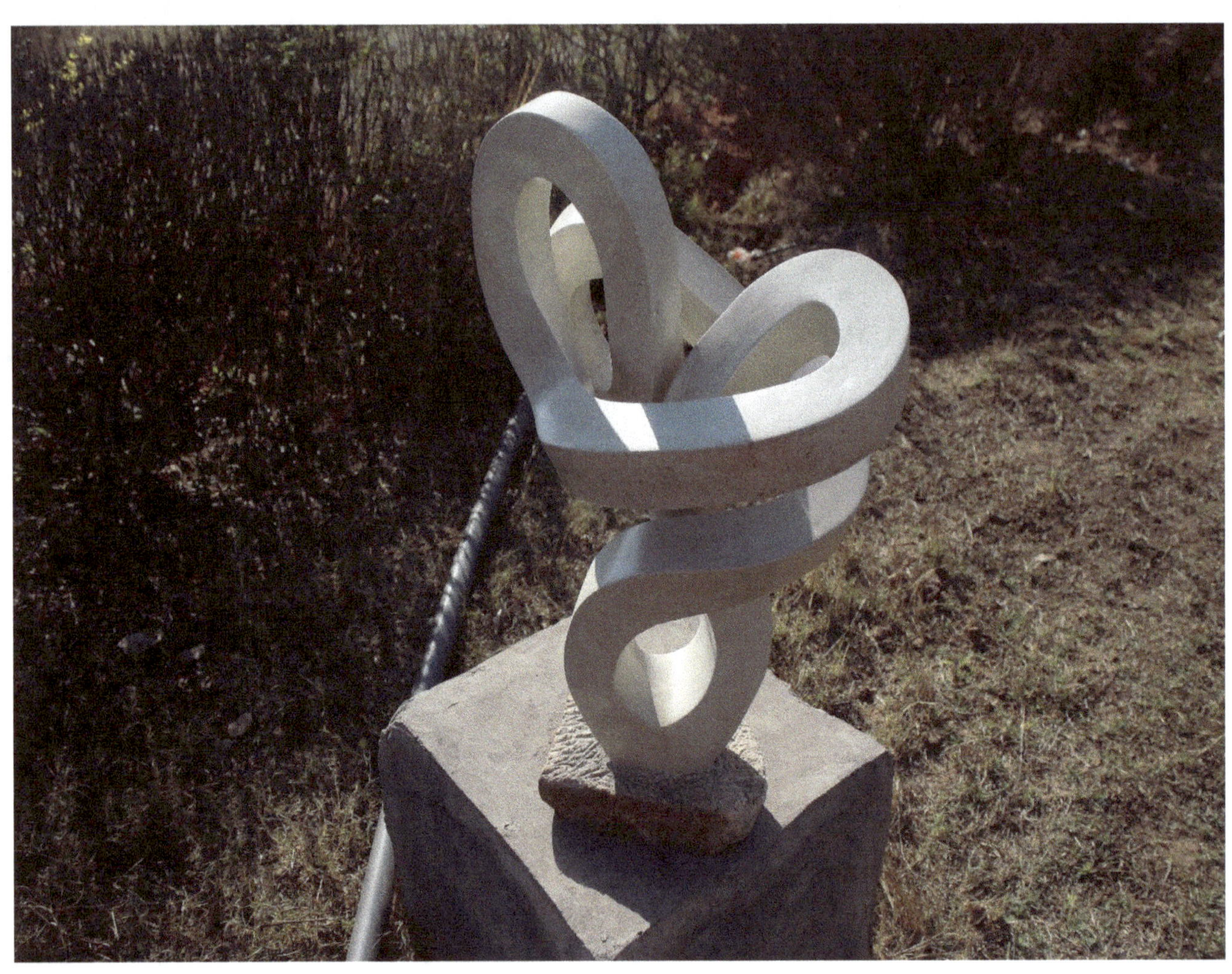

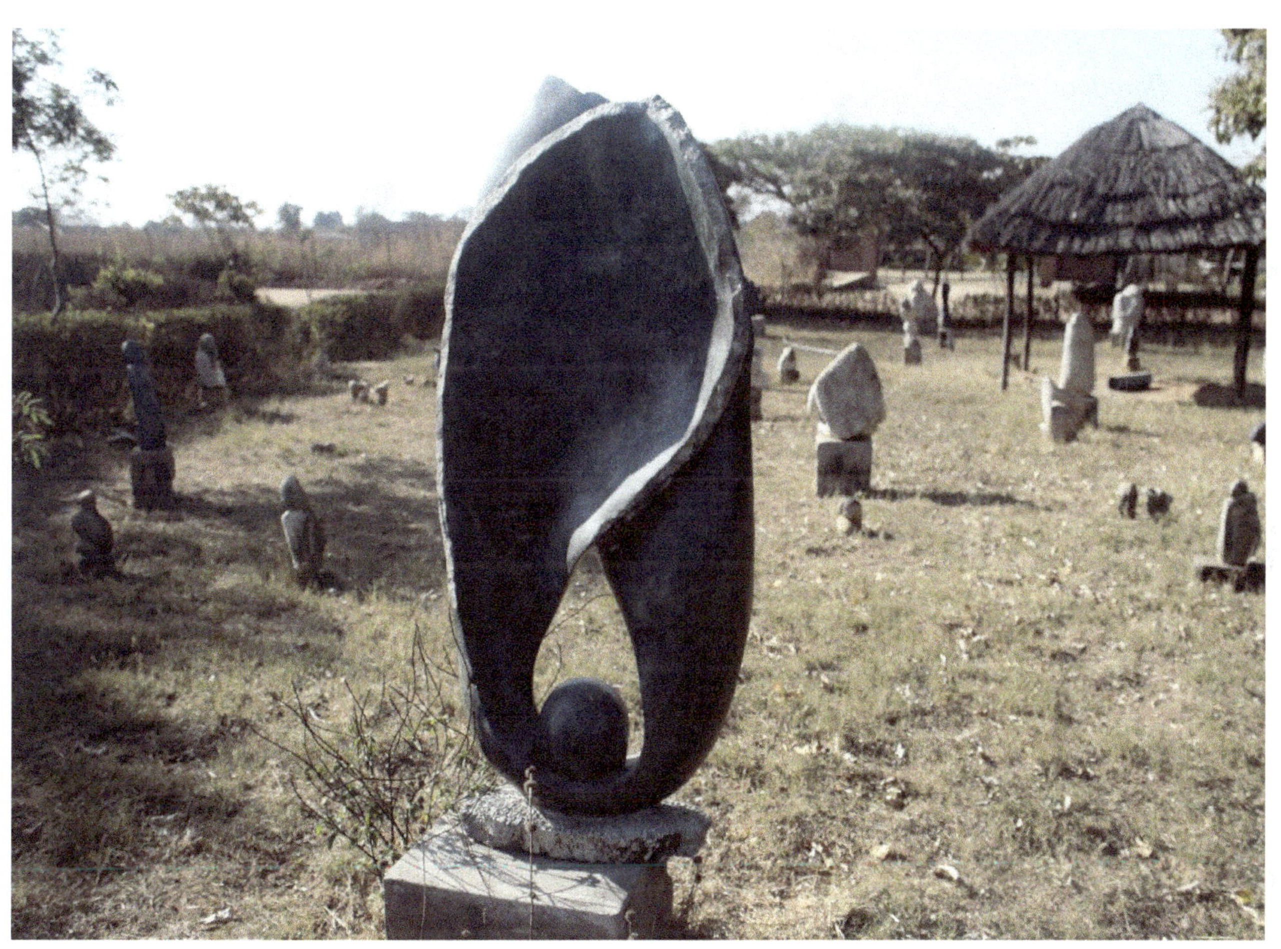

terse verse

Chenjerai Mhondera

my pen, stolen
was found broken
under his majesty -
king of farts' mattress;

blood, dry in its bones -
and the barrel, quarelling against
the verdict, to find self in a lake of fire!

this pen,
this ink;
a bold undertaker!

you snort and a braggart

Chenjerai Mhondera

i've never lived with pain
all the days of my life
because when pain was
coming i w'ld know that
here comes pain,
and i w'ld avoid it straight away

but today i'm a fool again,
i thought pain is just a cold, rough fool;
piercing relentlessly and selfishly into one's flesh,
unbeknown, sometimes it is as beautiful
and as adorable as the woman you love,
and give utmost care and attention -
even in the face of dejection

only for that pain in such beauty,
to spit at you, on you
and tell you, your time has
expired - you little, old fool -
you snort and a braggart!

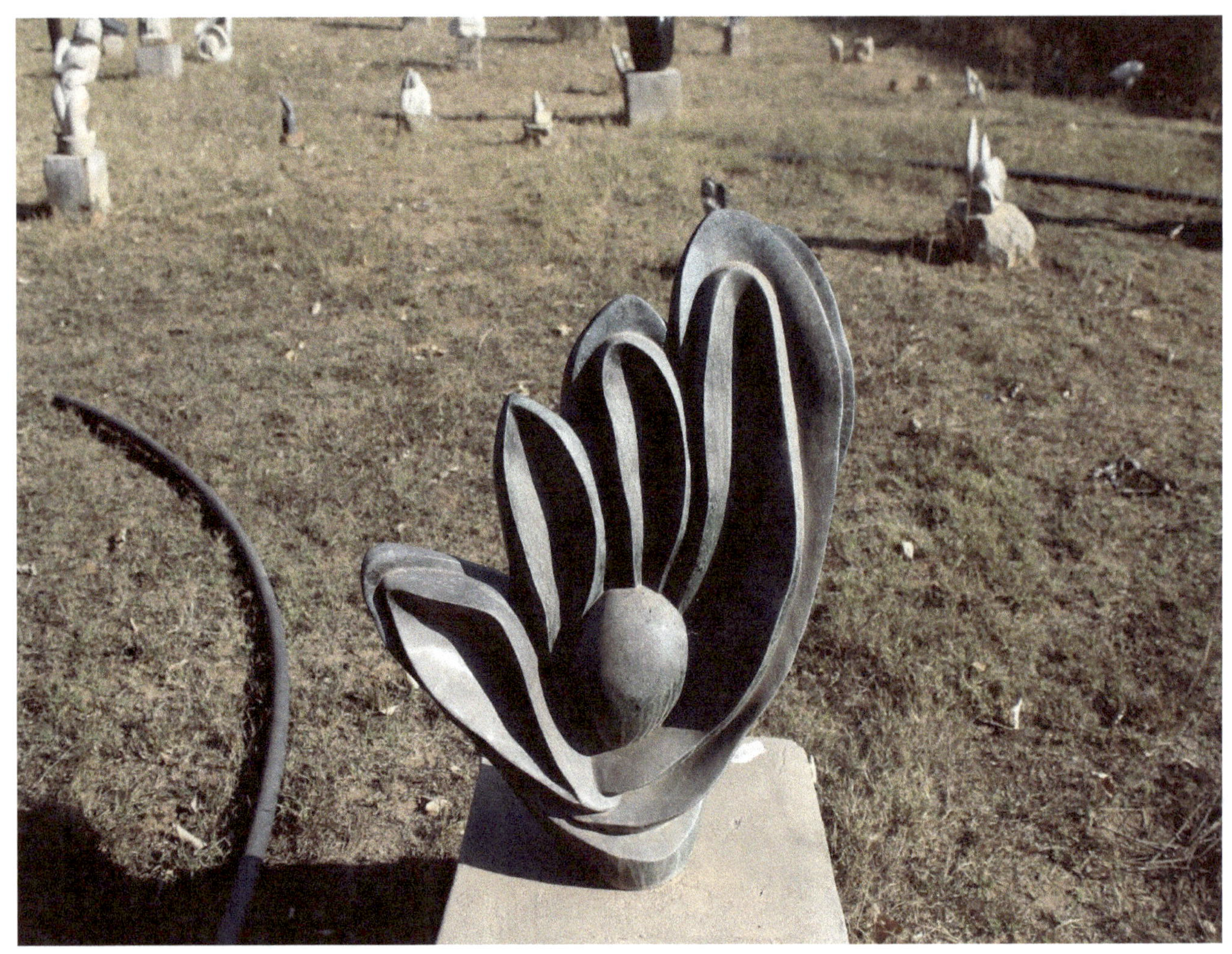

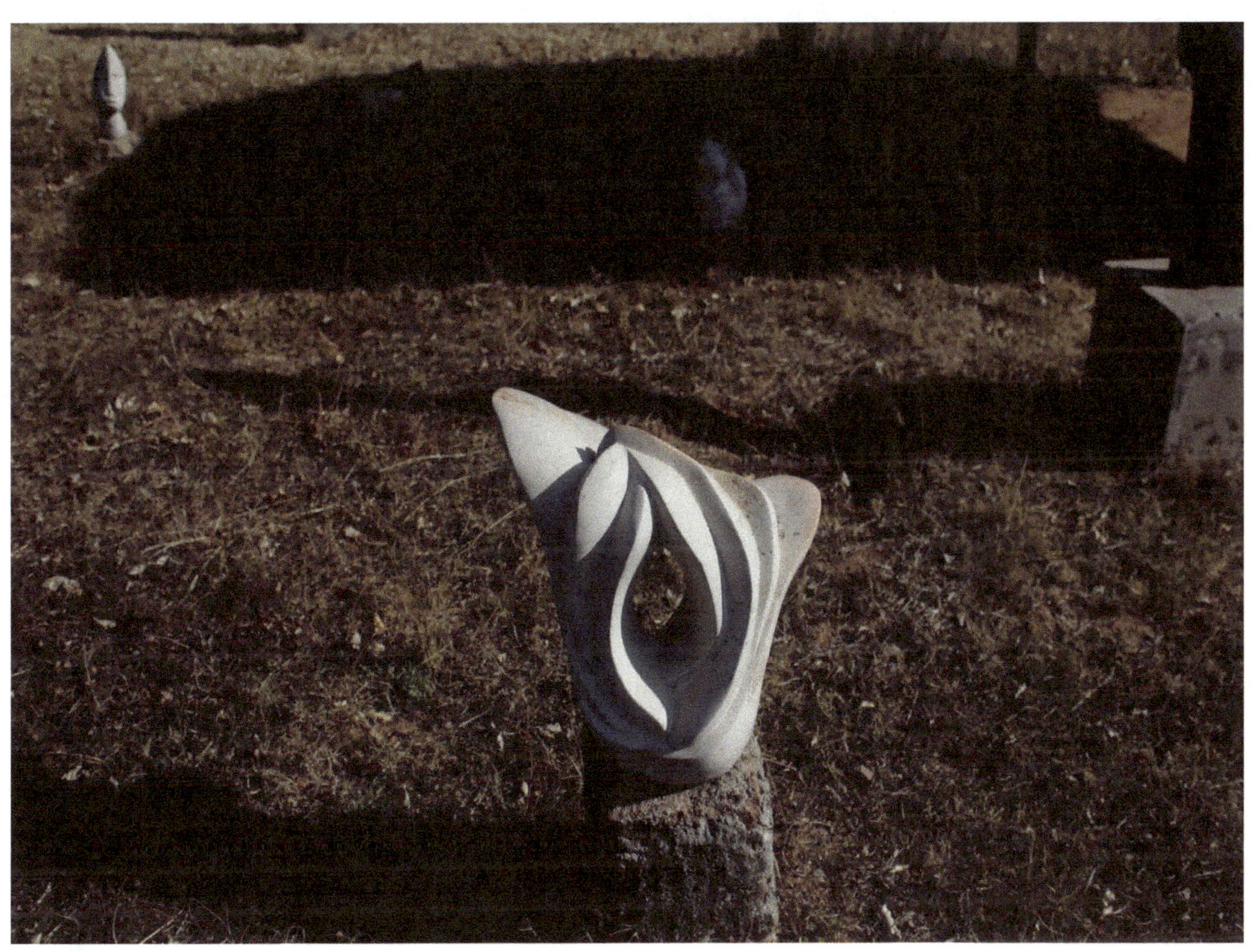

Izayeke zodwa

Qinisela Possenti Ndlovu

Loba kunyama kusesabeka, kuyasa kuyaphela okwethuka,
Ngiyikufa, Ngathatha Abazali,
NgingumZali kubantwana UMondli ongu Meli, uMeli onguMondli
Kimi lakubanawami.
Ukubumdala kwaba ngamabizo ami aphakathi.
Sisebatshinane Izihlobo ezingahlelekanga zasenza intandane,
Basimisa enyaweni zemfundo,
Bazibisela zihamba mbijana ngokungazi.
Kwaba yindaba kaFudu icinta uMvundla kumdlalo wabo wokugijima.
Loba kuleyezi elimyama iyaphuma imisebe yelanga.

Loba kunyama kusesabeka, kuyasa kuyaphela okwethuka,
Sadla okwakukhona, kungekho okwakudleka,
Ngabayisigqilikazi, senkosikazi enguMakhelwane.
Zehla ezimathonsi, ajuluka amaginqo.
Zahlatshelwa ingoma, sathuqhubeka singamabutho sithandaz.
Ngahamba ngodondolo,
Emifuleni, agcwele okungaziwayo okuyingozi
Kumumethe izilo zolwandle,
Saba lilitshe ngaphansi kwedala,
Inyawo ziyadidizela zigida ingoma zendulo,
Loba kuleyezi elimyama iyaphuma imisebe yelanga.

Loba kunyama kusesabeka, kuyasa kuyaphela okwethuka,
Loba lingangitshelanga ngiyamazi uBaba,
Ngimbona emaphutsheni.
Nyawo lami, dlalisa unyawo lami.
Njenga mabhiza ematha ngamasondo edabula indonga zeJericho,
Avulekile Amasango, Nansi i Jelusalema, ikhaya labangcwele,
Loba kuleyezi elimyama iyaphuma imisebe yelanga.

Loba kuleyezi elimyama iyaphuma imisebe yelanga
Iziqhephuqhephu zokudla zayifunza ingane ka Ma
Yahleka, Yajabula, Yalala,
Emhlane olubhalu lokucatsha,
Ngesimbanga, we Mama wesizwe.
Umninimuzi wathi okunge kazake ngikubone,
Lokhu yathetshulwa yingwe,
Ukholo olunje luyayifuqa intaba
Loba kuleyezi elimyama iyaphuma imisebe yelanga.

Loba kuleyezi elimyama iyaphuma imisebe yelanga
Wakhala, Wakhwaza.
Sancela uncedo Mama wesizwe,
Saluthola uncedo, saba ngabantu.
Upahla, izembatho, ukudla, Indlala yaba yinto eyedlulayo.
Kwajabula abaphansi, lenkanyezi zagida, lenyanga yabobotheka,
Izingelosi zathandaza,
Ithemba kalibulali,
Loba kuleyezi elinyama, Iyaphuma imisebe yelanga

Masks only
Qinisela Possenti Ndlovu

No matter how hectic was the night there was a peaceful dawn.
We were death, robber of your parents,
We were Parents to children, Female Father, Male Mother,
To my and their siblings.
Responsibility was my and their middle names.
At a tender age, Irresponsible family members, made us orphans.
Stopped the footsteps of Education,
Replaced it with slow tracks of ignorance.
The ancient story of Tortoise, Winning the race from The Hare
Every dark cloud had a silver lining.

No matter how hectic was the night, there was a peaceful dawn.
Ate what was there, nothing to eat.
Became a slave girl to a Woman; our Neighbour,
Tears flowed, sweat flooded.
Songs were sung, we soldiered, prayed.
Walked with walking stick,
In rivers, full of unknown dangers,
Flooded with sea creatures.
We were a stone under a rock,
Feet busy, danced to ancient hymns.
Every dark cloud had a silver lining.

No matter how hectic was the night, there was a peaceful dawn.
No matter we were not told my and their father,
We knew him, had seen him in dreams,
My feet and their feet played,
Like Horses gallop that tore ancients walls of Jericho.
Heavens opened, Oh! Jerusalem, the land of the holy.
Every dark cloud had a silver lining.

No matter how hectic was the night, there was a peaceful dawn.
Crumbs of food, feed mothers child,
Laughed, rejoiced, Slept,
On my and their backs, cared to hide.
In surprise, wow, Mother of the nation.
Until kingdom came, I had not seen such faith
Faith moved mountains.

Every dark cloud had a silver lining.
No matter how hectic was the night, there was a peaceful dawn.
Begged for help, Mother of the nation,
We received help, we became people.
Roof, clothes, food, Hunger became a past tense,
Ancestors rejoiced, Stars danced, Moon smiled,
Angels prayed.
Earth moved mountains.
Every dark cloud had a silver lining.

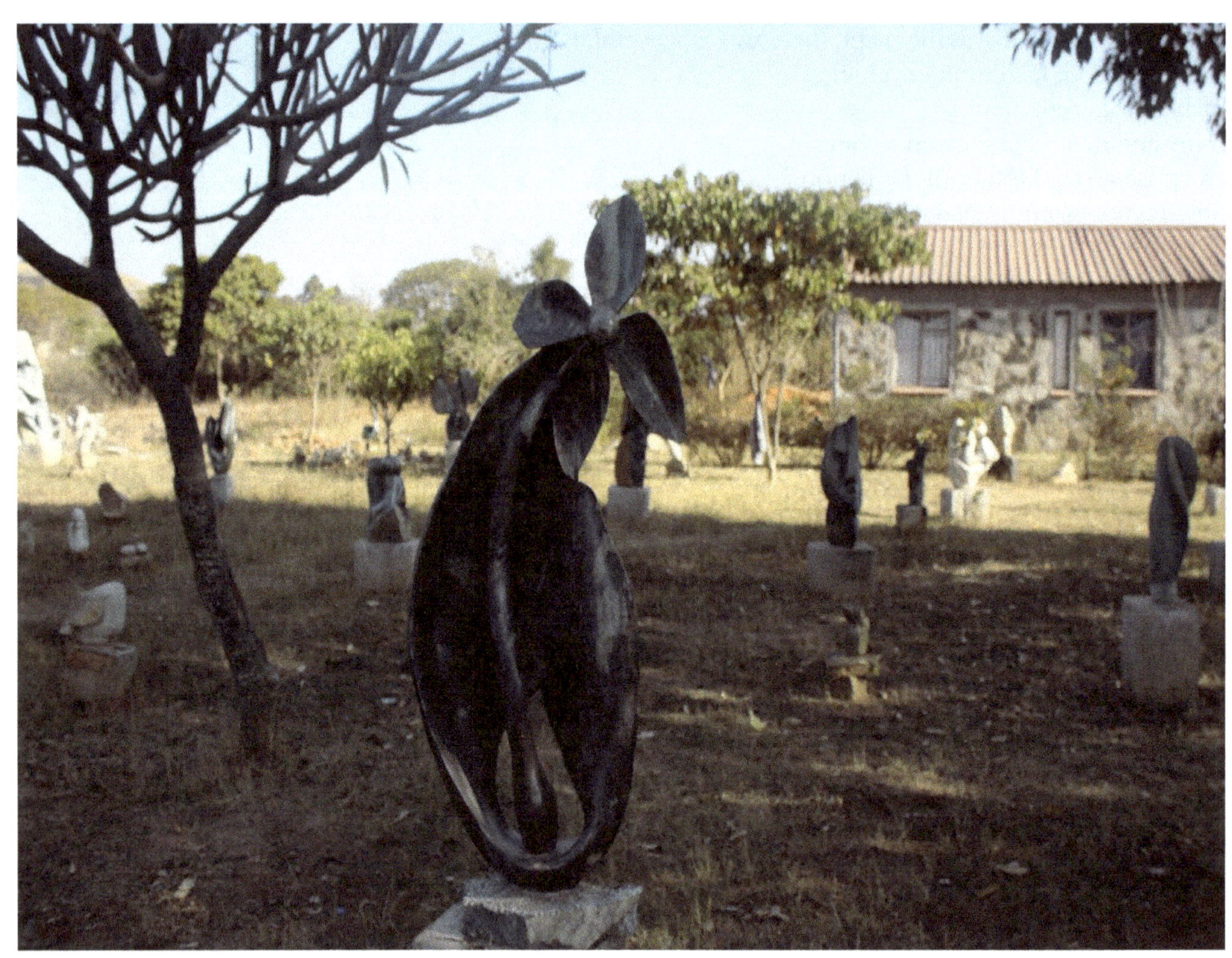

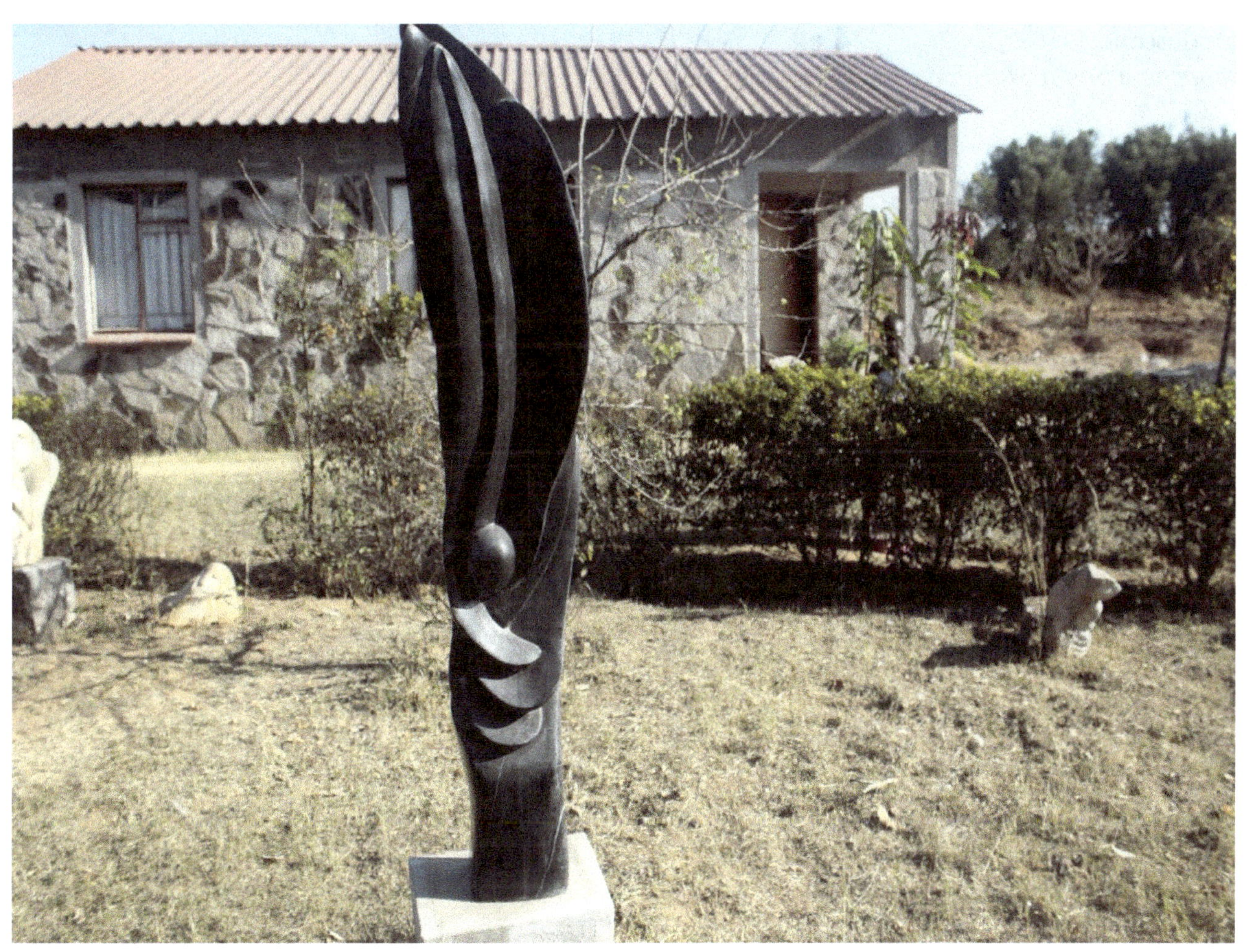

Kaleidoscope

Gamuchirai Susan Muchirahondo

Everything to me expresses itself in colour.

When I'm alone I feel yellow.

Around people I'm orange...vibrant and free and bright...but not as yellow.

Being with him was army green, unpleasant but necessary.

Loving him was a constant fade between pink and black...a grey tainted by meekness of a sort.

Freeing myself from him was a lively green...an echo of pure white painted across the wind...

Releasing him was purple and pale... pleasant but unnecessary...

Looking in the mirror now is clear and beautiful... rainbows shooting from the corners of my mind.

Kenan Blue

Gamuchirai Susan Muchirahondo

He's like ...kenan blue
I have no idea what that is, but it fits him too
Delicate arms
Strong, manly
Fragile heart
Loving fiercely

My lover sits by the stairs at dusk as he boils over with emotion
Bathing in apricity

Will it be like this forever?

I want to take my lover some place quiet
To a town only him and I know
A place where I let my hand engulf his and my lips follow
Dripping in all consuming desire

Whatever the wind is
It's meant for me and him
To carry us on its wings
And bring us to sudden glee

Where no eyes wander
And the flowers dance about us

Where I am my lover's
And he is the tree in my forest that isn't forbidden
And the winter sun isn't something he squints at
He bathes in the glow and in me
Too

Binary Love

Gamuchirai Susan Muchirahondo

Let me stalk you
You'll never wake up to an empty chatroom ever again
Let me fill your mind with giggles and full laughs
Let me exhaust your storage with images of me

Let me write you paragraphs that could have been two sentences
Let me immerse myself in your inbox
Segregate me from the masses and pin me
Pin me against the wallpaper of your galaxy or apple

Take a bite or two and get back to the screen
Scroll me and scroll all over to find me on every platform
Haunting your digital universe
This century has seen great things and will see better or worse
Make me the center of your metaverse

Would we be without these ones and noughts?
I wrote you so many poems in my notes
I sang you along to every song on my playlists
I read you in every audiobook

Would we meet anywhere outside of this binary world?
Would time tiktok the same,
Would you pinterested in me?

I love you more than numbers could count
I love you beyond this digital curtain
Beyond these frail screens
Turn off.
Switch off and I'd still be very on for you
Right here

Where the sun shines

Sombre
Gamuchirai Susan Muchirahondo

In sombre times, the heart sings
It speaks
Of a million infinities
That have gone by without notice
It cries out in ache
To have you look up and watch the world spin

To call your attention to the victories that came before this fall
The love as you await its fall
Or yours
Into the petals of a Neverland known only to man and you
Will you see it in the mile or right there beside you?
When your destiny calls and the stagnancy tears, when the stars fall into place as the world wears

Will you hear it
Will you hear it?

Sunflower
Gamuchirai Susan Muchirahondo

I danced like a mad person
Hands all over the air
Spinning out of control
Throwing my head back and forth
And
Harry keeps going

I've got your face hung up high in the gallery

I pull my dress up and down
My legs show themselves time and time again
The heat in my stomach
Sending glistening all over my body

The guitar solo dropping beads of sweat down my bossom
The way music takes over my soul
Possesses my being
Makes me feel like water that can take any shape anywhere
Illuminates me, my soul and deludes me
Into thinking the sun only shines for me
Sunflower

Sculptures by Rangarirai Makunde
Photography by Tendai Rinos Mwanaka

Rangarirai Makunde is mostly interested in human figures. His work like his son's is displayed near Domboshava hills and caves monument.

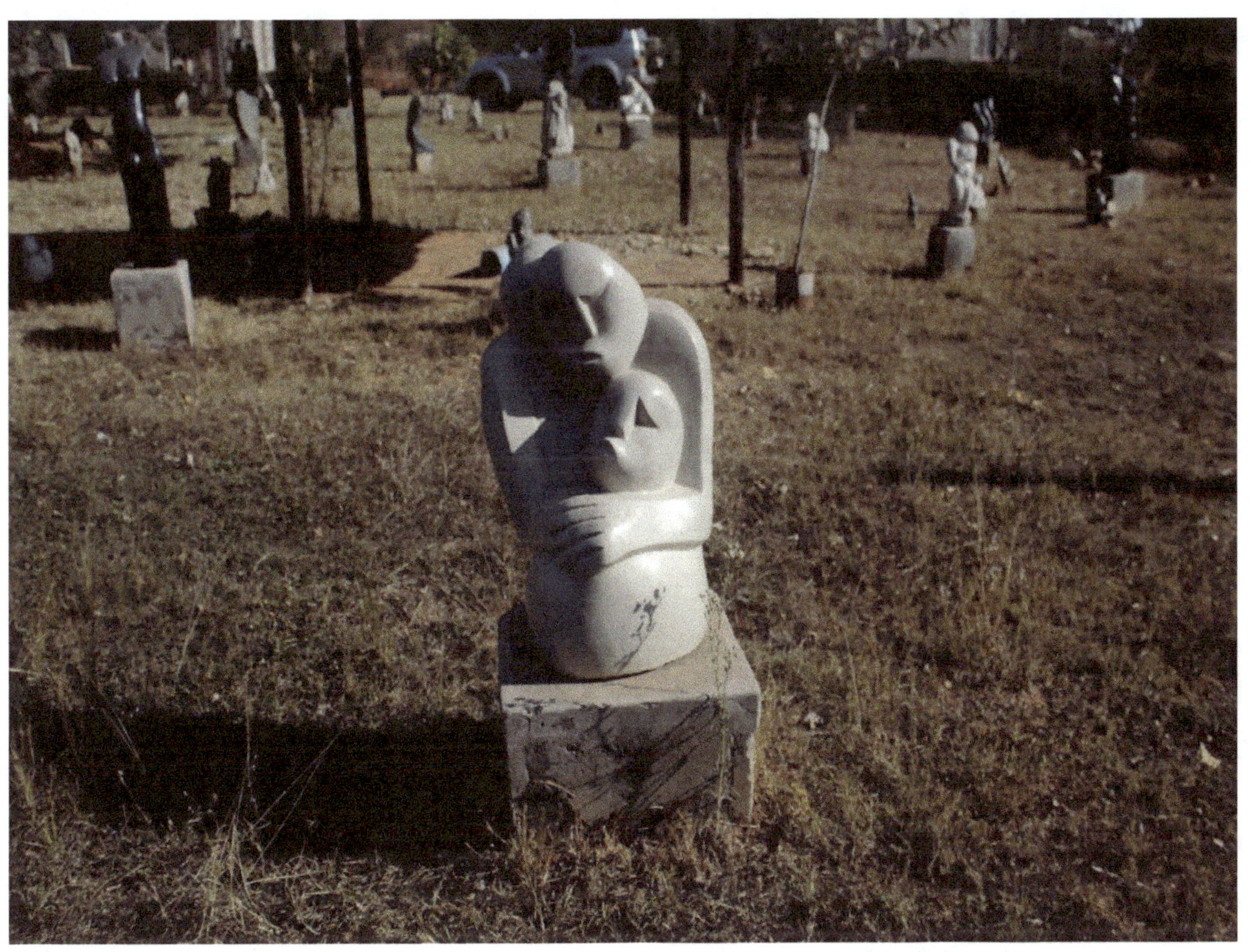

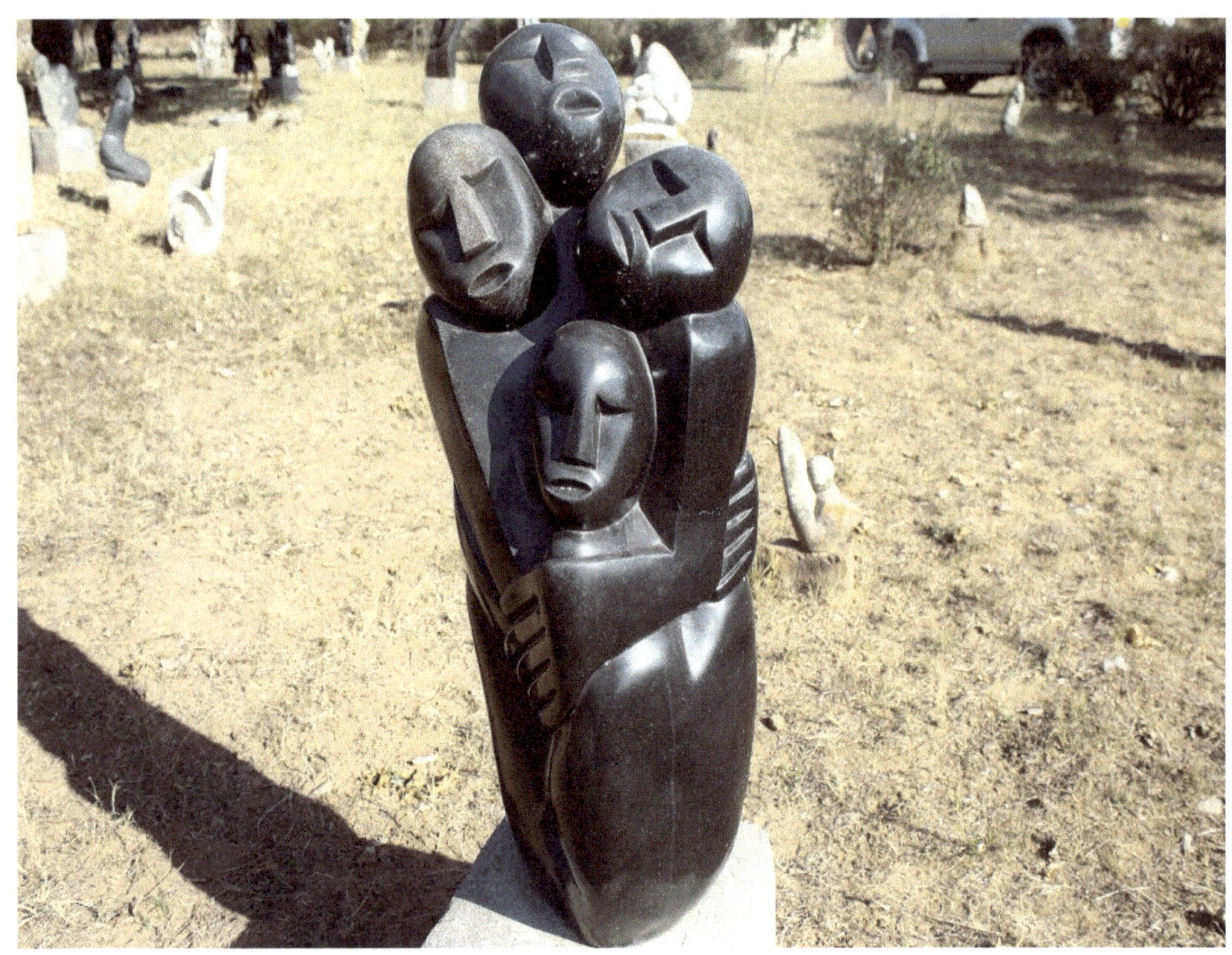

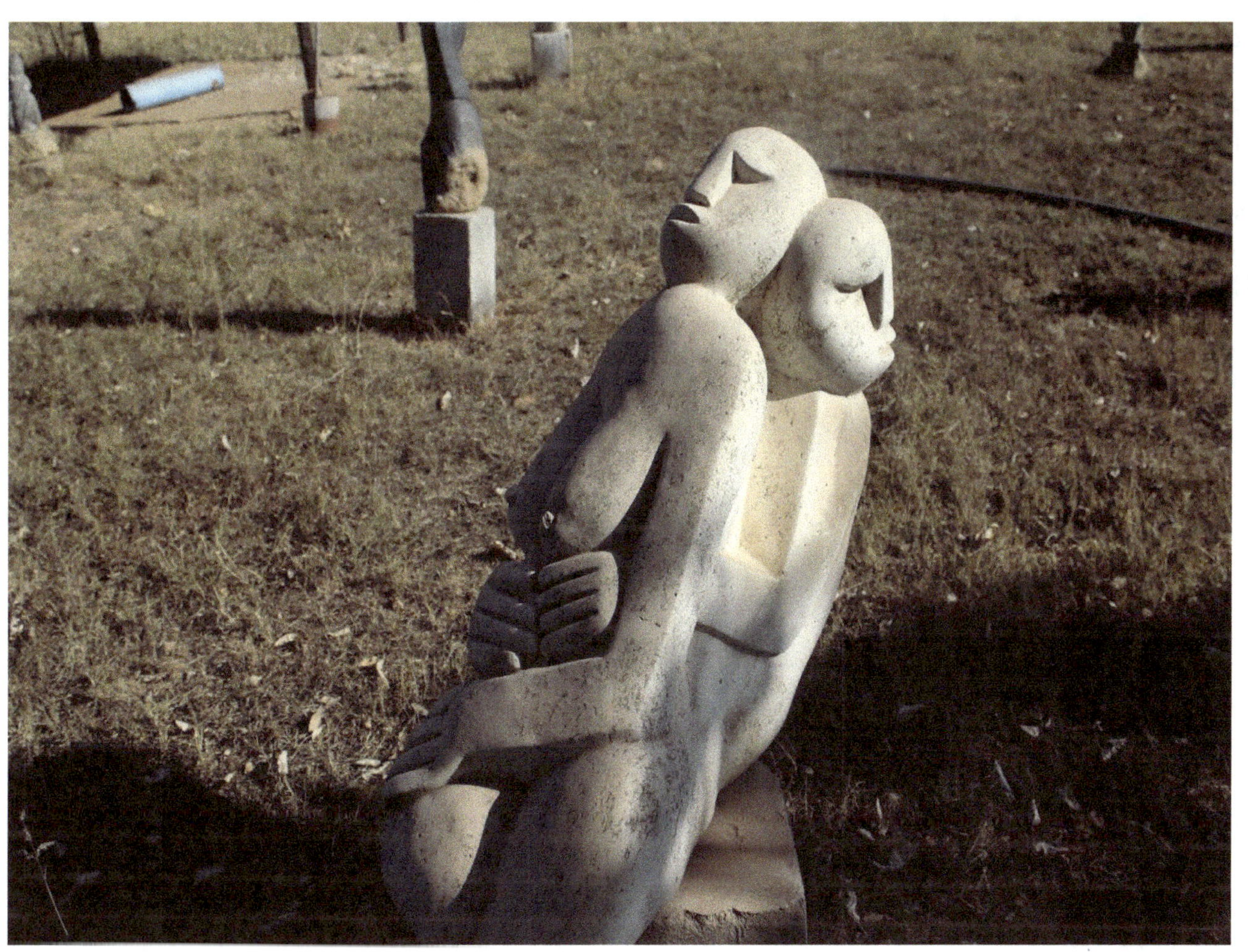

The bed

Oscar Gwiriri

Father was the last to wake up,
He rotated the pillowtop mattress,
Did the bed in a well done manner.
Mother later remembered some bed issues.
Removed sheets and also rotated the mattress,
The mattress position was back to square one.

Gallup-poll

Oscar Gwiriri

The questionnaire
Is about a billionaire
Whose golden Will
Had nothing else,
But his will to be buried
In a recovery position.

Waterbodies sustainability

Oscar Gwiriri

Amongst shells of cowries
Gathered used pet bottles,
Twined hooks and motherboards,
From damn neglect fishers,
Rich poor engineers and maybe
Pollutive beach tourism bitches.

Sacrificial Mama

Oscar Gwiriri

Mother was a loving mother
Though I can't recall my nestling times,
But I can really remember very well
When she assisted me with homework.
Coached by my teacher in her bedroom.

When I couldn't get a place at a boarding school,
Mother invited the principal home for negotiations.
Of course I had low grades for boarding school,
But mother broke the barrier by her bedroom,
Finally the poor me got to the prestigious school.

My academia was never impressing at all,
No employer dared look at my filthy certificates,
Mother negotiated for my employment,
With the prestigious CEO in her poor bedroom.
For real, the poor graded me is at work right now.

Despite my skills incapacitation and dull mind,
I am dilly-dallying and getting paid a salary.
Mother is still negotiating for my promotion,
Possibly for a bigger post as she endeavours.
She just needs more negotiating time in the bedroom.

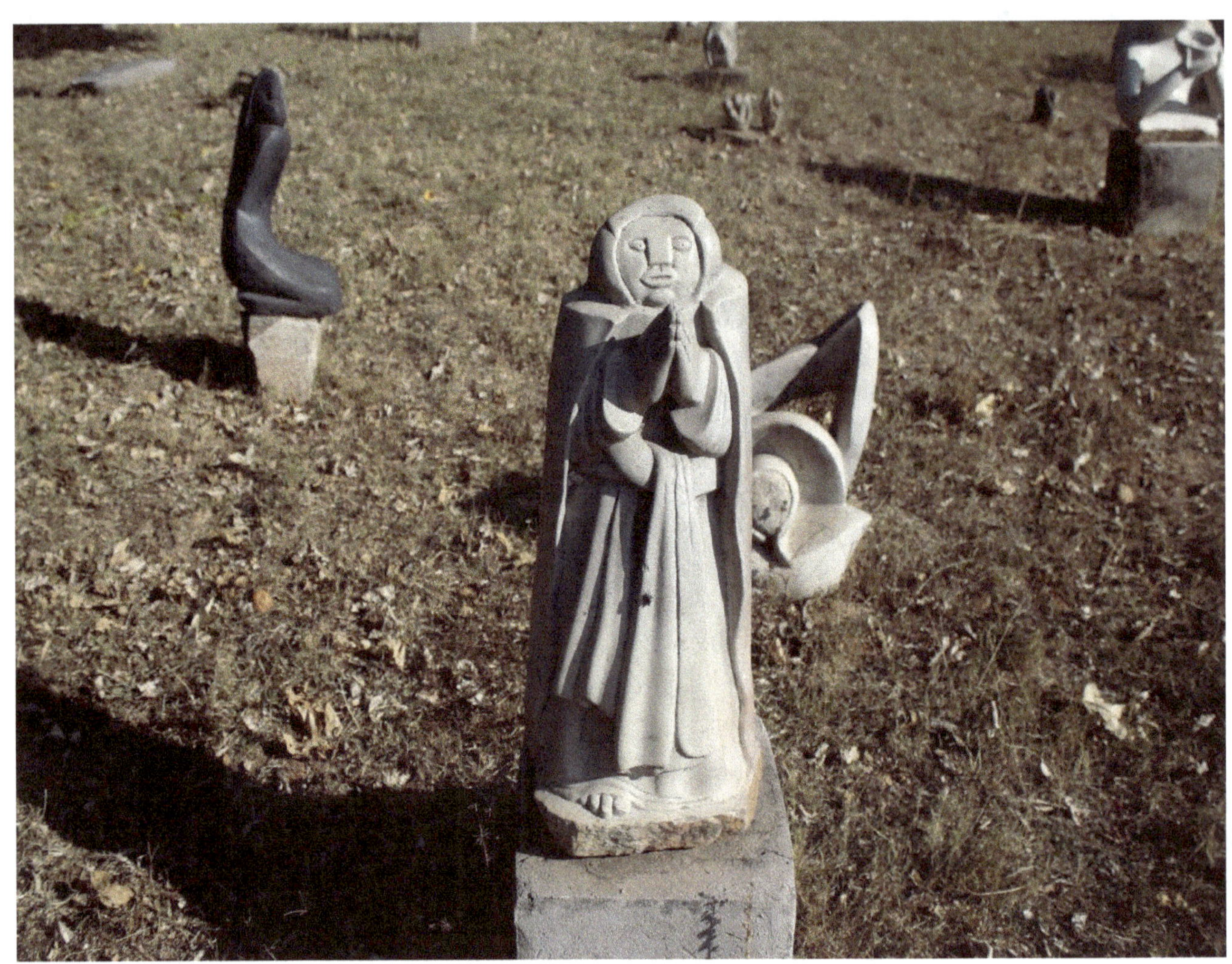

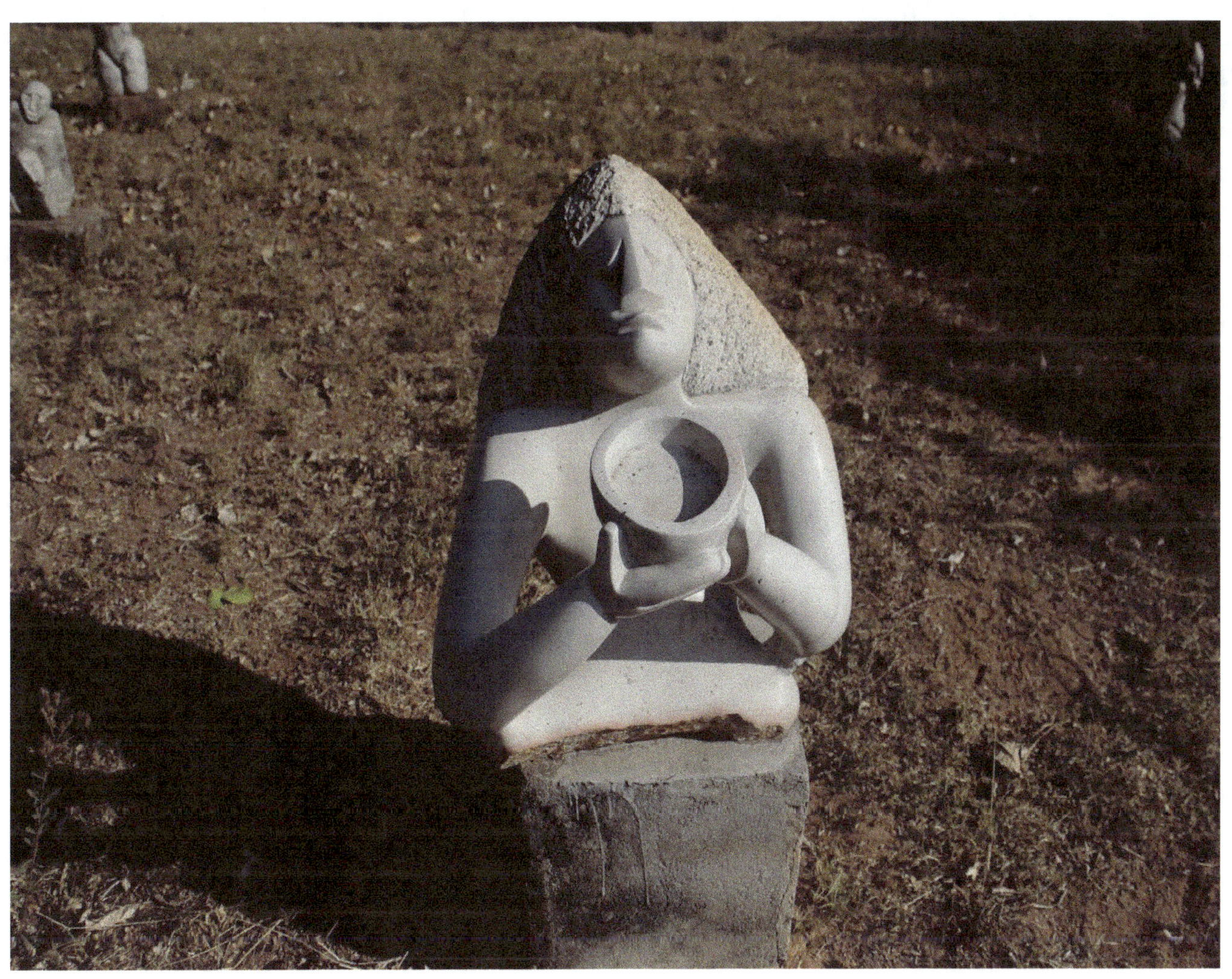

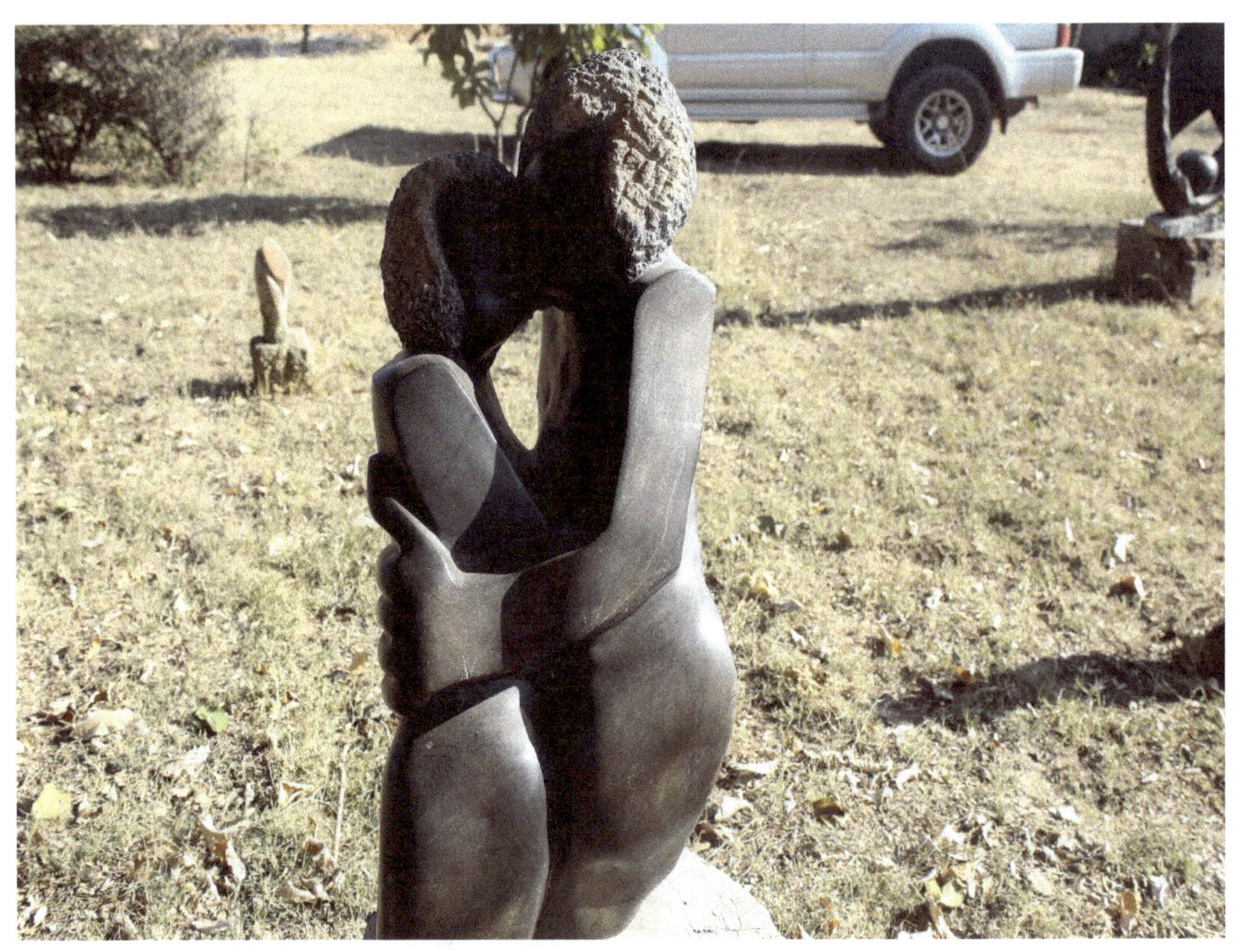

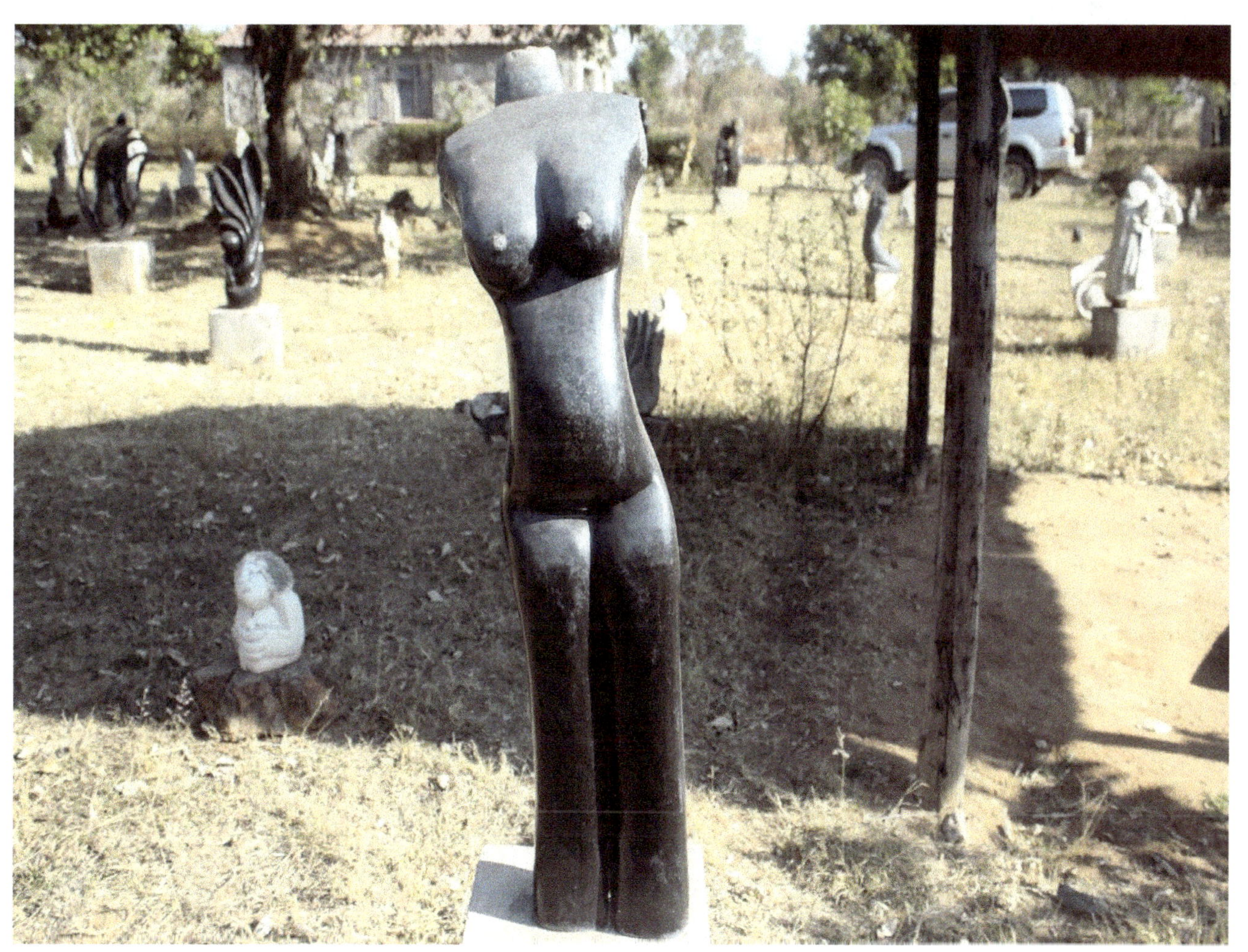

Roller Coaster

Jabulani Mzinyathi

The lightning of tantrums
The emotional blackmail
Operation mind control
Trying to create automatons
That manipulation resisted
Tears of a control freak flow
Desiring demonic total control
This X ray mind's eye sees it all
Seeing through the manipulation
The daggers drawn from scabbards
This bird refusing to be caged
Like an eagle soaring through open skies
This tiger fish is not aquarium bound
Swims upstream in the Zambezi river
Pretence cannot find room here

When you are gone

Jabulani Mzinyathi

When you are gone
The lingering memories
Of the steamy love making
Which you call smack down

When you are gone
Those items left inadvertently
Perhaps territory marking at work
That the sovereign is in charge

The single earring left
The lotion left here too
The umbrella left here too
The memories, when you are gone

When you are gone
Engulfed by floods of memories
The smile pleasantly sprouts
That is when you are gone

Running away

Jabulani Mzinyathi

That prophet from that Island
That question stands today
"Can you run away from yourself?"

The melanin in me speaks today
Speaking to the melanin in you
Sever those self-rejection chains

It is not only the skin bleached
The mind continually bleached
Can you evade your shadow?

That kinky hair they envy
For your skin they sun tan
Yet you try to flee from yourself

Your rich firm posterior and boobs
For that, fortunes are forked out
The melanin in me sees your beauty

Woman set yourself free
Espouse those natural endowments
Kick out the eurocentric garbage

No Woman No Cry
Jabulani Mzinyathi

And the message is warped
To fit the misogynistic schemes
Tears fall from my eyes like rain
Excruciating is the pain now felt
As that song so full of immense hope
Is turned into a misogynistic anthem

Perhaps without the drum and bass
Perhaps without the soothing voices
The spoken word may lay it bare
That the singer, song writer was no hater
That the guitar wielding man was a lover

So, no woman do not cry, no don't
Please do not shed those tears
You my little darling no, don't cry
We will walk down memory lane
Remembering the good friends we had
Remembering too those we long lost
That government yard was no leisure park
So no woman don't cry, shed no tears
Woman, everything will be all right

That is the great intersection of genres
These lines may cast that bright beam
For the story never to be warped again
That the man had an abundance of love
That charmer in turn your lights down low
That man in the embrace of the mellowmood
That man who could ask her to stir it up
Unfathomable that he could advocate musogyny

That misogyny wrongly attributed to that song
No woman do not cry, please shed no tears.

****Inspired by Bob Marley song lyrics*

BURNT OFFERINGS: Artworks by Lin Barrie and Johnson Zuze
Photography by Tendai Rinos Mwanaka

This consisted paintings and wire installations from Lin Barrie and Johnson Zuze respectively, exhibited by Pikicha Gallery, Harare. I managed to attend the closing interactive ceremony of this exhibition. It also included poetry readings, music performance, fashion show and film screening by Kelli Barker. Some paintings from Lin Barrie are accompanied by poetry vignettes from the artist

Burnt Offerings, Re-Invention, Taking Flight: Lin Barrie, Fine Artist, Artist Statement

Fire has terrible beauty, a dual nature, destructive and creative at the same time...alluring and frightening, real and metaphorical. We have suffered two domestic fires in our lives. I have been driven to collect burnt memorabilia; creating a 'burnt offering' of artworks.....Burnt Offerings. Nature is an inspiration; the seeds of many plants need the passage of flames to fully regenerate themselves.....Re-Invention. As a Phoenix rises from the flames and ashes, so we lift ourselves from the travails of life, physical or emotional.....Taking Flight. Along with my paintings and installations, I join with Johnson Zuze, who also suffered a housefire in his life, and who creates recycled, winged, wire works (using snare wire that I have gleaned from anti-poaching efforts in the south east lowveld of Zimbabwe) and my daughter Kelli Barker, make up and body artist, who has created an art film "Burnt Offerings" with her co-creators Sébastien Lallemand-Steemans, cinematographer, and Faz, aka The Faz Pixels, photographer, plus so many more Zimbabwean creatives, including Hope Masike and Ivhu Tribe; all filmed in the gorgeous She of Earth venue in Harare). Kuda Chakwaz was curator for this exhibition, held at Pikicha Gallery, Emagumeni, Helensvale July- September 2023. Challenges abound in all our frail lives, shaping us in often unexpected ways. Community conservation and culture, oral traditions and myths, storytelling and poetry, painting, and film, music and sculpture, connect us as we use our Burnt Offerings, Reinvent ourselves, and Take Flight. We are uplifted and empowered by the collaboration and spirit of our fellow Zimbabwean creatives. Thank you ALL!

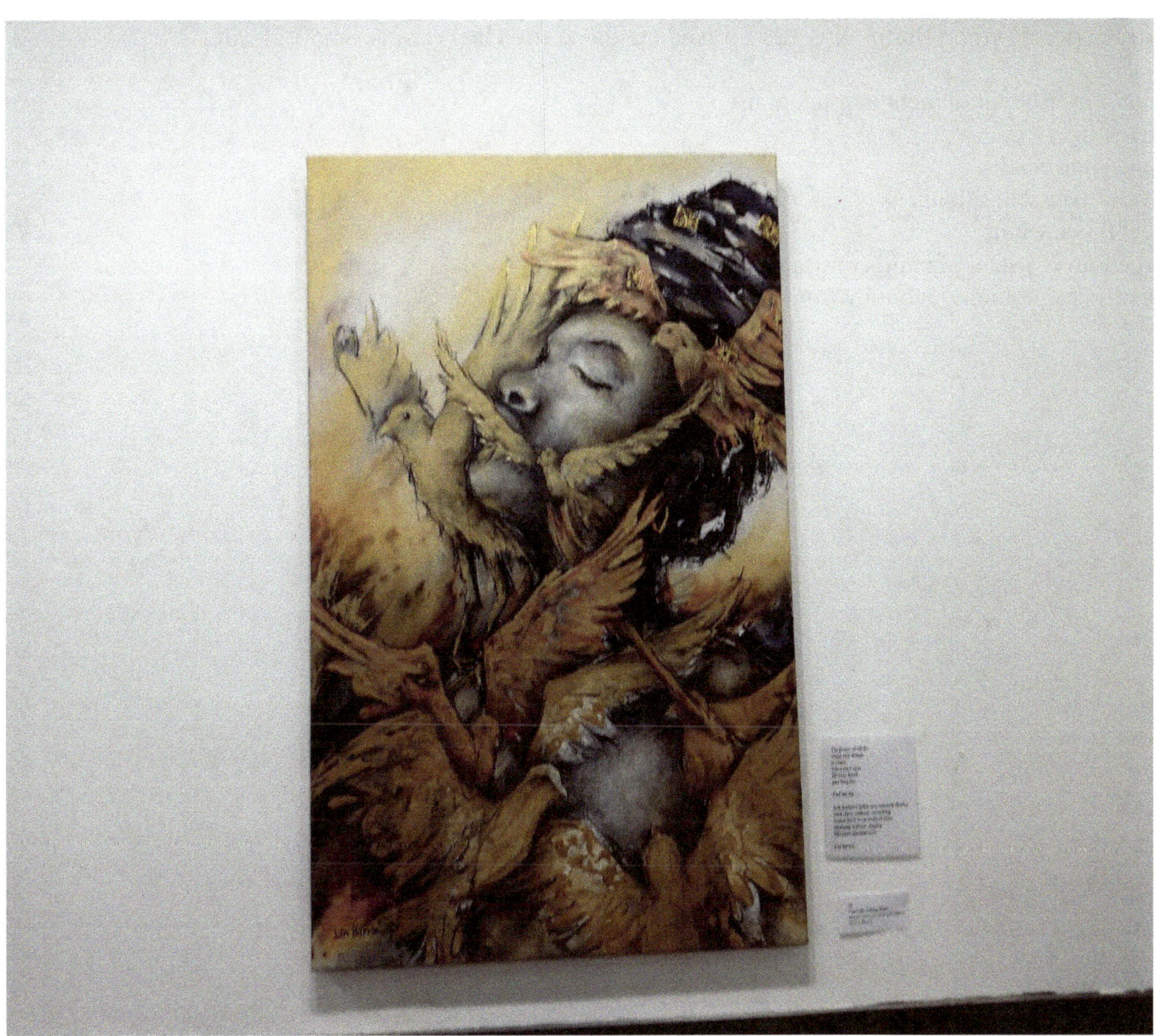

Lin Barrie, "Portrait, Burnt Offerings", mixed media on stretched canvas, 84,5 x 60 cm

The power of entrapment is yours to use
or resist.
Bow your head
give of yourself, submit.
Feel the tension...
Freedom is a state of mind constrained not only
by physical boundaries but by your mind.

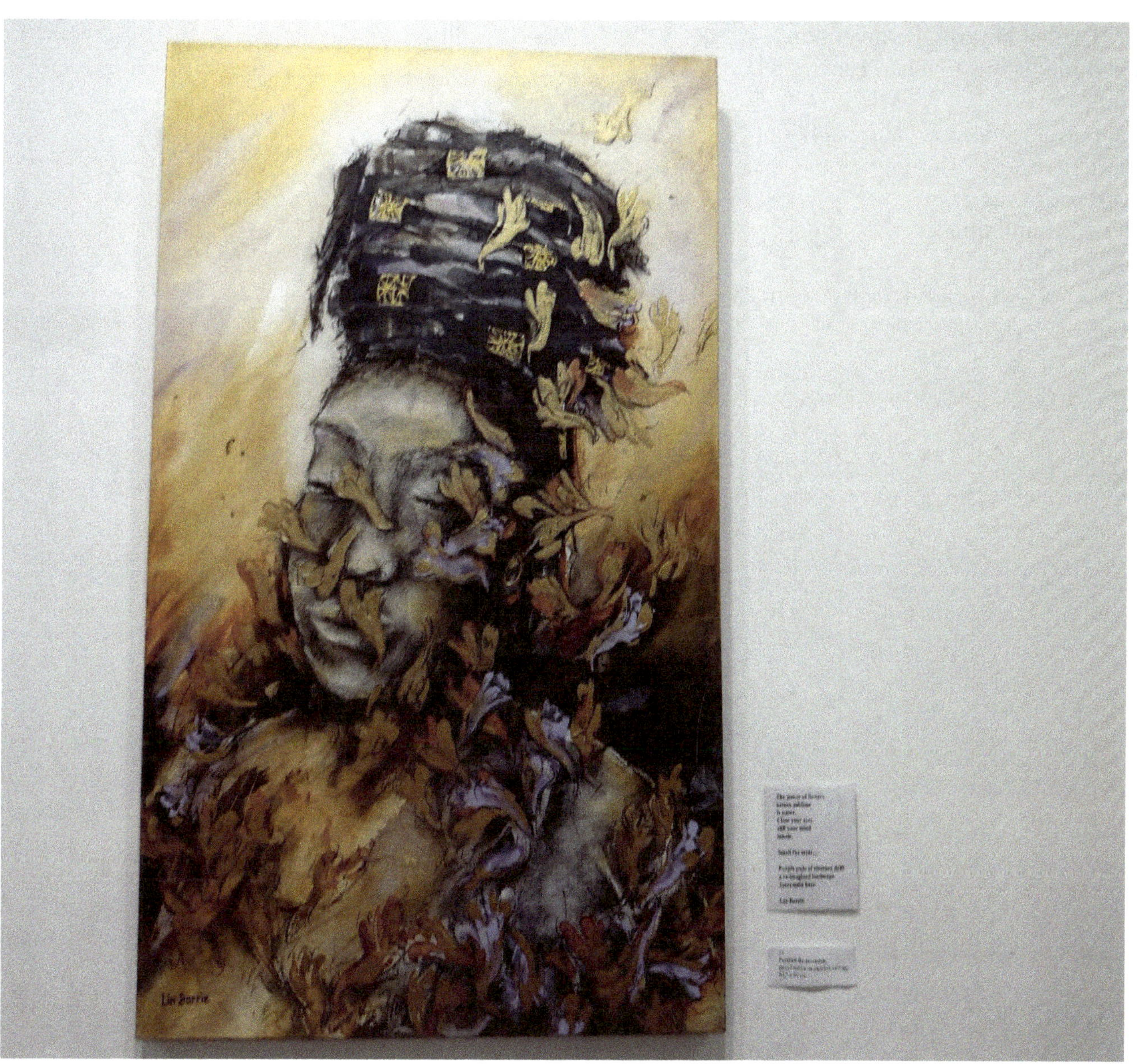

Lin Barrie, “Portrait, Re-invention”,
mixed media on stretched canvas, 84,5 x 60 cm

The power of flowers nature sublime
is yours.
Close your eyes
still your mind inhale.
Smell the scent…
Purple pods of pleasure drift a re-imagined landscape Jacaranda haze

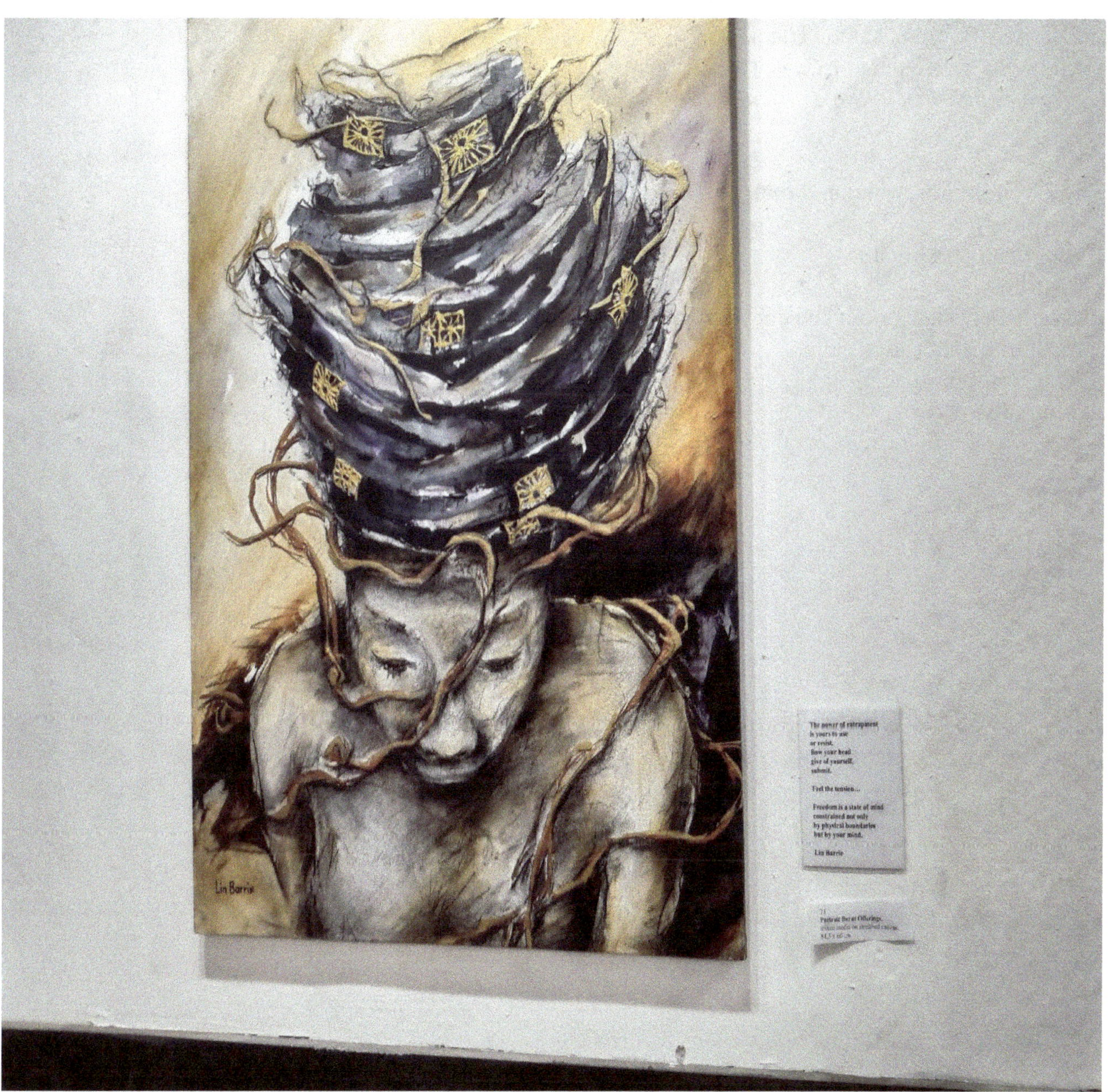
Lin Barrie
The power of entrapment
is yours to use
or resist.
Bow your head
give of yourself,
submit.
Feel the tension...
Freedom is a state of mind
constrained not only
by physical boundaries
but by your mind.
Lin Barrie

Lin Barrie, “Portrait, Taking Flight”,
mixed media on stretched canvas, 84,5 x 60 cm,
(Has been published in the Tesserae anthology 2023, Carnelian Heart Publishing)

The power of birds, wings and things, is yours.
Close your eyes
tilt your head, just breathe.
Feel the lift....
Soft feathers tickle tear-tracked cheeks; kind claws without scratching
scrape hurt from bruised skin;
birdsong without singing
fills your anxious ears.

A seed of my heart

Onward Mutapurwa

She wore a petal smile,
She says marry me,
I bestow her a pretty ring
She says age with me,
I say we will be together even if life melt like sugar,
Even if this pen of life run out of ink,
With my indelible pen I will write our life
Even if the dagger cut deep through my heart,
Be a second Jesus to your own Lazarus
If I'm penniless account me with papers
Like farmers, dug wells
Plant trees, roses
Cash crops in my deserted heart, maybe we can enrich our poorness.

If the moon can feel my pain

Onward Mutapurwa

If the moon can feel my pain,
Why not the sun see my struggle
Days after another, some questions still remains will you be my destiny
Unhealed lesions as hot ashes to my mind,
I'm in agony sharing emotions with the ghost of you
In this uncertainty hope I smile with a cry
Of cause I was a beautiful mess
I played only mates to appease myself, but now in a tears night I'm searching for a star to show me the reason why love is both hell and paradise
I'm still waiting for you like an obedient sun to her harlotry day who fall for the moon,
I know by dawn you will see the reason it takes pain to love than hate and you will see my
Crystal love is a fountain

Days when the future lies

Onward Mutapurwa

We were sitting on a hill,
We were happy souls with a luscious life,
Somewhere over the space, we rest upon greener pasture of love,
Everywhere I go, you were my red carpet
And like festive fruits,
The world feel our freshness,
Drought was no more for we loved what we have,
We bask on satisfaction, but unfortunately like farmers we get robbed of our crops,
We die of hunger, we blame ourselves on all and break it like clay pot

Love Lies

Onward Mutapurwa

Fed up in sorrow, hungry days I drink my
Tears
I say, when I marry you,
I thought you will be merry and I thought I will show you the world
I will give you its fantasies,
I will take you to Paris,
You will see the Eiffel, the world's most amazing, but now it's all about rubbed memories of a deceased heart.
Turn on your lights I'm looking for you

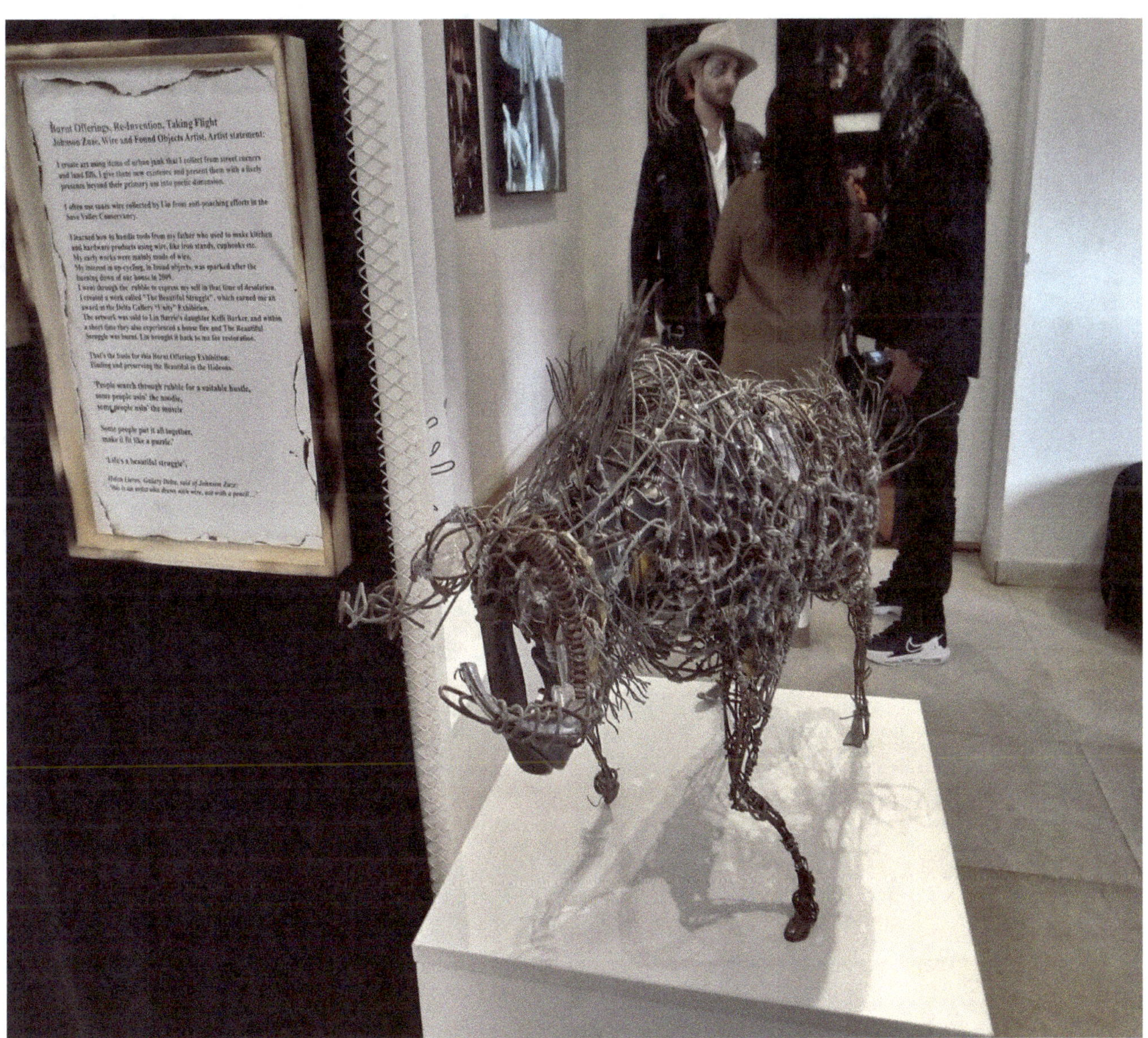

Johnson Zuze "wildebeeste"

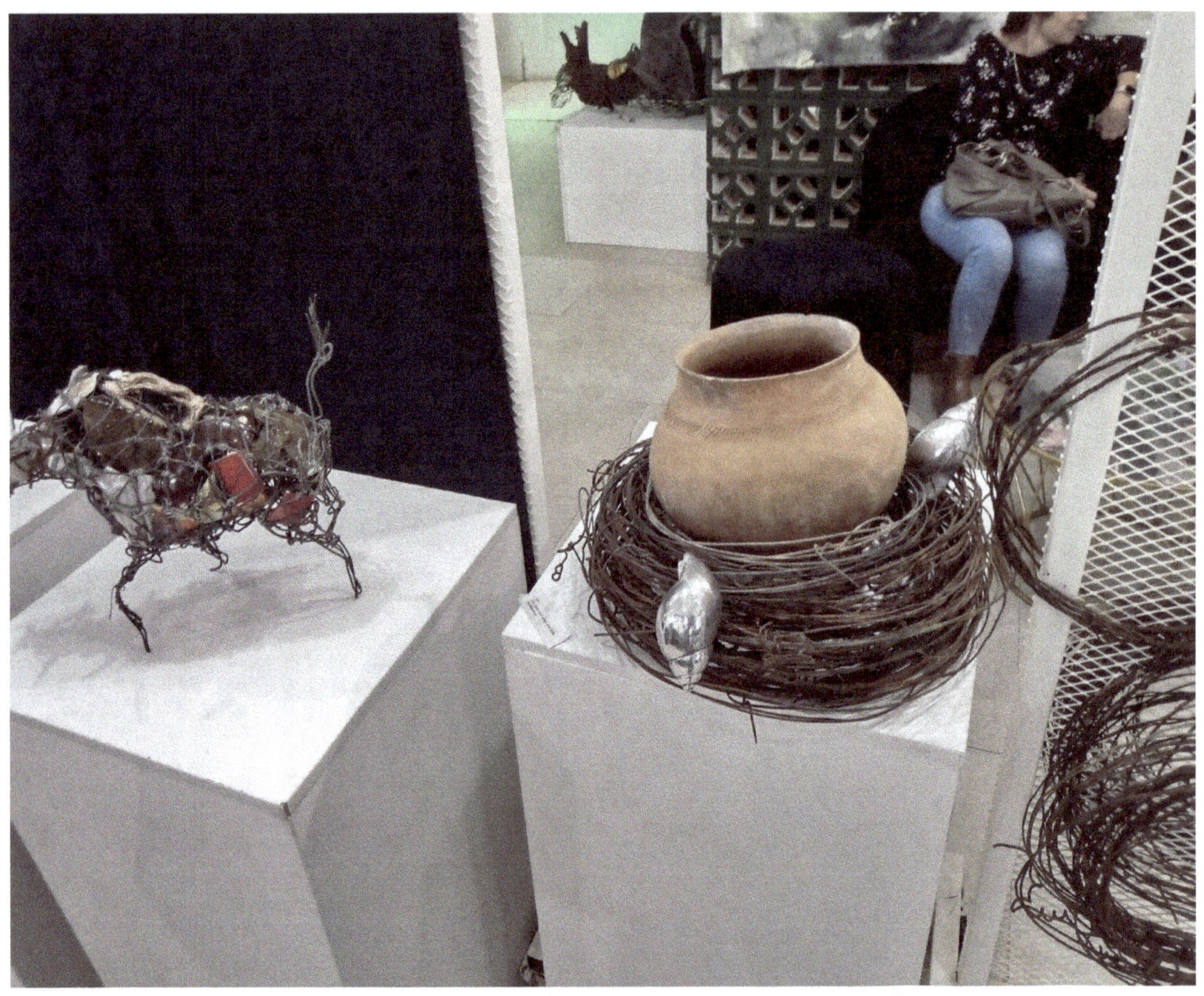

Johnson Zuze, “Warthogs” and Lin Barrie, Clay pot hata snare wire and shell installation

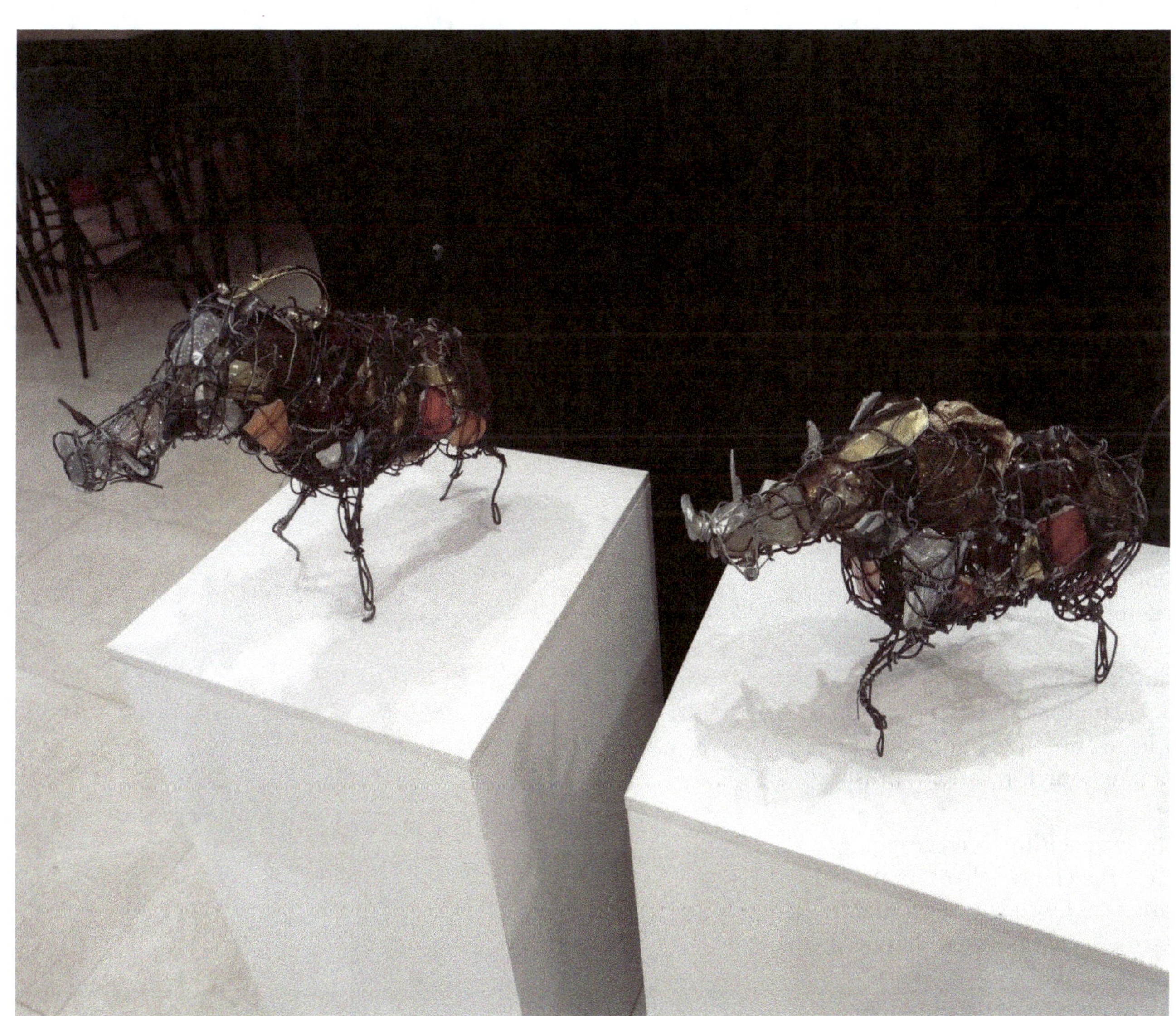

Johnson Zuze, “Warthogs”

Abominations

Jeremiah Maengedze

When freedom is delictuous,
Is there a concrete need
Of touting tainted democracy,
Reeking like burst raw effluent

When scribes are analphabetic,
Pens spit ink in dire defiance
Wrecking virgin pages with gobbledygook,
Presstitution fed to emaciated masses

When the musician is dead dumb,
The insane parrot oppressor's jingles
Incurious to nauseating discord,
Sickening praise wails

When the blind leads the trail,
Buckle up for cliff bottom landings
Or losing up one's infirm mind,
Stuck in eerie forest underbrushes

Why evangelist peace's gospel,
When the clergy is frost mum
Nursing a distended, sewn mouth,
disarmed, immobilized shepherds

When the clergy gulps hot-ten tots,
Ebriated sermons hijack sober podiums
Daubing parishioners ale stinking gospel
To gulp dregs of spurious testimonies

When the sheepdog dines with wolves,
Pasturelands become terror fields
Where ominous shrubs have sly eyes,
And turfs scan depraved minds

They face jeering goliaths,
Gladiators of mortal duels
To pick the Bible or sword,
Incinerated refuting voices

Who will oversit their shenanigans,
Anointed, hands under table judges
Shrewd oligarchs of porous courts,
Impaling the poor on pickets of lies

When children invert house roles,
Flogging forbearers for admonishing
Castigating them for wise reprimands;
A curse lingers for generations.

Rod Of Thorns

Jeremiah Maengedze

I went there to Oz,
One gloomy summer vacation
To nurse a nagging infirmity,
To jolt tortured mind to sanity

There, I beheld them,
Darty-eyed, anorexic adults
Pale faced, cornered prey;
Bewildered ghosts in daylight

They walk gorilla style,
Spent, gruffly creaky peasants
queuing to endorse mounting penury
in fallacious polls of fishy outcomes;
Incurious, fatigued electorate

Sulky, rotund tummied youngsters,
Skeletal wrecks cowering at strangers
Drench in tamed, reeking slimy puddles,
Oblivious, incurious innocents

Aside dusty, ware-choked pavements,
Enervated vendors market fading wares
Apathetic clients scampering for basics,
Here, they ply trade in everything,
Sharp elbowed, covetous merchants

Bloated wives hustle at chaotic markets,
Vigilant itinerant greenback predators
Emaciated counterparts brooding at home

Rumor-mongering in porous shades,
Whining for merited compulsory upkeep

Bleaky streets host wretched youth,
Chits mutating into monsters overnight
Tethered to drugs to dodge reality,
Broken teens of a crunchy era
Eternal idlers in comforting mirages

I was there in Oz,
Where hope lies yonder in afterlife
Naive masses taken for bumpy rides
On rigid seats in parachronic vans,
Daring blind entrusting shrewd escorts

I was there in Oz,
Where they toil on grim stretches
Bonded to perpetual, nauseating penury
Silently bearing unpalatable daily doses,
Of lashes from the rod of thorns.

Spooky Basements
Jeremiah Maengedze

If you brace for the chilling tour,
Down stale, stuffy passages
In the bosom of sodden earth,
Hold tight thy bosom

Mind bumping into them there,
Cobwebbed, sitting skeletons
Protesters of bitter exits,
Remnants in sealed basements

Down pitch, eerie corridors,
They endure unruffled sleep
Dreams the living repudiated,
Portraits boxed in stuffy cabinets

They lie in clouded limbo,
Creepy ghosts of sinister gloom
Aping ancestors time outpaced,
In winding queues for the long wait

I heard them down there,
In acrid hoarse whispers
The untold, sombre stories,
From obsolete colossal chests

They chill to the marrow,
Testimonies of contrite spirits
unaccounted for silent echoes,
On blood epigraphed, cold walls.

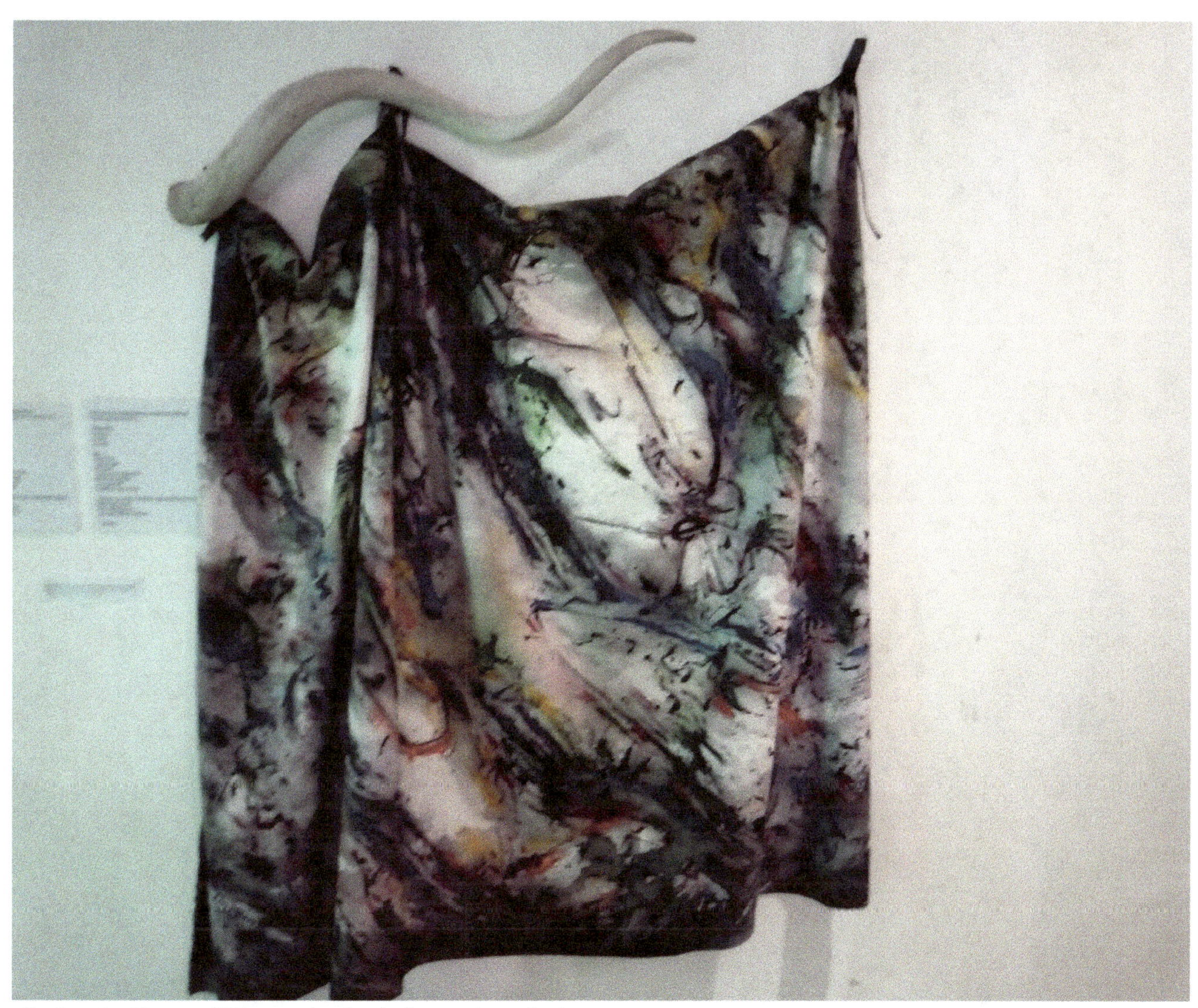

Lin Barrie, Fire and Water plus kudu horns installation

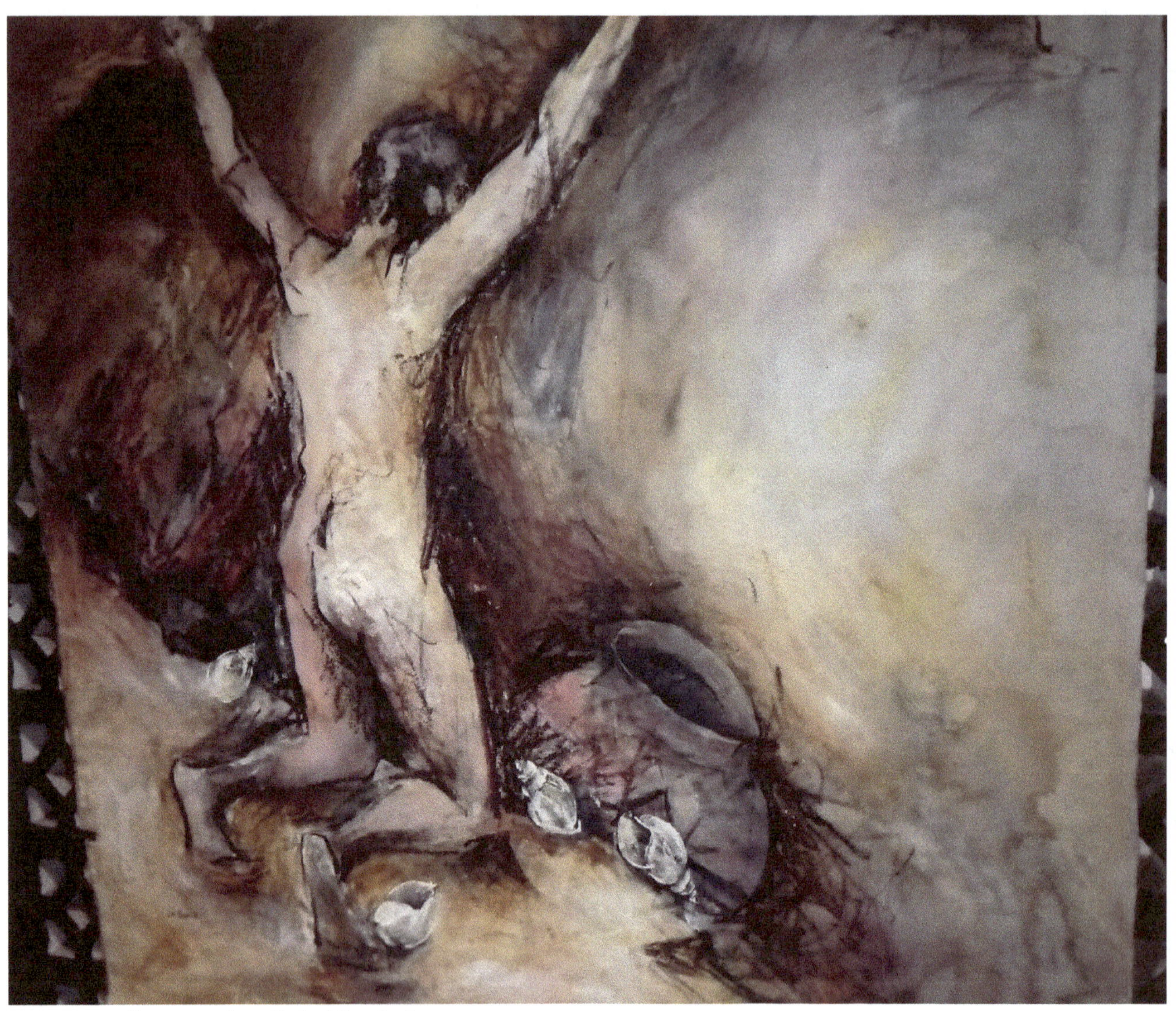
Lin Barrie, “Man and snail shell” painting

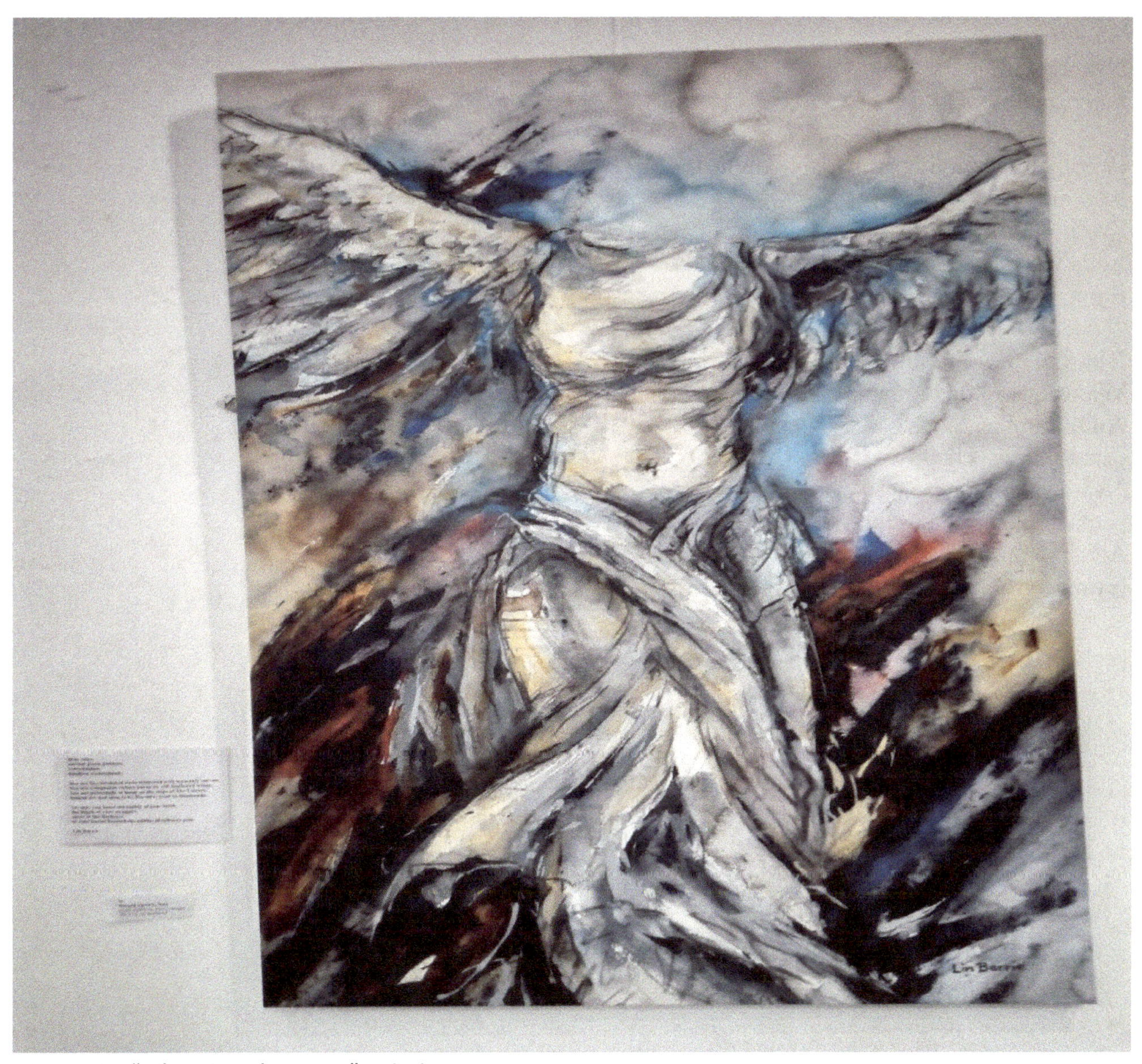

Lin Barrie, "Nike winged woman" painting on camvas

Nyarawo Iwe!

Chengetai Nyagumbo

Pako pamuromo hapamharwi nenhunzi,
Kudini ikoko!
Zvose unoda kuzviziva chete,
Kana waziva wochifamba nazvo handiti ka!
Kana wazvifambisa wowaneyi?

Nhasi mota racho ndoritushura chete
Wanyanyisa kunyumbira!
Ndinokuona zvangu kakawanda.
Ehe tozvireva chete.
Nyaya yako ndeyeyi chaizvo?
Kana uchida zvemawoko ndozvigonawo futi.
Aikaka, munhu wepi!
Nyarawo mhani iwe!

Zvazopera!
Chengetai Nyagumbo

Mimba yenzou iya yazoponwa.
Kudhamba tanga tanzwa hedu,
Zuva nezuva tichiudzwa ma a,e,i,o,u ,
Tanga takaura nawo.
Kumwiswa guchu remapiritsi chaiko!
Mapiritsi makuseni, chitsama chaowo masikati,
uye ekuwanda manheru.
Chero nguva here?
Chero varwere vegomarara havamwi nemwero wakadai.
Manje takavhiyiwa nezuro hameno kuti tinopora here nhasi?
Regayi tichimbofema,
Timborohwa nemhepo chaiko!
Pazvichadzoka pamwe tinenge tava kunyikadzimu,
Vapenyu munenge muripo muchanzwirira henyu zvakare.
Totenda Samatenga,
Kuti vazodai kupera.

Vazukuru!!
Chengetai Nyagumbo

Vazukuru iiii ndazoshaya chekureva ini.
Ndava kushaya chimiro ini muno mumana.
Kungoti kwangu pote mahong'era acho ndinomanzwa.
Zviri kundishaiisa hope siku nesikati.

Hunhu rudziyi hwamunoiita imi?
Ndakuunganidzayi kuti ndikurumeyi nzeve.
Poshi, zvibateyi.
Mafambiro enyu haana kunaka, gadzirisayi.
Piri mapfekero enyu ngaange akatsigawo.
Zvihwishu ayewa kwete.
Kudembedza mabhurugwa ayewa bodo.
Gerwayiwo zvakanaka ,handina kuti iswayi muparavara handina kumbodaro ini.
Gezayiwo muchipfeka.
Zvinodhakwa pasi nazvo...
Maazvinwza here vazukuru?

Hazvisi zvangu..

Chengetai Nyagumbo

Ndaiitozvidawo.
Kutozvichemera chaiko.
Kutozvinyima kudya zuva rose.
Kuzvinamatira.
kutozvirwira.

Zvakazondikandisa mapfumo pasi imi.
Kundigadzika mudhishi zvangu.
Izvi zvakandipedza simba.
Vamwe makazvigona seyiko?
Zvongoperera mupfungwa here?
Iiii Nyadenga akandirwadzisa ini.
Veduwee ndofira munhanga here chokwadi?
Vezera rangu vava nedzimba inga wani.
Chero vasina asi vana vanavo.
Zvino iniwo ndobva ndashaiwa zvose.
Haaa veduwee hazvichaiita kani.
Ndava nezita remadunhurirwa rondodamwa nepwere.
Hutsikombi hwangu hwazokomba zvino.
Ndozvidawo kani!
Ndatozvigamuchira hangu kuti hazvisi zvangu.

Sarapavana

Chengetai Nyagumbo

Kugona kushoropodza kuti vakwasha ngavauye nenhumbi dzehumai kana majazi chete ndizvo zvakangwaririrwa paduri sehuku.Kuzoti mombe dzedanga kana dzehumai dzinogarotaurwa nezvadzo zuva nezuva.

Kuchemedza runhare hunzi pakati pangu parwadza isayi mashereni muecocash ndizvo zvinogonekwa chete.

Kuuya kuzoona vazukuru kurembedza maoko chete.
kana tudovi kana mangayi muchibepa kana.
Muri vanhu rudziyi imi.
Aah mandigona ini.
Kuti makanyatsoti kwesere here imi?

Kwenyu zviriko here izvi?
Zvinosiririsa.
Zvinochemedza izvi.
Chiyiko nayi vana sarapavana.

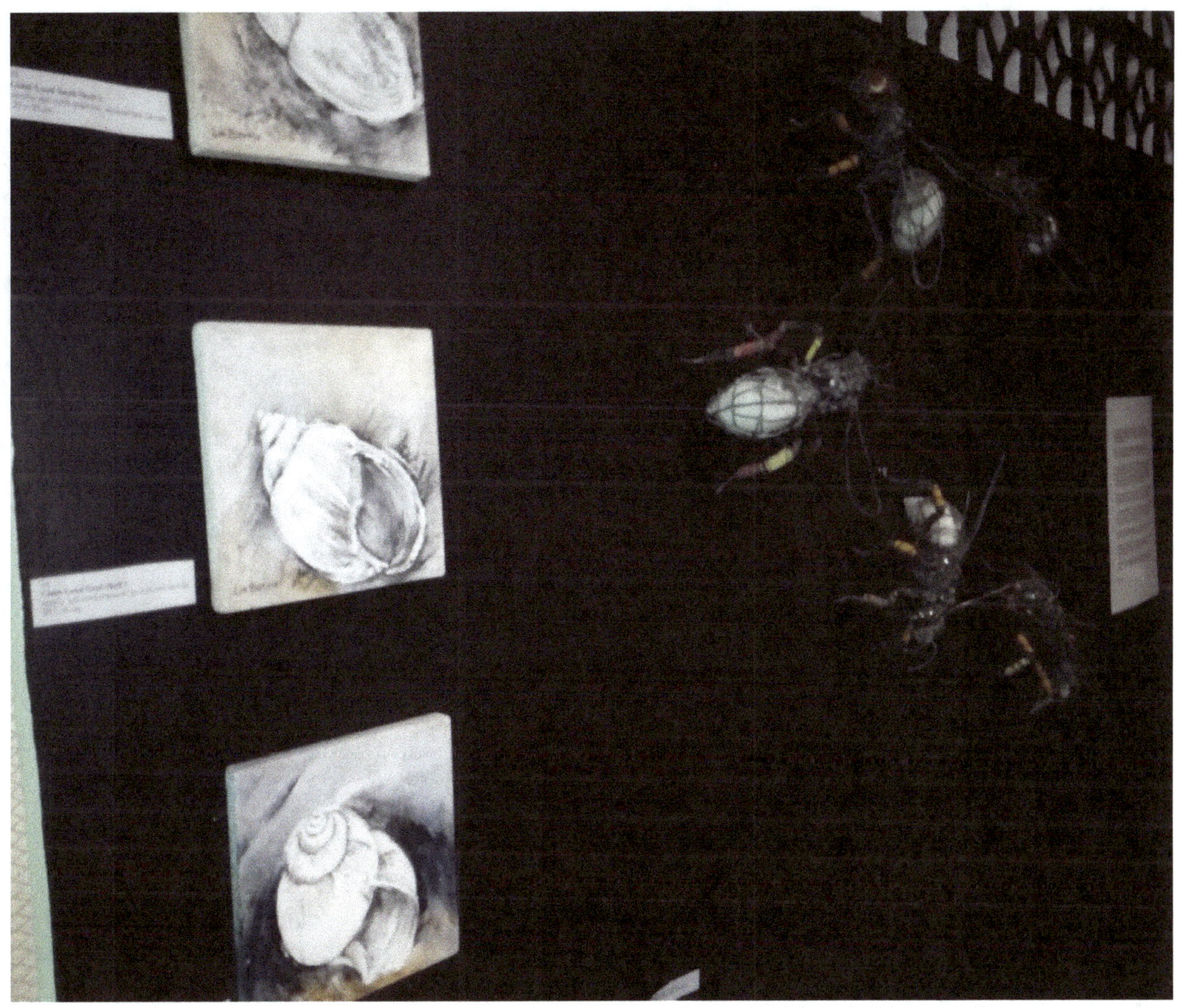

Lin Barrie "Snail shell" paintings and Johnson Zuze "shell wasps" wire and found objects sculpture

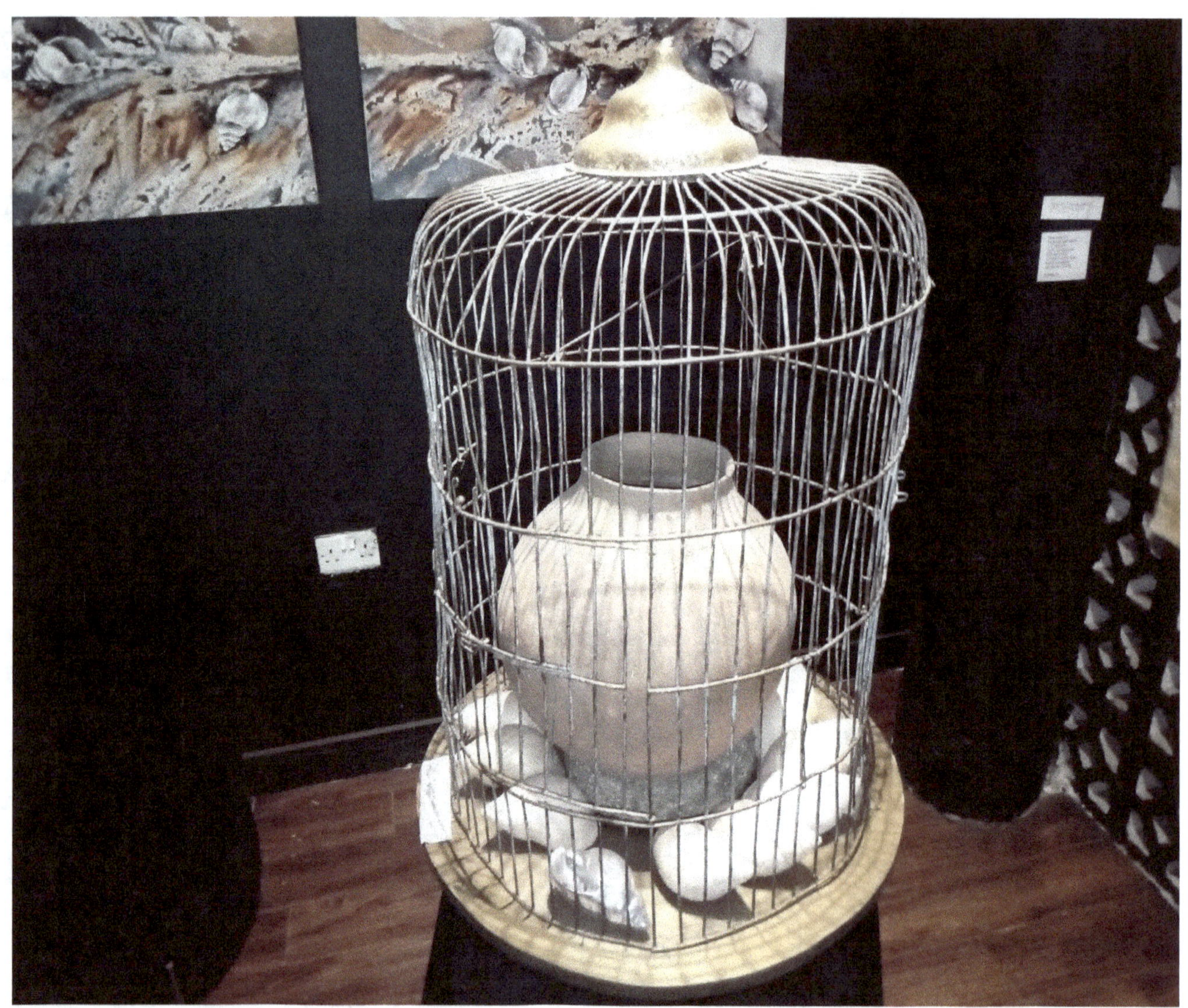

Lin Barrie, Caged culture installation and Lin Barrie painting snail diptych in background

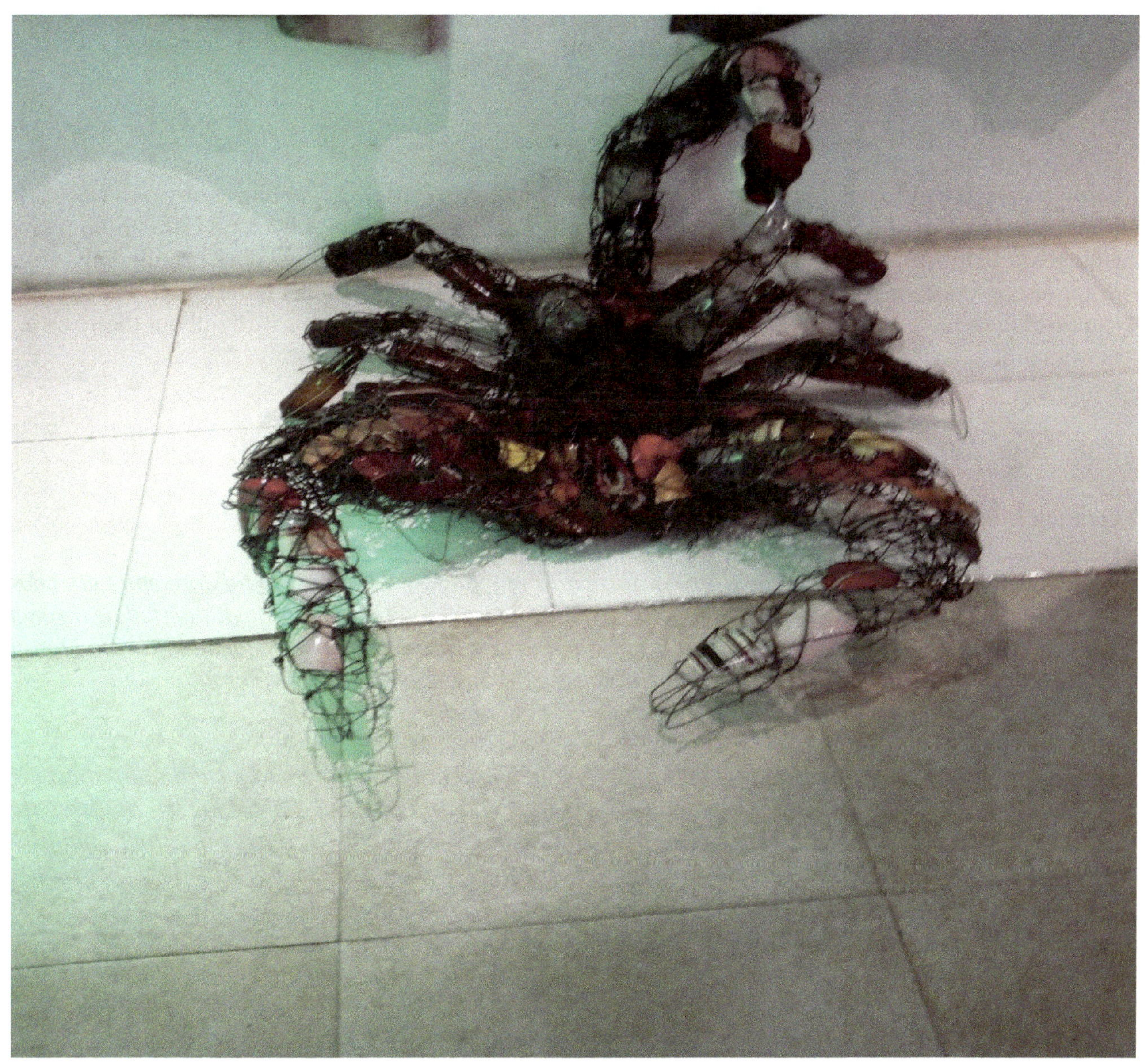

Johnson Zuze “scorpion woman” wire and found objects sculpture (Garden of Eden)

The New Voices in Zimbabwe's Publishing Arena

Matthew K Chikono

Gone are the days when if one fancied a read they would find themselves a public library or a bookstore where a wide range of books by local writers would be available. Books by Chenjerai Hove, Shimmer Chinodya. F. Ribeiro, P. Chakaipa, M.A Hamutyinei, Aaron Chiundura Moyo were prominently displayed on book shelves. Most of those bookshops are gone and even fewer libraries are still open to cater for the general public but those books are still in circulation. More books are still out there, with newer names.

The New Voices

Stephen Mupoto

Writing has always been within me from my formative years. I loved listening to folklore and fairy tales from my mother. When I was in Grade 3, the art in me started manifesting through storytelling through pictures. I would do pictorial stories before I decided to pen my first short novel entitled Crime Doesn't Pay. My primary school teacher, Mrs. Annah Nyarwendo then identified the writer in me and encouraged me to start writing. That is how my journey started.

When I was older, publishing did not come easy. Now I have done both traditional and self-publishing. When I went traditional publishing, the process was long and arduous. Self-publishing has not been that difficult because I only incurred printing and cover design costs. First I sent my manuscript to publisher for assessment. The publisher accepted my manuscript and gave me a quotation. The publisher then started editing my manuscript upon payment of all the publishing fees.

When my first book came out, I was not satisfied. The publisher did shoddy work. No dummy was ever sent to me. I then read through the manuscript and it was riddled with errors. On my second book I felt I parted ways with money for no reason. The publisher did not do much to improve the manuscript. I had to rework on it on my own and had other peer writers to peer edit it.

Our local Zimbabwean market has not been so rewarding to me and everyone else involved. A lot of people wanted to buy the book but at shamefully low prices. Publishing and printing costs are exorbitant.

I haven't tried online selling but I am considering selling my book on Amazon soon. I have published more than nine books that include Who Killed Laura? Faulty Lines, Medusa's Lair (The above three are called the Laura trilogy and should be read in that order). Mission Blade, the Signature, Mission Blade and the Lost Transcripts, the Midget Mafia, Bleeding Sands and Dashed Dreams.

Tafadzwa Chiwanza

My desire to write poetry would have been nothing without the ability to do so. How long I tittered in the shadows, afraid to take up a pen and speak! As a young lad in high school, I wrote a few hundred works of poetry that had neither the words nor the meaning to make them worthy pieces. But they helped me shape myself into a stone. The poems were free, happy and could transform in ways I could never do now! My gratitude goes to my best friend, who not having the modicum of knowledge of what poetry ought to be, read each of those pieces like they were the words of Wordsworth himself.

My poetry took a significant turn when I met Dr Chidora in 2018. By that time I had enrolled at the University of Zimbabwe majoring in Accounting. I was beginning to make use of the university's special collections section. My poetry could not remain immune to the works I was reading; it got better in delivery but terrible in identity. Each poem was an awkward mixture of influences from Dambudzo Marechera to Sylvia Path. Meeting Dr Chidora altered my path. He brought to me the confidence necessary to write in my own voice and skin. He brought freedom and identity to my work. He remained instrumental in the publication of my second poetry collection.

After I finished the draft of my first poetry collection, I allowed myself to feel good about the script by letting it mellow for a while. A month or so. The objective was to distant I from the writing process so that I could look at the work with a clearer perspective and by that I mean the eyes of the potential reader. After doing this, I then made edits to the script before I gave it to a few friends who could proffer me with some necessary critique. Then I did some more rewrites.

I submit my completed manuscript to an independent publisher. The publisher did marvelous work turning it into a magnificent debut. I was happy with the result. However, the reception of the book was lukewarm. This had nothing to do with quality. The general populace didn't care enough for poetry. I have learnt a lot from the publication of my debut collection No Bird Singing Now, and I hope to do better on my second titled The rest is silence.

The above writers are not the only new voices on the local scenery. Some new writers are doing well whilst some are finding the craft and the industry not so easy going.

The Arena

Most of the books that filled our bookshops were imported or locally published by few traditional publishing houses such a College Press, ZPH, Longman, Mambo, and Weaver Press. With the situation as it is in our motherland Zimbabwe, the economy and stuff, most of these publishing houses are dead or at least not operating at quarter best. Small publishing houses have been born in recent years and they have taken up the mantle when the local industry crushed and burned both publishers' and writers' livelihood with it. This new-era publishing houses have managed to keep the industry from totally sinking into oblivion. However most of these houses don't offer traditional publishing but hybrid or self-publishing services.

These scores of publishing houses have helped hundreds, if not thousands, of Zimbabwean writers fulfill their dream of getting published.
These houses are doing a great job but most of them face a number of challenges including inadequate technology advances and low sales caused by poor performance of our economy and reduced readership because of ever changing education curricular and the death of reading culture.

Tinashe Muchuri

We have conventional or traditional publishing houses and self-publishing service providers. These two are different in their operations.
They first embark on solicitation of works from identified authors and or authors submit works for consideration. In this category the writer submits the work all the publication costs are taken care of by the publisher. The author is paid royalties of between 10-20% quarterly or twice a year. This category

tries by all means to produce quality work as they employ qualified editors. Publishers in this category are driven by profit, however they are aware that quality work gives them returns.

Publishers in the second category help those who want to self-publish produce their books. Some of them are editors in one language and struggle with others. They do not outsource editing services. They print and supply first drafts in some instances marred with spelling errors.

This is so because they are mainly fond of collecting funds from the aspiring writers and some renowned writers. The volumes render their services poor in some circumstances. Their services include: editing, isbn, acquisition, cover design, content page, layout printing, binding and finishing. The author pays for all these services to the service provider and sometimes the authors get disappointed when given a poor print of the manuscript. To serve money the service provider may engage the cheapest providers of the above services. The quality is not up to standard. The binding and the print sometimes is faint and fonts sometimes change with each page or in the middle of a paragraph.

John Gambanga

The standard has dropped noticeably. Some publishers lack money to hire top editors to assess and edit copy. As a result quality is often compromised. Manuscripts that should not be published due to a number of reasons are released. Quality control is critical in book publishing in my honest view. Some publishers are overworked and therefore strained and this compromises quality. A manuscript must be read by at least two people for assessment before acceptance. The assessors or gate keepers must be thorough in their work. It's better to publish a few good books than scores that are below expected standards. Bad books should not be published. Bad writers must be assisted so that their work is good and not condemned.

However, most of the new age publishers point out that the quality has remained the same or even better. The number of the books nominated on NAMA awards in the last few years is the testament of their unwavering quality books being published. It's not only about local awards but hundreds of these books are finding homes all over the world in top university libraries.

A Roar from the terraces

Buying of books, especially literature and poetry, is considered a luxury for most in this country. Most local writers, both new and old, have found it difficult to sell their books both in print format and soft copies. Family, friends and workmates fill in as the best customers. Numerous stakeholders in the publishing industry have tried to revive but this death doesn't seem to be only affecting the Zimbabwean industry.

Book readership has slumped over the years. Younger generations spend more time on social media and televisions, leaving little time for academic reading and none for general reading.

The Norton Children's Books Festival

The Norton Children's Books Festival is an initiative that Aleck Kaposa came up with in order to give children a platform to recite poetry, display artistic talent through drawing and colouring as well as many other activities that involve creative writing in general with the main aim to read books. The festival was also a platform to make children read and enjoy books as well as develop their artistic talent.

He staged the first edition of the Festival at Katanga Open Space in 2018. More than 15 schools from Norton, Harare and surrounding areas took part in the event. The festival has continued over the years. Tried and tested players in the book industry were gradually replaced by emerging first timers and new voices that have done well with the new trend in the publishing industry. In a way the festival have managed to capture the young people back to the culture of reading books for the nourishing of the minds

Comexposed Converge

Comexposed Converge started out as a Convention purposed to revolutionize the way Africans and Zimbabweans in particular view themselves through Comic books and comic art. Now, Converge has evolved to transform not only that but the way Zimbabweans and African view themselves, but how they live their everyday lives, by showing them how to harness the power of digital arts and technology. Writers have found a way to change with it. Not only are comic books displayed but books across genres are finding a platform to be revealed to the world. Writers and readers have find themselves a lounge.

Founded by Eugene Ramirez Mapondera and Tinodiwa Zambe Makoni the converge has been held annually since 2015 in Harare. Through Converge, the duo have created a space where the experts, enthusiasts and novices alike can be completely immersed in the world of innovation for a day. Their hope is that the knowledge and experiences they gain, will empower them to go out into their spaces and transform those spaces, not only for their benefit, but for the benefit of our country and continent

Notes

Tendai Mwanaka

"Publishing is now just an act of love. I don't know any publisher publishing literary books at my level who is doing well in terms of sales. There is a reason the likes of Weaver press, ZPH, College press and others stopped publishing literary writing." Tendai Mwanaka from Mwanaka Media and Publishing said. His publishing company, which is also part of the African Books Collective, has published over hundred titles under its belt.

Aleck Kaposa

As a publisher I have made a little contribution to the Zimbabwe literary landscape in that I have edited or published NAMA award-winning books, one university set text, and more than 100 other titles. Some of these titles have been hugely popular with readers. Our books have been featured in newspapers, on the radio and television. We have given hope to hundreds of emerging writers who have found a home at our stable. Personally I have been nominated and in some cases won different awards. I have mentored one or two publishers over the years.

Judging by the sales at book launches and bookshops, we have had good response. We are always printing about 10 titles regularly with at least 30 copies each. I think that's fairly good but we would be happy to increase that a hundredfold.

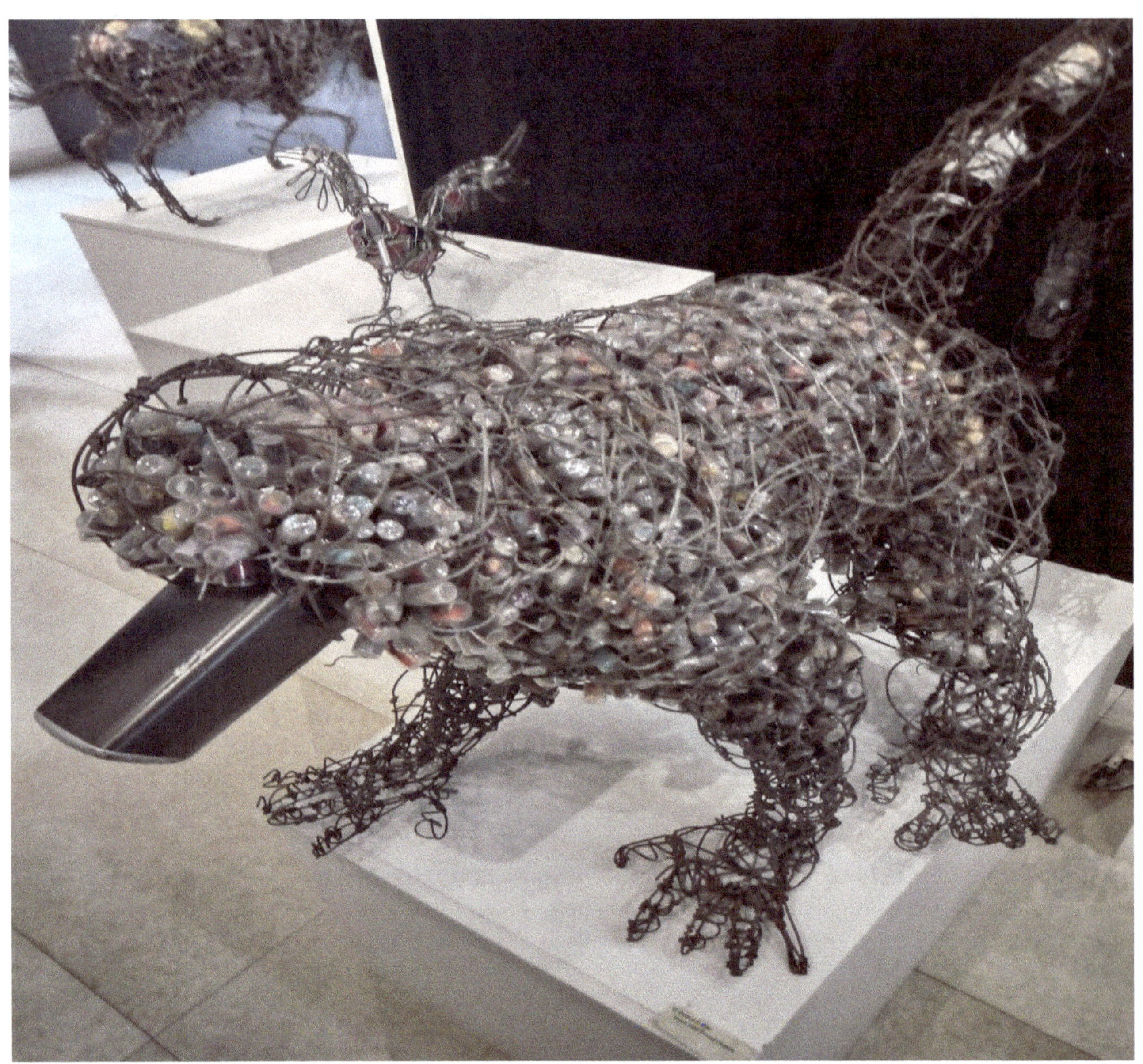

Johnson Zuze, “Gudo”, wire and found objects sculpture

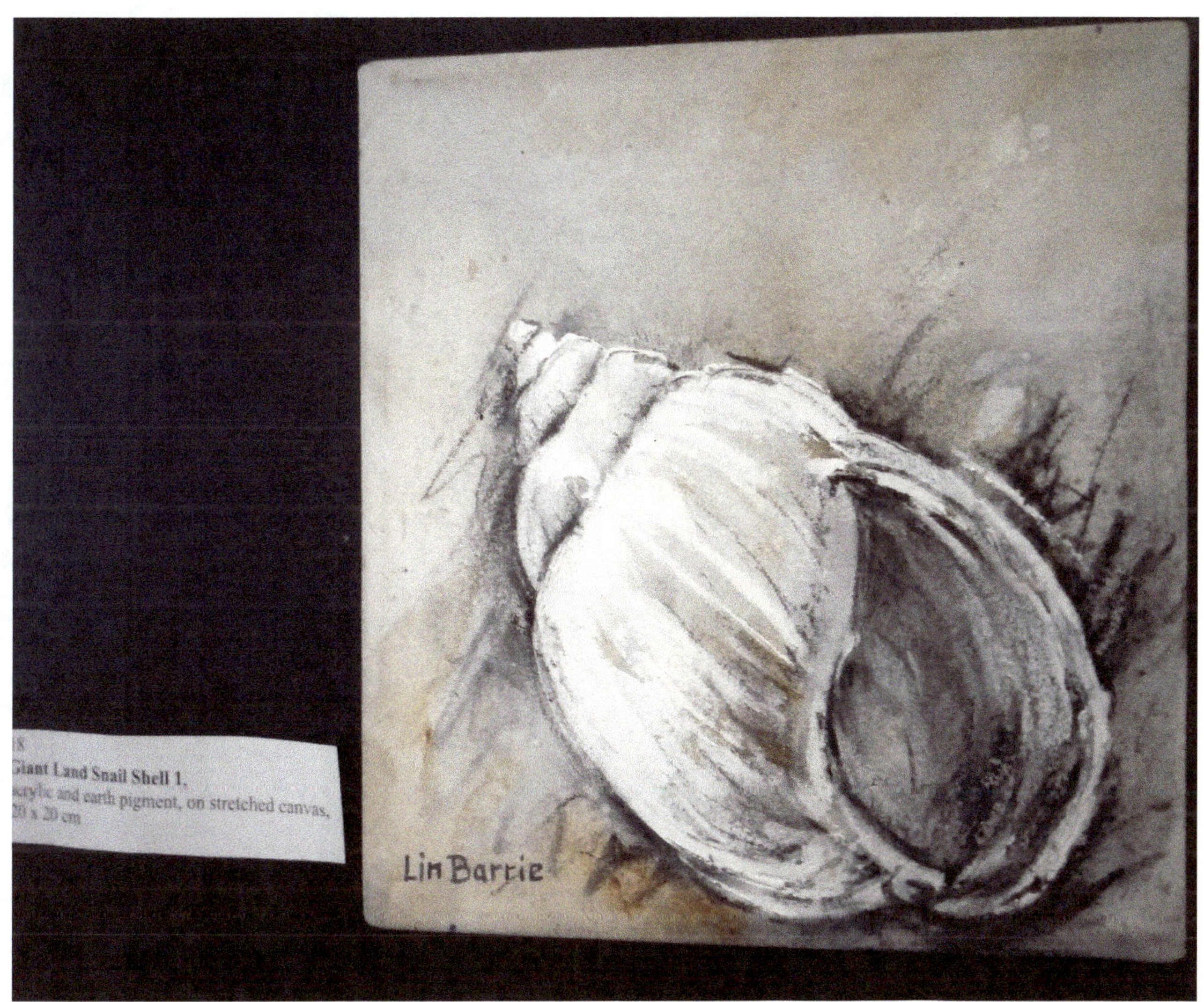

Lin Barrie "snail shell" painting on canvas

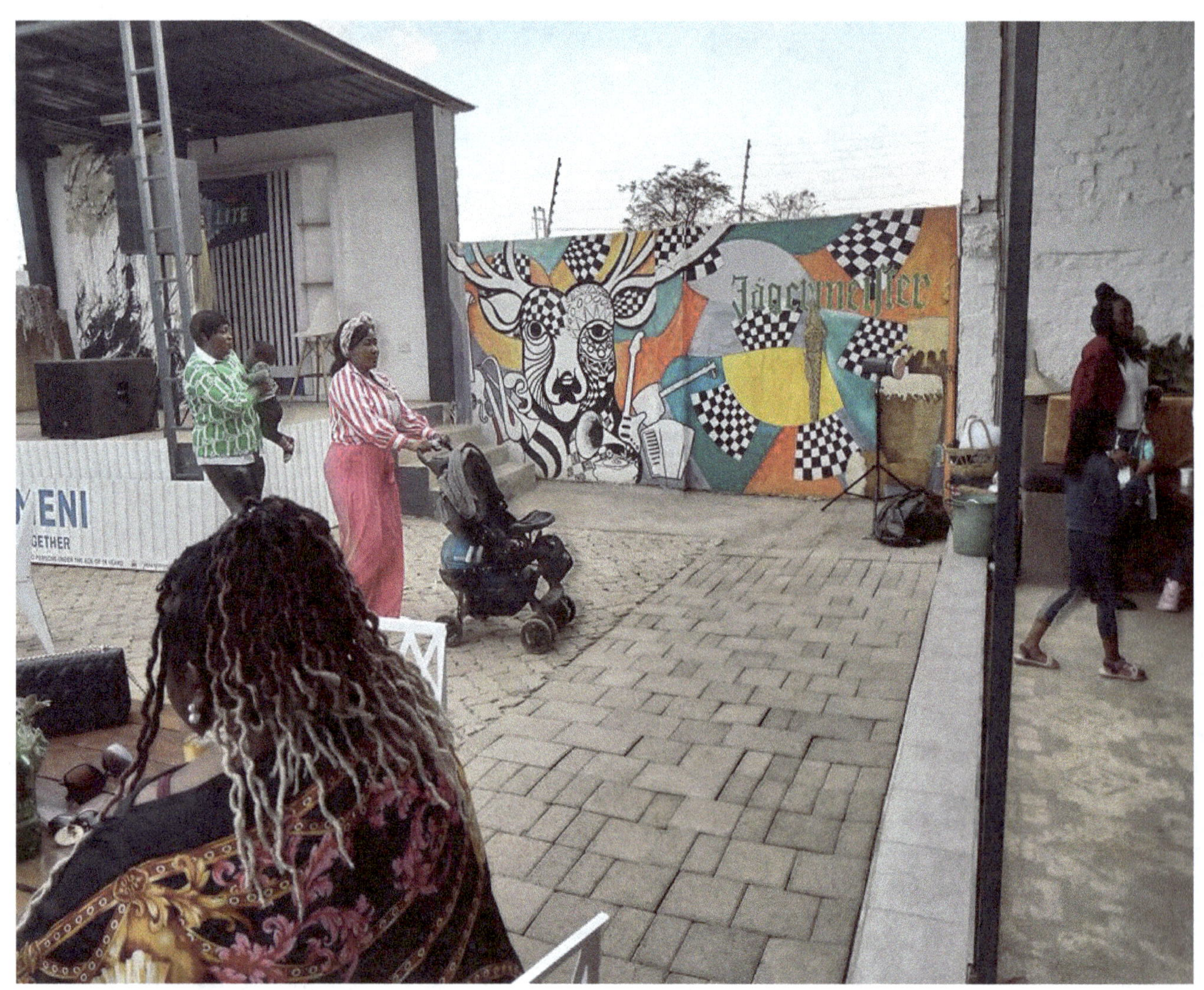

Emagumeni courtyard

Mmap Multi-disciplinary Series

If you have enjoyed *Zimbolicious Anthology Vol 8*, consider these other fine books in the **Mmap Multi-disciplinary Series** from *Mwanaka Media and Publishing:*

Africanization and Americanization Anthology Volume 1, Searching for Interracial, Interstitial, Intersectional and Interstates Meeting Spaces, Africa Vs North America by Tendai R Mwanaka
A Conversation..., A Contact by Tendai Rinos Mwanaka
Africa, UK and Ireland: Writing Politics and Knowledge Production Vol 1 by Tendai R Mwanaka
Writing Language, Culture and Development, Africa Vs Asia Vol 1 by Tendai R Mwanaka, Wanjohi wa Makokha and Upal Deb
Zimbolicious: An Anthology of Zimbabwean Literature and Arts, Vol 3 by Tendai Mwanaka
Drawing Without Licence by Tendai R Mwanaka
Writing Grandmothers/ Escribiendo sobre nuestras raíces: Africa Vs Latin America Vol 2 by Tendai R Mwanaka and Felix Rodriguez
Tiny Human Protection Agency by Megan Landman
Ghetto Symphony by Mandla Mavolwane
A Portrait of Defiance by Tendai Rinos Mwanaka
Nationalism: (Mis)Understanding Donald Trump's Capitalism, Racism, Global Politics, International Trade and Media Wars, Africa Vs North America Vol 2 by Tendai R Mwanaka
Ouafa and Thawra: About a Lover From Tunisia by Arturo Desimone
Zimbolicious: An Anthology of Zimbabwean Literature and Arts, Vol 4 by Tendai Mwanaka and Jabulani Mzinyathi
Chitungwiza Mushamukuru Anthology by Tendai Rinos Mwanaka
The Day and the Dweller: A Study of the Emerald Tablets by Jonathan Thompson
Zimbolicious: An Anthology of Zimbabwean Literature and Arts, Vol 5 by Tendai Mwanaka
Robotics Anthology, Africa vs Asia Vol 2 by Tendai Rinos Mwanaka
Shaping Up by Tendai Rinos Mwanaka
Zimbolicious Anthology Vol 6: An Anthology of Zimbabwean Literature and Arts by Tendai Rinos Mwanaka and Chenjerai Mhondera
Registers of Loss: PhotoTalking to the Baobab Trees of Nyatate by Tendai Rinos Mwanaka

The Trick is to Keep Breathing: Covid 19 Stories From African and North American Writers, vol 3 by Tendai Rinos Mwanaka
Fixing Earth: An Anthology of Ireland, UK and Africa Writers, Vol 2 by Tendai Rinos Mwanaka
Zimbolicious: An Anthology of Zimbabwean Literature and Arts, Vol 7 Tendai Rinos Mwanaka and Tanaka Chidora
WRITING WOMAN ANTHOLOGY: Poetry and Visual art by Tendai Rinos Mwanaka, Abigail George, Sue Zhu and Monalisa Jena
WRITING WOMAN ANTHOLOGY: Personal Essays and Short stories, An Anthology of African and Asian Writers, Vol 3 by Tendai Rinos Mwanaka, Abigail George, Sue Zhu and Monalisa Jena
WRITING WOMAN ANTHOLOGY: Drama and Scholarly Essays, An Anthology of African and Asian Writers, Vol 3 by Tendai Rinos Mwanaka, Abigail George, Sue Zhu and Monalisa Jena

https://facebook.com/MwanakaMediaAndPublishing/

www.ingramcontent.com/pod-product-compliance
Lightning Source LLC
LaVergne TN
LVHW081251100826
845148LV00009B/1191

* 9 7 8 1 7 7 9 3 3 1 6 6 3 *